A Primer on American Labor Law

Other books by William B. Gould IV

Black Workers in White Unions: Job Discrimination in the United States.
Cornell University Press, 1977.

Japan's Reshaping of American Labor Law. MIT Press, 1984.

Strikes, Dispute Procedures, and Arbitration: Essays on Labor Law. Green-
wood Press, 1985.

Labor Relations in Professional Sports (with Robert C. Berry and Paul D.
Staudohar). Auburn House, 1986.

A Primer on American Labor Law
second edition

William B. Gould IV

The MIT Press, Cambridge, Massachusetts, and London, England

This edition was set in Baskerville by the MIT Press Computergraphics Department from computer diskettes provided by the author, and was printed and bound by The Murray Printing Co. in the United States of America.

Library of Congress Cataloging-in-Publication Data

Gould, William B.
  A primer on American labor law.

  Bibliography: p.
  Includes index.
  1. Labor laws and legislation—United States.
I. Title.
KF3369.G68   1986   344.73′01   86–3011
ISBN 0–262–07098–7   347.3041
ISBN 0–262–57063–7 (pbk.)

For Ed, who always wanted me to write a book that would reach a large and diverse audience.

Contents

Preface to Second Edition

There have been a number of significant developments in labor law since 1982, when the first edition of this book was published. In industries confronted with deregulation or with foreign competition, the advent of concession bargaining (coupled, in some instances, with new limitations on management's prerogatives) has changed the labor-management landscape. Numerous decisions—many too inconsequential to be mentioned in a book such as this—have been issued by the National Labor Relations Board (whose composition and outlook changed dramatically before the end of President Reagan's first term) and the Supreme Court. Indeed, the labor movement's disillusionment with the NLRB prompted AFL-CIO president Lane Kirkland to opine about the desirability of repealing the National Labor Relations Act.[1]

The decline of the labor movement to approximately 19 percent of the work force has led to unprecedented soul-searching on the part of labor.[2]

An interesting by-product of the decline of organized labor has been the growth in the importance of the rights of individual employees outside the union environment. Wrongful-discharge litigation initiated by nonunion employees has become the most discussed issue in the field of labor law.

As I have reflected on the changes for this second edition, I have found the comments and criticisms of Reinhold Fahlbeck, Professor of Law at the University of Lund and the Stockholm School of Economics and Visiting Fellow at the Stanford Law School, particularly insightful. Professor Fahlbeck, a Swedish labor lawyer with expertise in American labor law, has been both generous and unrelenting, and I am most grateful to him.

I am also grateful to Joseph Costello and Elizabeth Smith of the Stanford Law School for providing material for the notes, and to Mary Ann Loughram and Maxine Emery for their skillful typing.

Preface

The idea of this book grew out of lectures that I gave in the early 1970s at the AFL-CIO Labor Studies Center in Washington, D.C., and at the University of Illinois Institute of Industrial Relations in Champaign, Illinois. The audiences were trade unionists (mostly local officers and shop stewards), and the subject was labor law and labor arbitration. The discussions were lively and the questions stimulating. I became aware that many people had an institutional incentive to learn about labor law, and I quickly realized that the existing literature was not reaching them; in fact, there really was no book aimed specifically at such an audience. This impression was confirmed by a series of talks that I gave to similar audiences at the Institute for Industrial Relations at the University of California at Berkeley. My contact with corporate representatives at some of the institute's functions made it clear that both sides of the bargaining table were interested in obtaining a basic outline of the labor-law system, one that would not be so encyclopedic as to be intimidating.

In the mid 1970s I began to lecture on American labor law to labor academics, American-studies specialists, trade unionists, employers, and government officials in various countries in Europe, Asia, Africa, and Latin America. In most of these countries I was asked to recommend a book that provided foreigners with an outline of American labor law. My inability to recommend such a book finally induced me to write *A Primer on American Labor Law*. Structured seminars sponsored by the United States Department of State and the United States International Communications Agency in such countries as India and Brazil and lectures given under the auspices of the Kyoto American Studies Seminar helped organize my thinking for this book, as did some of my lectures to my Labor Law I classes at the Stanford Law School.

There are other books on American labor law that are more detailed and involved than this one. Readers who wish to go farther should consult the lengthier volumes aimed at university students, such as *Labor and the Law* by Charles O. Gregory and Harold A. Katz (third edition), or those written for American academics and lawyers, such as *Basic Text on Labor Law* by Robert A. Gorman and *The Developing Labor Law*, edited by Charles Morris. Those who desire to explore employment-discrimination problems further may wish to consult my *Black Workers in White Unions: Job Discrimination in the United States*. The most encyclopedic text in this area is *Employment Discrimination Law* by Schlei and Grossman. The best case book aimed at American law students as of this writing is *Employment Discrimination Law: Cases and Materials* by Arthur B. Smith.

A Primer on American Labor Law is more descriptive than analytic. It is intended for those who would not otherwise be exposed to the American labor-law system: labor and management representatives, foreigners, neutral parties involved in labor dispute resolution and having a special interest in the United States or industrial relations, general-practice lawyers who occasionally represent a union or a company but are not specialists in the field, students of labor relations and labor law, and even practicing labor-law specialists who have some interest in a brief comparison with foreign systems.

Many people have helped make this book a reality. My audiences and classes made me think and rethink my material and its presentation. William Keogh of the Stanford Law School, Robert Flanagan of the Stanford Business School, and the late Norman Amundsen of the University of California's Institute of Industrial Relations read and commented on my drafts. I am grateful to the Stanford Law School students who provided valuable research and note material: Debra Roth, Todd Brower, Alan Reeves, and Karen Snell. I am particularly appreciative of the work done by Mr. Reeves, who suggested some textual changes and shouldered the major burden of the notes. And it would have been impossible to produce this work without the extremely valuable and skillful typing and organizational work of Clarie Kuball and Mary Enright.

The research for this book was supported by the Stanford Legal Research Fund, which was made possible by a bequest from the estate of Ira S. Lillick and by gifts from Roderick E. and Carla A. Hills and other friends of the Stanford Law School.

Finally, I could not have completed the book without the patience of my wife, Hilda, and my three sons, Bill, Tim, and Ed, during my long absences abroad and in my office at the Stanford Law School.

A Primer on American Labor Law

1

An Overview

American labor law and the American industrial-relations system have a symbiotic relationship, and neither can be understood without reference to the other. This should come as no surprise; after all, law, lawyers, and litigation play a major role in our society. Our collective bargaining system has been devised predominantly by labor and management, however, not by the government and the courts. In fact, we often forget—and foreign observers fail to grasp—that our most important tool in the resolution of labor disputes is our private arbitration system, which operates outside the formal legal system of courts and administrative agencies. Before examining the history and substance of American labor law, then, let us begin with their impetus in the American industrial-relations system: organized labor.

As a result of the evolution of the industrial-relations system in the United States, the unions have a remarkably different attitude toward law than, for instance, those in Britain. This is not to say that American trade unions do not have a healthy and often well-founded distrust of lawyers; one can see this attitude manifested in countless ways. But the unions are not against the law here. And this is because the American unions—especially the industrial unions that emerged during the Great Depression of the 1930s—obtained political power before industrial power. They were willing and eager to look to the law as a useful adjunct to their growth and the achievement of recognition and bargaining relationships with employers.

Trade unionism came late to the United States. There were stirrings among American workers toward the end of the nineteenth century (particularly in the 1880s)—first under the banner of the Knights of Labor, which attempted to organize unskilled as well as skilled workers (a venture doomed to failure). The second major effort was by the American Federation of Labor, initially led by Samuel Gompers, who espoused an approach to trade unionism that focused on what labor could achieve at the bargaining table. The AFL, a central federation to which various unions were attached, strove to avoid becoming formally affiliated with a political party as the European unions had. Gompers's refrain, "We shall reward labor's friends and punish its enemies," reflected a philosophy that involved labor in the political process with political parties but did not provide for formal affiliation. To this day, however, the AFL-CIO, the umbrella organization for national unions, plays an active political role; except in 1972, the AFL-CIO has supported every Democratic Party presidential candidate since Adlai Stevenson.

At the turn of the century, the power and prestige of Gompers and of the AFL were being used on the behalf of skilled craftsmen organized on an occupational basis. The masses of workers, who had often been shunned by the craft unions as unorganizable, were not affiliated with major industrial unions (or with unions of any kind) until the 1930s. At that juncture new unions, such as the United Auto Workers, the United Steelworkers, and the United Rubber Workers, came forward. They sought to organize and represent production workers and skilled tradesmen under the umbrella of a new federation, the Congress of Industrial Organizations (CIO), and they grew with the law. To some extent their structure was shaped by the law as the National Labor Relations Board, operating under the National Labor Relations Act, fashioned units or categories of job classifications, for the purpose of bargaining on an industrial basis, that permitted the inclusion of semiskilled and unskilled workers in the same bargaining unit with tradesmen.[1]

All of this is in contrast with the history of organized labor in Britain, where great general unions that organized workers without regard to job classification or industry reached out to organize the semiskilled and the unskilled through the "new unionism" of the 1880s. In Britain the unions had industrial power before political power, and so they used their position and strength to fend the law off and to keep it out of their affairs. This was a central thrust of labor legislation in the first Asquith Liberal government, in which the trade unions had some influence. The Trades Disputes Act of 1906 was designed to create immunity in the courts for trade-union activities.[2] In the United States a similar policy of laissez-faire was adopted at the time of the Norris-LaGuardia Act[3] but was quickly abandoned in 1935 with the passage of the National Labor Relations Act, which provided for the right to engage in collective bargaining. For better or for worse, to this day the American trade unions continue to look to the law, and to the National Labor Relations Board in particular, for sustenance.

Another important feature of the American industrial-relations system is that it is (again, particularly by European standards) a decentralized bargaining structure. In Europe, particularly on the continent, the pattern is multiemployer or industrywide bargaining. In Germany, the primary function of the unions since World War II has been to bargain regional tariffs or agreements establishing a minimum rate for a geographical area of the country. In Sweden, wage bargaining takes place on a centralized basis—initially between the Central Labor Federation (LO) and the Swedish Employers Federation—and along industrywide lines with the involvement of the major industrial unions.[4] Industrywide bargaining is also the rule in Britain, although to a lesser extent. In all of these countries there is a local organization to represent employees, but the local entity usually does not possess nearly as strong a presence or as much contact with the national trade union as in the United States. In Britain, shop stewards bargain for pay rates and sometimes for other conditions of employment—often in committees that are independent of the national trade-union structure. In Germany, *Betriebsrate* (shop committees, or works councils) are involved by statute in a wide variety of employment decisions and sometimes have veto power over employers' decisions.[5] In recent years German unions, particularly in the metals industry, have come to play a more substantial role in the plant and to be more integrated with the system of works councils as a matter of law. In Sweden there are local clubs (roughly equivalent to American local unions) that operate on a plant basis, but many plants are too small to have one.

In the United States the percentage of eligible workers who are organized into trade unions is lower than the percentages in Europe and Japan.[6] Where organization exists, though, it is clear that a plant-level presence tied to the national union structure is much stronger in the United States than in any of the other industrialized countries. The local union, which has a formal affiliation in its dues-sharing structure with the national or international union, is often organized at the plant level. Depending on the number of members and the amount of dues, some of the officials of the local, such as the president and the secretary-treasurer, may be employed full-time by the local and paid out of the workers' dues. However, in many locals all of the officials are full-time employees of a company; when they are involved in negotiations or grievance handling, their wages may be paid either by the company (the collective bargaining agreement often provides for this) or from the local union's treasury.

Most collective bargaining agreements in the United States are negotiated at the plant level, with the involvement of the local union. The agreements are relatively detailed and comprehensive. One of the most important functions of locals relates to the processing of grievances over an agreement's interpretation. Locals are sometimes involved in the final step of the procedure, arbitration. The local usually pays the union's share of the costs of arbitration, and if the local and the employer are particularly disputatious this can be a considerable drain on the local's treasury. However, because most disputes are resolved at the lower steps of the process, the local is quite dependent on members of grievance committees, which are composed of full-time employees. Similarly, the local depends for grievance processing on the shop stewards, who also are full-time employees involved in a vital function on behalf of the union.[7]

Another structural variation arises from the union's basis of organization and its organizing rationale. So far, we have only considered locals that are organized on a single-plant basis. Locals may also be organized on a multiplant or a multicompany basis ("amalgamated locals"). More broadly, they may be affiliated with a national craft, industrial, or general union. General unions are somewhat exceptional in the United States; the best example is the International Brotherhood of Teamsters, the largest American union (which does, however, have a base in one industry: transportation). Officials of national unions may be involved in the bargaining of the agreement, but most of the negotiating staff will be local officials.

In such industries as automobiles, steel, and rubber, unions have negotiated companywide agreements—but even there, local-plant supplemental agreements are negotiated on certain issues.

Today most unions are affiliated with the merged AFL-CIO, which was formed in 1955. This federation has a no-raiding agreement that is binding on its affiliates. The craft unions play a dominant role in its leadership and policy. The Teamsters are not affiliated with the AFL-CIO; they were expelled in 1957 because of a controversy relating to corruption in their unions. The United Mine Workers and the International Longshoremen and Warehousemen (the West Coast dockers) are also unaffiliated. In 1968 the United Auto Workers withdrew because of dissatisfaction with the AFL-CIO's policy and leaders, but in 1981 they returned to the fold.[8]

Another important aspect of the American system is the wage consciousness of the trade unions.[9] Historically, American trade unionism has been hard-hitting in its economic demands. In part, this is thought to be attributable to the lack of class solidarity among many American workers. Because a labor organization cannot appeal to workers on a class basis, the appeal must be based on wages and fringe benefits. This has helped produce what some have called "business unionism" or "bread and butter unionism."

Many of the matters handled by labor and management at the bargaining table in the United States are dealt with legislatively in Europe. This is particularly true of fringe benefits, such as vacations and vacation pay, holidays, unemployment compensation, medical insurance, and hospitalization benefits.

Traditionally, protection against dismissal without cause, and compensation of workers laid off or dismissed because of plant closure or the contracting out of work, have been addressed by collective bargaining in the United States. In Europe "unfair dismissals," whether for economic reasons or on disciplinary grounds, are dealt with through legislation. But recently a number of state courts, following the lead of the Supreme Court of California,[10] have held that employers cannot dismiss employees without just cause or arbitrarily or in bad faith.[11] (Chapter 11 contains a more thorough discussion of this development.) Some states have enacted legislation regulating plant closures and layoffs attributable to them.[12] In Japan, in contrast to both America and Europe, lifetime employment for "permanent" workers in large companies is guaranteed under a system that is promulgated unilaterally by the companies, outside the collective bargaining system.[13]

Thus, the number of subjects to be discussed and resolved through collective bargaining is considerably greater in the United States than in Europe and Japan. Without a welfare-state system like those in Europe, and without paternalism like that in Japan, American unions must (or should) be active in their negotiations with management. The appeals that the unions make to recruit workers cover many items. The American system encourages unions to push for more at the bargaining table. It encourages management to install labor-saving devices to increase productivity (a phenomenon that seems to have declined in recent years). The decentralized system of bargaining and the wage-conscious behavior of unions also encourage American employers to resist union organizational activities. Accordingly, there are many more organizational and recognition disputes than in other industrialized countries. Anticipated labor costs and potential competition problems promote such resistance, which is in part responsible for the heavy caseload of the National Labor Relations Board. Most of the more than 40,000 unfair-labor-practice charges per year[14] that have been processed by the NLRB involve allegations of discriminatory discipline and discharge of workers, frequently during organizational campaigns. The NLRB is engaged in more litigation than any other federal agency.

In Germany or Scandinavia, a dispute can be resolved on an industrywide basis and the parties are bound to the solution. But in the United States, essentially the same kind of dispute can come before the NLRB again and again, because different employers and workers see their situation as slightly different from that considered in an earlier decision, and they are not bound by any adjudication or decision on an association or industrywide basis. Moreover, because most of the cases involve discipline or dismissal, they are essentially questions of fact, and no general rule can dispose of most of them.

The American industrial-relations system has myriad characteristics. Which of those touched on here are primary, secondary, and so on has been debated extensively, but few would debate that our body of labor law rests firmly on the system's fundamental characteristics. How has that come to be?

2

Industrial Relations and Labor Law Before Modern Legislation

In the United States and in Europe the Industrial Revolution brought competition between employers for distant markets. This created an environment in which labor was increasingly treated as a raw material or a commodity, and it is therefore hardly surprising that a profound sense of discord was generated between workers and their employers. This historical development cannot be divorced from any consideration of industrial relations and labor law in the United States today.

American and European workers sought to band together and to protect themselves against the attempts of business combinations, trusts, and monopolies to reduce labor costs. The courts in the United States and the parliament in England, through their "anti-combination" statutes, sought to brand such worker combinations as unlawful conspiracies in restraint of trade—a restraint that might diminish free competition between employers. In the United States the law of conspiracy was criminal law, and indictments were obtained against combinations of workers trying to raise wages. The leading case in which the criminal conspiracy doctrine was applied was the Philadelphia *Cordwainers* case of 1806.[1]

Certain issues raised in the *Cordwainers* case remain with us today:

- How could individuals who had no "permanent stake" in the business become substantially involved in making decisions relating to it? As the prosecution said in *Cordwainers*, "Will you permit men to destroy it [business] who have no permanent stake in the city; men who can pack up their all in a knapsack or carry them in their pockets in New York or Baltimore?"

- What is to be the proper and appropriate sphere of interest for workers? What could be regarded as a management prerogative with which employees could not interfere? Very much involved in any consideration of this question was the Tory idea—promoted by America's first secretary of the treasury, Alexander Hamilton—that private organizations such as unions interfered with the rapid increase in manufacturing and therefore with national prosperity.

- How could prices of products be set safely if the workers were to wait until order books were swelled to capacity—when the time would be propitious—to put pressure on employers for higher wages? How could commercial contracts be negotiated in distant markets under such circumstances?

- What was to be done about the emergence of these new combinations of private societies and their pressure on individuals to comply with the combination's notion of the collective interest? As Job Harrison testified in the *Cordwainers* case, "If I did not join the body, no man would sit upon the seat where I worked . . . nor board or lodge in the same house, nor would they work at all for the same employer."

These were but some of the issues raised in *Cordwainers*. The case did not decide definitively whether the combination itself was an unlawful conspiracy or whether it was necessary to prove that its object was the improvement of wages and working conditions, but it served as a legal weapon for employers and thus stultified union growth.

Numerous judicial decisions in the nineteenth century made efforts by workers to improve their wages and working conditions through combinations an unlawful criminal conspiracy. In 1842 a landmark decision heralded a new judicial approach to the control of union activity. The Supreme Judicial Court of Massachusetts, in *Commonwealth* v. *Hunt*,[2] enunciated a test that was to figure in the debate about the role of the judiciary in labor disputes during the twentieth century. It rested upon an assessment of tactics, motive, and intent. In *Hunt* the court approved the closed shop, which requires a worker to join the union prior to employment, as a lawful objective. Said the Court:

The manifest intent of the association is to induce all those engaged in the same occupation to become members of it. Such a purpose is not unlawful. It would give them a power which might be exerted for useful and honorable purposes, or for dangerous and pernicious ones. If the latter were the real and actual object, and susceptible of proof, it should have been specially charged. Such an association might be used to afford each other assistance in times of poverty, sickness, and distress; or to raise their intellectual, moral, and social conditions; or to make improvement in their art; or for other proper purposes. Or the association might be designed for purposes of oppression and injustice. . . . An association may be formed, the declared objects of which are innocent and laudable, and yet they may have secret articles, or an agreement communicated only to the members, by which they are banded together for purposes injurious to the peace of society or to the rights of its members. Such would undoubtedly be a criminal conspiracy, on proof of the fact, however meritorious and praiseworthy the declared objects might be.[3]

Although the *Hunt* decision was a break from reliance upon the criminal-conspiracy doctrine as a vehicle to thwart union growth, and although it did not abolish the doctrine, the court refused to assume that the objectives of workers were improper. The criminal-conspiracy doctrine began to fall into disuse. But other legal theories were used against the unions.

The rule followed by the courts in the civil arena was the "*prima facie* tort" doctrine: that the intentional infliction of economic harm upon another party is a tort, and thus unlawful, unless justifed by a legitimate purpose. This meant that a labor union was liable on the face of it in damages for losses sustained by virtue of a private wrong done to another party (economic pressure through strikes and picketing by the union aimed at an employer).

But was the self-interest of the workers a legitimate purpose, or was a judicial balancing of competing economic interests (workers, employers, and the public) required? All too often the courts opted for the latter standard. With no defined guidelines to be followed, the courts were able and willing to use their own social and economic predilections to determine what constituted "legitimate purpose." As Cox, Bok, and Gorman have said, "On the civil side . . . the volume of labor litigation sharply increased, and although it is impossible to reconstruct the legal atmosphere of the post Civil War period, it seems fair to say that when the labor disputes engendered by the conflict over union organization were taken to the courts, the judges were substantially free, despite the scattered precedents, to create new law appropriate to the new occasion, guided only by the vague 'principles' which emerged from rulings upon more familiar situations."[4]

In 1896 the Supreme Judicial Court of Massachusetts granted an injunction against picketing or "patrolling" because such conduct had the effect of interfering with freedom of contract and the right to employ an individual at a price agreeable to the parties.[5] Such interference with business, in the court's view, was a "private nuisance" and, accordingly, enjoinable. This meant that the judiciary prohibited the unions from patrolling, and that disobedient individuals could be fined or imprisoned. Justice Holmes, dissenting from the decision, argued that patrolling did not necessarily carry with it the threat of unlawful activity or bodily harm:

There was no proof of any threat or danger of a patrol exceeding two men, and as of course an injunction is not granted except with reference to what there is reason to expect in its absence, the question on that point is whether a patrol of two men should be enjoined. Again, the defendants are enjoined by the final decree from intimidating by threats, expressed or implied, of physical harm to body or property, any person who may be desirous of entering into the employment of the plaintiff, so far as to prevent him from entering the same. In order to test the correctness of the refusal to go further, it must be assumed that the defendants obey the express prohibition of the decree.[6]

Moreover, Holmes argued against the "justifiable conduct" test (that only economic pressure or picketing whose object is justifiable in the court's judgment is protected from an injunction): "The true grounds of decision are considerations of policy and of social advantage, and it is vain to suppose that solutions can be obtained merely by logic and general propositions of law which nobody disputes."[7]

Holmes continued to dissent against the "*prima facie* tort" doctrine, simultaneously expressing skepticism about the ability of trade unions to obtain a larger share of wealth through collective pressure (except at the expense of the less organized workers[8]). This matter continues to generate considerable controversy,[9] but Holmes's basic theme was simply that the courts ought not to devise their own policies in the absence of instructions from elected legislatures.

Meanwhile, as the American Federation of Labor emerged beyond embryonic form, a new judicial weapon against the growth of trade unions was developed. Its statutory basis was to be found in the Sherman Antitrust Act of 1890.[10] The Sherman Act, a reaction to the abuses of trusts that had achieved prominence and strength in the wake of the Industrial Revolution and the westward migration, had as its rationale the prohibition of conduct suppressing competition between businesses. Soon after its enactment, some employers argued that unions and their economic pressure achieved the same objectives and therefore violated the statute. Restraint of trade had been attacked by the courts before the Sherman Act, but the approach taken was a judicial refusal to enforce contracts that, for instance, provided for the boycott of an employer departing from an industry practice or agreement on allocation of markets or prices. The statutory scheme of the Sherman Act provided that unlawful conspiracies could be attacked in the courts.

During the debate about the Sherman Antitrust Act, Congress had not really addressed the statute's applicability to labor. At common law the phrase "restraint of trade" had meant aggregations, pools, or combinations whose object was to control the supply and price of products in order to suppress competition among companies shipping goods across state lines and thereby establish a monopolistic position in the industry. At common law, proving restraint of trade required evidence of motivation to harm or restrain others in the pursuit of their occupations.

The first test of the applicability of antitrust legislation to labor came before the Supreme Court in 1908 in the case of *Loewe* v. *Lawlor*,[11] or *Danbury Hatters* as it became more popularly known. This case involved a secondary boycott engaged in by the United Hatters of North America, which had called a strike against the D. E. Loewe Company for the purpose of unionizing the company. The union attempted to get consumers to boycott the company's hats in various states across the country. The union and its allies, the American Federation of Labor and other affiliates, attempted to boycott not only the company but any person who patronized the company. Because the union's efforts were aimed at parties other than the employer with which the union had a dispute, the tactics were referred to as "secondary" activities. The Supreme Court concluded that the antitrust laws applied to labor. Said Chief Justice Fuller, speaking for the Court: "The records of Congress show that several efforts were made to exempt, by legislation, organizations of farmers and laborers from the operation of the act and that all of these efforts failed, so that the act remained as we have it before us."[12]

The impact of *Danbury Hatters* was devastating for organized labor. The unions and many others felt that the statute had been interpreted improperly, inasmuch as organized labor was not the focal point of congressional debate that took place prior to the enactment of antitrust legislation. Moreover, because the Sherman Antitrust Act provides for treble damages rather than the actual amount of the losses incurred (as well as criminal sanctions), the final judgment after fourteen years of litigation in *Danbury Hatters* awarded a substantial amount of money ($250,000). What was particularly troublesome about the judgment was that the members of the union were individually and personally liable. Though the case was settled in 1917 for slightly over $234,000 and the AFL was able to obtain $216,000 in voluntary contributions from union members, the fact that labor had to "pass the hat" to avoid the foreclosure of members' homes made the case unforgettable.

Immediately after the Supreme Court's decision in *Danbury Hatters* in 1908, the labor movement began a campaign to reverse the decision and the applicabiity of the Sherman Antitrust Act to trade unions. In 1908 the Democratic Party promised to amend antitrust legislation so as to reverse the Court's decision, and in 1912 it did so again in the following language: ". . . labor organizations and members should not be regarded as illegal organizations in restraint of trade."[13] After Woodrow Wilson was elected president in 1912, these efforts culminated in the Clayton Antitrust Act of 1914, which Samuel Gompers immediately characterized as labor's Magna Carta and Bill of Rights and the most important legislation since the abolition of slavery. The two key provisions of the Clayton Act were found in sections 6 and 20.

Section 6 stated that "the labor of a human being is not a commodity or article of commerce. Nothing contained in the antitrust laws shall be construed to forbid the existence and operation of labor . . . organizations, instituted for the purposes of mutual help . . . or to forbid or restrain individual members of such organizations from lawfully carrying out the legitimate objects thereof; nor shall such organizations, or the members thereof, be held or construed to be illegal combinations or conspiracies in restraint of trade, under the antitrust laws."[14] Gompers said that section 6 constituted "sledgehammer blows to the wrongs and injustices so long inflicted upon the workers," and that "this declaration is the industrial Magna Carta upon which the working people will rear their structure of industrial freedom."[15] But what did section 6 mean? Only one theme emerged clearly: Antitrust laws were not to be deemed to forbid the existence and operation of labor organizations, and therefore, although such organizations are by definition anticompetitive in that they seek to suppress competition between workers in the same plants, companies, wider geographical areas, and ultimately throughout the nation, they were not to be regarded as illegal.

Supplementing this approach was section 20 of the Clayton Act, which Gompers had characterized as the "Bill of Rights" portion. Section 20 stated that no restraining order or injunction should be granted by any U.S. court in "any case between an employer and employees, or between employers and employees, or between employees, or between persons employed and persons seeking employment, involving, or growing out of, a dispute concerning terms or conditions of employment" unless a showing of irreparable injury was made and there was therefore no adequate remedy at law. A restraining order or an injunction is designed to force a person or entity to do something. Injunctions often had been—and still are—designed to force a union to stop striking, picketing, or engaging in other forms of economic pressure against the employer. Section 20 also prohibited injunctions where workers struck, or peacefully picketed, or urged individuals to cease patronizing "any party to such dispute." The language was broad, yet section 20 did not explicitly address the question of what kinds of union economic pressure were to be appropriate. Because the statute did not limit restraining orders to disputes between an employer and *his* employees, one might assume that secondary boycotts were not to be regarded as unlawful. But when the Court did confront this issue, in *Duplex Printing Press Co.* v. *Deering*,[16] organized labor and Samuel Gompers received a rude surprise indeed.

The Supreme Court's decision in *Duplex* destroyed most of the hopes and expectations of organized labor about the Clayton Antitrust Act. *Duplex* arose out of a suit for injunctive relief to restrain a secondary boycott against a printing-press manufacturer in Battle Creek, Michigan, employing about 200 machinists in the factory in addition to some office employees and others. The company followed an "open shop" policy, purportedly refusing to discriminate against either union or nonunion men. The union, which had as its goals a closed shop in which only union members could be employed, the eight-hour day, and the union scale of wages, called a strike at the factory. When only a few of the workers joined in the union's efforts, the union attempted to boycott the company's products by warning customers that it would be better for them not to purchase from the company, threatening customers with sympathetic strikes, and inciting the employees of customers to strike against their employers. It also notified repair shops not to do repair work on Duplex presses and threatened union men with the loss of their union cards if they assisted in the installation of Duplex presses. The Duplex company brought an antitrust action against the union for unlawful restraint of trade.

The Court stated that a distinction between a primary and a secondary boycott was material to the question of whether union conduct was immunized by virtue of the Clayton Act. The Court first examined section 6 and stated the following:

The section assumes the normal objects of a labor organization to be legitimate, and declares that nothing in the antitrust laws shall be construed to forbid the existence and operation of such organizations, or to forbid their members from *lawfully* carrying out their *legitimate* objects; and that such an organization shall not be held in itself—merely because of its existence and operation—to be an illegal combination or conspiracy in restraint of trade. But there is nothing in the section to exempt such an organization or its member from accountability where it or they depart from its normal and legitimate objects and engage in an actual combination or conspiracy in restraint of trade.[17]

The Court then focused on section 20 of the Clayton Act, noting that that provision specifically forbade the issuance of restraining orders or injunctions in U.S. courts where there was a labor dispute between an "employer and employees" and that the first paragraph's prohibition of orders in such circumstances "unless necessary to prevent irreparable injury to property, or to a property right" where there was no adequate remedy of law (that is to say, where the wronged party could not be adequately compensated through damage) was merely "declaratory of the law as it stood before."[18] Said the

Court: "The first paragraph merely puts into statutory form familiar restrictions upon the granting of injunctions already established and of general application in the equity practice of the courts of the United States."[19] The Court noted that the second paragraph referred to cases where the parties were "standing in proximate relation to a controversy" of the kind designated in the first paragraph. Noting that the majority of the circuit courts of appeals had previously concluded that the words "employers and employees" should be treated as referring to "the business class or clan to which the parties litigant respectively belong," the Court nevertheless concluded that any construction of the statute that would preclude employer relief where union secondary activity was involved against employers "wholly unconnected" with the Battle Creek factory was a statutory construction "altogether inadmissible."[20] With a somewhat selective glance at legislative history, the Court rejected the "views and motives of individual members" of Congress and relied on committee reports that it recognized were not "explicitly" addressed to the question of whether secondary as well as primary boycotts were to be permitted. Significantly, the Court made clear its condemnation of the damage done to "many innocent people"—secondary employees and employees who were "far remote" from the "original" dispute.[21]

Justice Brandeis, in a strong dissent in which he was joined by two other justices (including Holmes), stated that the contest between the Machinists' Union and the company involved "vitally the interest of every person whose cooperation is sought." Said Brandeis: "May not all with a common interest join in refusing to expend their labor upon articles whose very production constitutes an attack upon their standard of living and the institution which they are convinced supports it? Applying common-law principles the answer should, in my opinion, be: 'Yes, if as a matter of fact those who so co-operate have a common interest.' "[22] Brandeis noted that "centralization in the control business brought its corresponding centralization in the organization of workingmen," and that a single employer might threaten the "standing" of the entire labor organization and its members. When it did so, said the dissent, "the union, in order to protect itself, would naturally refuse to work on his materials wherever found."[23] Addressing the antitrust-law question, Brandeis noted that the Clayton Act was the "fruit of unceasing agitation, which extended over more than twenty years and was designed to equalize before the law the position of workingman and employer as industrial combatants."[24] The dissenting opinion noted that use of the "malicious combination" doctrine, which had made actionable trade-union activity that judges had deemed harmful and therefore unlawful.

The ideas of the proponents of new legislation had been "fairly crystallized" by 1914, said Justice Brandeis, and the principal theme that had emerged was a desire to remove the judiciary from involvement in labor disputes and consequent determinations based on their own social and economic viewpoints. Part and parcel of this view was that workers had suffered as a result of judicial involvement and that considerable confusion about the demarcation line between lawful and unlawful union conduct had ensued. Brandeis then noted that the Clayton Act had not referred to employers and employees in the employ of the same employer, and that under strict technical construction the statute could have no application to disputes between employers of labor and workingmen, "since the very acts to which it applies sever the continuity of the legal relationship."[25] That is, if a work stoppage was commenced, the striker was no longer in the employ of the company and could be replaced. Thus, under a technical statutory interpretation, primary strikers who had a dispute with no one other than their own employers could be excluded from the act's protection.

In conclusion, Justice Brandeis noted that although his view of the law was that each party could conduct an industrial struggle in its own self-interest, no "constitutional or moral sanction [should be ready to attach] to that right."[26] The overriding theme of the dissent was that the intent of Congress had been to remove the judges from defining what constituted "self-interest" and therefore appropriate action.

Organized labor's hopes were once again dashed by the majority opinion in *Duplex*. Indeed, the implications of *Duplex* were even more devastating than those of *Danbury Hatters*. In the first place, the Clayton amendments now provided employers as well as the U.S. government with the authority to sue for injunctive relief against unlawful labor disputes. This posed a considerable problem toward the end of the 1920s. Second, *Duplex* and its progeny represented the apogee of the "unlawful objectives" test. Justice Brandeis's concerns that judicial involvement meant that the judicially imposed social and economic predilections of a pro-entrepreneur judiciary were soon to be realized. And the result of *Duplex* clearly was that the language of section 20 of Clayton was mere surplussage at best.

The difficulties of applying the "unlawful objectives" test articulated in *Duplex*, the opportunity for judicial bias, and the artificial nature of judicially fashioned boundary lines became apparent in *Coronado Coal Company* v. *United Mine Workers*.[27] The opinion was written by Chief Justice Taft. Evidence established that a strike had been prompted by the "keen competition" between nonunion employers and employers that had bargaining relationships with the union, and the Court concluded that this demonstrated an unlawful attempt to prevent the manufacture and production of goods and to restrain control of their supply entering into interstate commerce. Consequently, the Court held that where a union was engaged in a primary or local strike against an employer, unlawful intent within the meaning of antitrust laws could be demonstrated through specific evidence, because the restraints on trade was "indirect." However, where the union activity was secondary inasmuch as employers whose employees were not directly involved in the dispute itself were the subject of pressure, the restraint was direct and unlawful intent could be inferred from the economic tactic.

The road was thus open to the very kind of judicial meddling and abuses that had created "unceasing agitation" of the kind described by Justice Brandeis. Particularly ominous in this regard was the above-noted availability of injunctive relief to employers (as well as the government) by virtue of the 1914 Clayton statute. Employers used this tool with increasing frequency in the 1920s, encouraged by the sympathetic response of the judiciary. Frankfurter and Greene have chronicled the many abuses that came to be associated with this aspect of the judicial process in their classic book *The Labor Injunction*. What follows here is a brief summary of their study and the comments of other scholars.

Employers filed motions for injunctive relief, or orders requiring organizations and industries to do certain things whenever strikes or picketing occurred at plant premises. (Generally, the economic pressure was for the purpose of securing organization or some collective bargaining relationship.) The basis for obtaining such relief was not testimony and exhibits in a formal proceeding where witnesses could be subjected to cross-examination as well as examination, but generalized affidavits which were simply altered in minor respects to suit the details of the case. Moreover, injunctive relief was usually sought and obtained on an *ex parte* basis; the union's attorney was generally not present.

Generalized orders fashioned by the courts prohibited any individual from striking and picketing on the grounds that irreparable harm (harm that could not be compensated through a damage award) would be caused to his employer. In this connection, the courts often formulated a doctrine of vicarious responsibility under which the union could be held liable for the acts of any individual without regard to any showing of relationship between the union and the individual's conduct. Moreover, since most motions for injunctive relief were aimed at enjoining union efforts that were effective in the sense that they were likely to inflict immediate harm upon the employer, the motions were obtained expeditiously. The injunction would be in the form of a temporary restraining order. A temporary restraining order, which can be dissolved after a period of time or converted into a permanent injunction restraining the strike, was rarely if ever reversed at the time that the permanent injunction was sought. But the significant element of restraint was not only the failure to reverse but the granting of the injunction without thorough fact-finding. As Frankfurter and Greene said:

The injunction cannot preserve the so-called *status quo*; the situation does not remain in equilibrium awaiting judgment upon full knowledge. The suspension of activities affects only the strikers; the employer resumes his efforts to defeat the strike, and presumes them free from the interdicted interferences. Moreover, the suspension of strike activities, even temporarily, may defeat the strike for practical purposes and foredoom its resumption even if the injunction is later lifted. Choice is not between irreparable damage to one side and compensable damage to the other. The law's conundrum is which side should bear the risk of *unavoidable* irreparable damage. Improvident denial of the injunction may be irreparable to the complainant; improvident issue of the injunction may be irreparable to the defendant. For this situation the ordinary mechanics of the provisional injunction proceedings are plainly inadequate. Judicial error is too costly to either side of the labor dispute to permit perfunctory determination of the crucial issues; even in the first instance, it must be searching. The necessity of finding the facts quickly from sources vague, embittered and partisan, colored at the start by the passionate intensities of a labor controversy, calls at best for rare judicial qualities. It becomes an impossible assignment when judges rely upon the complaint and the affidavits of interested or professional witnesses, untested by the safeguards of common law trials, personal appearance of witnesses, confrontation and cross-examination.[28]

Beyond these problems was the fact that judges, without the presence of juries, often imposed contempt penalties in the same cases in which they had issued the injunction initially. (Contempt penalties—sometimes fines, sometimes imprisonment—are imposed by the courts on parties who disobey or are contemptuous of the court's orders.) Contempt problems arose regularly, sometimes because of liability that was imputed to the union by conduct of other parties through the "vicarious responsibility" doctrine.

All of this created an environment in which respect for the law and the judiciary, a critical prerequisite for a functioning modern democracy, was increasingly undermined. The concerns expressed by Justices Brandeis and Holmes in previous opinions became increasingly vexatious after the *Duplex* decision and the increased popularity of the labor injunction. Again, partly because of the efforts of Frankfurter and Greene, Congress was lobbied to reform the law. Again, the proponents of reform were successful in obtaining legislation. But this time the legislative package was different.

In the Norris-LaGuardia Act of 1932, Congress attempted to learn from the past and to speak more unambiguously, and to protect the statute against a *Duplex*-type interpretation. This objective was to be accomplished in a number of ways, foremost among them the broad declaration that jurisdiction was to be denied to the federal courts in certain kinds of labor disputes. Section 1 stated that no federal court would have "jurisdiction to issue any restraining order or temporary or permanent injunction in a case involving or growing out of a labor dispute, except in a strict conformity with the provisions of this Act."[29] Section 13 went on to attempt to reverse the impact of *Duplex*'s narrow definition of "labor dispute." The new provision referred to nearly every kind of labor dispute,[30] and quite clearly secondary stoppages were included within the definition. Section 4, operating with the definitions provided by section 13, stated that in any case growing out of the labor dispute the federal courts were precluded from issuing any injunctions except where violence or fraud was involved. Even where violence or fraud was involved, an order restraining such a stoppage was to be available only after a hearing had been conducted and a finding of facts set forth—and the hearing was to be conducted with examination and cross-examination rather than with the kinds of affidavits to which the federal courts had become accustomed prior to 1932. Although temporary *ex parte* orders could still be allowed, they were made permissible for a period of time not to exceed five days and on showing of "substantial and irreparable injury" to the employer's property as well as the posting of a bond. The right to trial by jury was provided in connection with contempt cases, and the prohibitions contained in the injunction were required to be specific in defining the conduct forbidden as well as the parties who were affected by the order, thus presumably diminishing the number of cases that might go into such contempt proceedings.

Additionally, the Norris-LaGuardia Act addressed an issue that had been a matter of controversy for some time in the United States. The "yellow dog" contract, through which employers required workers to stay out of unions as a condition of employment, was declared to be contrary to the public policy of the United States and thus unenforceable in any federal court. The Norris-LaGuardia approach to the "yellow dog" contract reflects the statute's general philosophy. Though the law promoted the doctrine of freedom of association for all workers as a matter of public policy, it contained no machinery for implementing this freedom. Norris-LaGuardia was a laissez-faire approach to industrial relations, a strongly worded series of instructions to the federal courts to keep their hands off labor disputes because they had made a mess of things by intervening in the past. Their handling of labor disputes had been inexpert and insensitive to the concerns and expectations of workers in an industrialized society. The act represented a strong warning to the courts not to engage in dubious statutory interpretation so as to avoid what appeared to be the intent of Congress—a tactic in which many thought the Court had engaged in *Duplex*. The theme of this statutory approach, denial of jurisdiction to the courts, was consistent with laissez-faire.

One major problem was left unresolved by Norris-LaGuardia, and another was soon to appear. The first involved the question of what impact, if any, Norris-LaGuardia had upon criminal prosecutions and damage actions pursued by employers or the government under antitrust legislation. The remedies, as well as injunctions, were available under the antitrust statutes, but Norris-LaGuardia explicitly addressed the issue of injunctive relief alone. The second question related to the basic inequality between capital and labor in the United States in the early 1930s. Was it enough to simply reverse *Duplex* and deny the federal courts jurisdiction in labor disputes? Would it not be necessary to provide protection for organized labor, which was confronted with company-dominated and company-assisted unions, company spies, the blacklisting of union members, surveillance, and other forms of harassment as well as the dismissal of union organizers who were employees?

The Supreme Court dealt with the first of these two problems in *United States* v. *Hutcheson*, which dealt with a government criminal prosecution against a union that had been engaged in a jurisdictional dispute over work assignments with another union. Justice Frankfurter, speaking for the Court, concluded that the Norris-LaGuardia prohibitions had broader scope than the denial of jurisdiction to federal courts in connection with injunctions. Said the Court:

The Norris-LaGuardia Act removed the fetters upon trade union activities, which according to judicial construction [section] 20 of the Clayton Act had left untouched, by still further narrowing the circumstances under which the federal courts could grant injunctions in labor disputes. More especially, the Act explicitly formulated the "public policy of the United States" in regard to the industrial conflict, and by its light established that the allowable area of union activity was not to be restricted, as it had been in the *Duplex* case, to an immediate employer-employee relation. Therefore, whether trade union conduct constitutes a violation of the Sherman Law is to be determined only by reading the Sherman Law and [section] 20 of the Clayton Act and the Norris-LaGuardia Act as a harmonizing text of outlawry of labor conduct.[31]

The Court further stated that the relationship between Norris-LaGuardia and Clayton had to be understood in its historical context and not read as a "tightly drawn amendment to a technically phrased tax provision."[32] Accordingly, the statutes were to be regarded as "interlacing" and part of one body of federal labor law. Therefore, where the courts were denied jurisdiction in labor disputes for the purpose of injunctive relief, they were also restricted in connection with criminal prosecutions and damage actions designed to suppress the kinds of union activity at which Norris-LaGuardia was aimed.

What then was the range of activity that would be immune from antitrust law? The test, said the Court, was one of self-interest. In vivid contrast to the position taken in *Duplex* and some of its antecedents, the Court was at pains to state that what was to be regarded as "licit and the illicit" had no relationship to the "wisdom or unwisdom, the rightness or wrongness, the selfishness or unselfishness of the end of which the particular union activities are the means."[33] The Court stated that so long as the union acted in self-interest and did not combine with nonlabor groups, union activity could not be prohibited. The problem of antitrust liability for unions that combine with nonlabor groups for certain objectives remains a major issue in American labor law, but *Hutcheson* is significant because of the freedom it provides to trade unions to engage in strikes, picketing, and boycotts.

The second major break with the past took place three years after the passage of Norris-LaGuardia. The enactment of the National Labor Relations Act, which created a national administrative agency to conduct representation elections to determine whether a union could represent employees as exclusive bargaining representative and to determine whether certain unfair-labor-practice violations had been engaged in, was an event of vast significance for American industrial relations. This marked the end of a brief interlude of laissez-faire toward labor relations as reflected in the Norris-LaGuardia Act.

3

The National Labor Relations Act

The National Labor Relations Act of 1935 forms the basis of
legal regulation of collective bargaining in the private sector.
Other statutes, such as the Fair Labor Standards Act of 1938,
provide substantive guarantees for individual employees who
work for employers engaged in interstate commerce and a
"floor" below which workers should not fall.[1] In the case of
the FLSA, minimum wages and maximum hours are provided. The Walsh-Healy Act[2] and the Davis-Bacon Act[3] provide minimum conditions for employees of government
contractors. During the 1970s other federal legislation (referred to in chapter 11) was enacted. State legislatures have
enacted their own laws in this area.

Prior to the National Labor Relations Act, Congress had already provided for collective bargaining in the railroad industry through the Railway Labor Act of 1926.[4] Furthermore, the
National Labor Board (under the auspices of the National Industry Recovery Act,[5] the pre-NLRA National Labor Relations
Board, and an executive order of the president) had been
conducting elections, albeit under statutory machinery that
was unenforceable before the Supreme Court's holding that
the NIRA was unconstitutional.[6]

The constitutional basis for the National Labor Relations Act is the commerce clause of the U.S. Constitution: article I, section 8. This provision allows Congress to enact legislation when it regulates commerce between the various states of the union. The constitutional theory upon which the statute is predicated is that statutory regulation of labor and management is necessary to diminish industrial strife that could disrupt interstate commerce. The Supreme Court, at the time of the NLRA, had struck down a number of the Roosevelt administration's laws providing social and economic reform. But by a 5–4 vote, in *NLRB* v. *Jones & Laughlin Steel Corp.*,[7] it upheld the constitutionality of the act. This came at a time when the Roosevelt administration was attempting to expand the Court in order to change the drift of its decisions. Chief Justice Hughes joined the majority of the Court in *Jones & Laughlin* in declaring the statute constitutional. His previous involvement on the other side of similar issues prompted wags to say "A switch in time saves nine."

Whatever Hughes's motivation, the Court accepted the constitutional theory that Congress could regulate labor relations so as to avoid interference with the shipment of goods across state lines. Ironically, as so often happens in connection with great social movements, when expectations are on the rise, once the statute was passed the amount of industrial strife increased significantly.[8] Yet it is fair to say that, over more than fifty years, the Board's work has contributed substantially to the promotion of industrial peace in the United States.

The particular significance of the NLRA (which in 1935 was called the Wagner Act after its principal author, Senator Robert Wagner of New York) was that it provided for regulation of some labor disputes by an expert agency—the National Labor Relations Board, whose principal headquarters were and are in Washington, D.C. Congress had departed from the laissez-faire philosophy of Norris-LaGuardia, but it could not be said to be reviving traditional outside involvement and the potential for abuses associated with antitrust laws and the labor injunction—although the courts now had appellate jurisdiction over the Board.

The NLRB was one of a number of administrative agencies established under "New Deal" legislation promoted by the Roosevelt administration. The Wagner Act provided that employees were to be protected in their free choice to protest working conditions they deemed unfair, to organize into unions and select representatives, and to oblige management to bargain in good faith with the union that represented a majority of the workers in an appropriate group or unit. As noted above, these rights were to be enforced through representational elections in which the majority would vote on which (if any) labor organization would represent them and through unfair-labor-practice machinery through which the NLRB interprets the statute to determine whether management or labor has engaged in unfair practices. (Labor unions' unfair labor practices were added to the law through the Taft-Hartley amendments in 1947.) In contrast with the administrative agencies that preceded it, the focus of the new board was on the development of a body of case law that would govern large portions of the relationship between labor and management.

Orders issued by the NLRB (often referred to as the Labor Board or just the Board) are not self-enforcing. Enforcement of the Board's orders is obtained through the Circuit Courts of Appeals. There are eleven such tribunals in the United States (there will soon be twelve), and they are just below the Supreme Court in the judicial pyramid. In the event that labor or management does not comply with an order enforced in the court, contempt proceedings (which can result in civil and criminal penalties, although the latter are rarely invoked) take place before the circuit court and not the Board.

Just as the Great Depression promoted the idea of self-organization among workers, both as a balance against big business[9] and as a form of industrial democracy, so also the outbreak of strikes at the end of World War II—when the pent-up demands of labor manifested themselves in industrial warfare that disrupted a number of key industries—helped create an environment conducive to limitations on the rights of unions. Changes in the National Labor Relations Act were enacted through the Taft-Hartley amendments. In addition to the rules relating to appropriate units, the organization of the National Labor Relations Board and the unfair-labor-practice provisions were altered.

The National Labor Relations Board

The Board, which had been one entity, was split into two separate sections by the Taft-Hartley amendments. On one side, there is a five-member board with its principal offices in Washington, D.C. (the "judicial" side of the Board). On the other side, also with its principal offices in Washington, is the "prosecutorial" side of the Board, which is headed by the General Counsel. (It cannot be regarded as prosecutorial in the strict sense of the word because it cannot seek criminal penalties or sanctions.) The two offices were separated because it was thought to be unfair and inconsistent with due process to have the same party adjudicate and investigate. Quite obviously, when one party has already completed its investigation and made a decision to proceed with an unfair-labor-practice proceeding, that party may be less than completely objective in subsequent adjudication of the case.

The members of the Board and the General Counsel are appointed by the president with the advice and consent of the Senate. Officials on both sides—prosecutorial and judicial—work together in connection with the Board's functions relating to representational matters, including the establishment of appropriate units and the conduct of elections.

The Taft-Hartley amendments, which imposed a variety of legal obligations upon unions, created a split between the General Counsel and the Board for unfair-labor-practice cases because the authors felt that employers had been denied due process by a pro-union Board acting as prosecutor, judge, and jury. If the hearing is held before the prosecutor who investigated and who has a stake in obtaining the conviction, fairness has been denied the accused. This sense that the pendulum had swung too far toward labor in the period between 1935 and 1947 pervades other amendments that were made to the statute in 1947 and 1959.

Preemption and Primary Jurisdiction for the NLRB

In the Wagner Act and the Taft-Hartley amendments, Congress intended to define carefully the role of the courts and the NLRB in labor relations. The amendments make it clear that collective bargaining agreements are contracts enforceable in court but that most allegations of unfair labor practices may be heard only by the Board and ultimately by the federal courts.

Unions and employers can pursue allegations of breach of contract in state or federal courts. Before the enactment of the Taft-Hartley amendments, it was difficult for employers to sue unions in state courts for breach of contract because in many states the collective bargaining agreement was regarded as a "gentlemen's agreement" and not a court-enforceable contract, and because often the court insisted that unions, as voluntary unincorporated associations, be sued in the name of each individual member, which was difficult in practice. Ironically, although the statutory provision that made collective bargaining agreements enforceable in the federal courts was prompted by Congress's concern that unions were acting irresponsibly and often in violation of their collectively negotiated contract provisions, the fact is that the unions have made considerable use of this provision of the law by insisting successfully that recalcitrant or unwilling employers proceed to arbitration where there is a dispute over the meaning of the collective bargaining agreement.[10] Most of the actions relating to the enforcement of agreements have been brought by the unions—principally because they are actions to compel arbitration or to enforce an arbitrator's award.[11]

The peculiar federalist system of the United States is the wellspring of the doctrines of preemption and primary jurisdiction, which are applied in the National Labor Relations Act's unfair-labor-practice provisions. Congress's intention to create an expert agency for labor matters is apparent in the NLRB General Counsel's broad discretion over whether to issue an unfair-labor-issue practice complaint (and thus whether a hearing on the issue will be held) and in the exclusion of the courts as a forum for initiating unfair-labor-practice cases.

Where Congress has the constitutional authority to legislate, the federal law may be supreme—and state jurisdiction may be ousted completely—where Congress chooses. The supremacy of federal law springs from article VI of the U.S. Constitution. The courts have fashioned a doctrine of preemption that is based on the Supremacy Clause and the Commerce Clause.[12] Whenever Congress has legislated in detail, the courts consider whether Congress intended to deprive the states of jurisdiction in the particular field (as the courts put it, whether Congress intended to "occupy the field").[13] The reason for the doctrines of preemption and occupation of the field is that conflicting interpretations of a law by state courts may frustrate the objective of the national legislation. That is, even if the state courts interpret the very same National Labor Relations Act that Congress enacted, they may interpret it in a different way than the Board would.

Accordingly, the Supreme Court has held that whenever the subject matter involved in a labor controversy is "arguably" protected by section 7 of the NLRA or prohibited by the unfair-labor-practice provision applicable to both unions and employers in section 8, federal and state courts are deprived of jurisdiction.[14] In applying the doctrine of preemption of the NLRA, the Supreme Court has stated that usually the Board has primary jurisdiction to determine the question of whether the subject matter involved in a labor controversy is protected or prohibited by the NLRA before the courts intervene.[15] This is because the Board is the expert agency entrusted with special responsibility to interpret the statute, and, if the courts were to step in without the benefit of the Board's interpretation, their exercise of jurisdiction and interpretation of the statute and national labor policy could cause mischief for the uniform federal scheme Congress intended to apply in labor-management relations.

To be sure, there are exceptions to the preemption doctrine. For instance, where a suit is brought for breach of collective bargaining agreement, the state retains jurisdiction even where the subject matter also involves an unfair labor practice. Cases involving the duty of fair representation are another exception to the rule. Moreover, a series of Supreme Court decisions[16] have permitted the states to assume jurisdiction where actions are brought alleging libel[17] or harm suffered under statutes designed to protect an individual's emotional injury,[18] or trespass by union organizers seeking to impart their message to employees or to the public on private premises,[19] or violence or a threat to peaceful order. The Court has also inferred congressional intent to confer regulatory authority upon the states when federal statutes provide some room for state action on the subject matter in question.[20]

Recent decisions have cast some doubt on the continued viability of the strong pro-preemption posture taken by the

Supreme Court in labor cases.[21] However, one can still safely say that the states have been limited in dealing with labor controversies involving the portion of the private sector that is covered by the NLRA and the portion of those cases over which the Board has chosen to assume jurisdiction under its authority to regulate employers and unions involved in interstate commerce.[22] As a result of the 1959 amendments to the NLRA, the Board cannot decline jurisdiction over any cases over which it would have assumed jurisdiction under the standards as of August 1, 1959.[23]

Although the Board's jurisdiction over commerce is broad,[24] it does not extend to foreign crews employed by foreign ships operating under flags of convenience,[25] inasmuch as there must be an affirmative intention by Congress to regulate such employers given the delicate consideration of international relations involved. However, the Supreme Court has approved the NLRB's assertion of jurisdiction over foreign flag vessels where the dispute between labor and management focused upon wages paid to American residents who did not serve as members of the crew but rather performed casual longshore work.[26] Similarly, where the International Longshoremen's Association refused to load or unload cargo destined for or originating in the Soviet Union, in protest against that country's invasion of Afghanistan, the dispute was held to be in "commerce" and within the NLRB's jurisdiction.[27]

The significance of the two doctrines of preemption and primary jurisdiction for the Board in connection with the General Counsel's authority is enormous. The doctrines make it difficult for a substantial number of cases to be heard on their merits in an open hearing. In part, the disinclination of a substantial number of Americans to protest this state of affairs is attributable to the preference by labor and management representatives (especially the former) for the supposed expertise of the Board and the unease many Americans have about judicial competence in labor matters, given the historical experience.[28] The irony here is that the preemption doctrine has expanded because the Taft-Hartley amendments broadened the Board's jurisdiction. Thus, statutory provisions aimed at restricting labor have deprived what was in many instances a more hostile state judiciary of jurisdiction over labor—jurisdiction that could be devoted to restraining strikes, picketing, and other actions through damages and criminal prosecution.

Who is Covered by the NLRA?

The coverage provided by the National Labor Relations Act is narrow.[29] Public employees at the federal, state, and local levels are excluded, as are agricultural workers, domestic servants, and supervisory employees. This exclusion does not mean that it is illegal for such workers to engage in collective bargaining. Indeed, collective bargaining for public employees and legislation at the federal, state, and local levels protecting the right of the workers to join unions has become part of the American labor landscape. For example, although most states do not protect the right of farm workers to engage in collective bargaining, California has a comprehensive statute that is in many respects superior to the NLRA in the protection it affords to workers.[30]

There is no logical basis for the exclusion of the workers referred to above. Essentially, their exclusion from the NLRA's protection relates simply to the fact that they had little political clout when the legislation was enacted. American labor law has traditionally excluded large groups of workers from its coverage.[31]

Additionally, certain workers besides those mentioned above are excluded from the definition of "employee" within the meaning of the Act; for example, independent contractors are specifically excluded by section 2(3).[32] Because the First Amendment to the Constitution provides for a separation of church and state, the Supreme Court has held that lay teachers of religious and secular subjects are not covered by the NLRA in the absence of an explicit indication by Congress that it intended to give the NLRB jurisdiction over such individuals.[33] Although the statute does not provide explicit exclusionary language, the Supreme Court, in *NLRB* v. *Bell Aerospace Company*, has held that managerial employees who formulate and implement company policy are also excluded from the bargaining unit.[34] Such employees, of course, are not eligible to vote in NLRB-conducted elections.

In 1980 the Supreme Court held that, at least under certain circumstances, faculty members in universities are properly excluded from the definition of "employee" because they are managerial employees.[35] The Court's reasoning, expressed by Justice Powell's majority opinion, is based on a presumed identity of interest between the faculty and the administration. The decision, like *Bell Aerospace*, was by a vote of 5–4. One of the majority opinion's deficiencies is that it overlooks the frequent clashes of interests between faculties and administrations. Another problem is the failure to recognize that labor can be involved in both confrontation and cooperation, as the UAW's recent interest in having workers on auto manufacturers' boards vividly demonstrates. This inability of the Court to perceive the need of a union or any society to have a collective bargaining model that promotes cooperation is disturbing indeed.

Access to the Law's Protection

What benefits are provided by the National Labor Relations Act for workers who are covered by it? In the first place, workers, as well as labor organizations and employers, may file a petition with the NLRB requesting an election to determine whether a particular labor organization represents the majority of workers within an appropriate group of employees. Such an election is conducted by secret vote, and ballots are generally cast at the plant where the workers are employed. More than half of the workers who vote in the Board-conducted election must vote for the union if the employer is to be required to bargain with it.[36]

Although in some countries organizations seeking to represent workers must register and be screened, no such situation exists in the United States. However, in order for a labor union to file a petition requesting representation and to impose bargaining obligations upon management, it must be a "labor organization" as defined in the NLRA: an organization "of any kind, or any agency or employee representation committee or plan, in which employees participate and which exists for the purpose, in whole or in part, of dealing with employers concerning grievances, labor disputes, wages, rates of pay, hours of employment, or conditions of work."[37] So as to provide the greatest scope for freedom of association under the statute, this provision has been interpreted liberally so as to permit a wide variety of organizations to obtain the benefits of the statute. There is no requirement of involvement in any particular industry or company, and the collective bargaining experience of another (perhaps larger) labor organization does not freeze out an organization that may seek to represent workers in the same industry.[38]

But the statutory scheme is designed to confer exclusivity on a labor organization. That is, once an organization receives majority support in an appropriate unit, the employer is under a statutory obligation to bargain with no other organization for the workers in that unit. All workers covered by or included in the unit, whether they are members of the union or not, have their wages, hours, and working conditions regulated by the collective bargaining agreement between the union and employer unless the contract between labor and management states otherwise. In professional sports, where contracts allow for bargaining between employers and individual players, there are good examples of such special contracts between labor and management. Stars such as Fred Lynn, the Red Sox erstwhile centerfielder who has negotiated new contracts with both the California Angels and the Baltimore Orioles, are able to command handsome salaries on the basis of individual bargaining.[39]

The collective bargain itself will, in many circumstances, provide for a wide range of benefits to be negotiated in an individual contract of employment; the wage or salary is one such benefit. But the situation in professional sports is not representative of most collective bargaining, in which wages as well as other benefits and conditions are shaped by unions and employers on an almost totally bilateral basis. And even in sports it is the collective agreement that sets minimum salaries and addresses the question of when players become free agents so that they may bargain with other teams. Indeed, the union representing soccer players in North America has the authority under its collective agreement to veto individual contracts. The National Football League Players' Association has proposed (without success) collective negotiation of maximum as well as minimum salaries. But the National Basketball Players' Association has agreed to a salary "cap" or limit that each club cannot exceed. Also, players' unions have become concerned about, and sought to regulate, some of the practices of agents who represent athletes.

The Appropriate Unit

What is an appropriate unit of workers? An appropriate unit is to be established by the NLRB among a group of workers who have a "community of interest" with one another. The principal forum for collective bargaining in the United States is an appropriate unit of workers established at the plant. But the statute and numerous decisions of the Board and the courts make it clear that an appropriate unit can be established at the company level and sometimes—where there is consent on both sides—on a multiemployer or industrywide basis.

The principal considerations that the Board and the courts use in determining what constitutes an appropriate unit are the following:

- whether the employees are under common supervision,

- whether the employer's bookkeeping relating to employee concerns, payment of wages, and other benefits is organized on a plant, a multiplant, or a multicompany basis,

- the basis on which the employees have communicated or bargained in the past,

- whether the employees have contact with one another at the workplace and whether, for instance, they clock in and clock out at the same location,

- if there is a dispute relating to whether the unit is appropriately multiplant in scope, the extent to which employees are transferred between plants (temporarily or otherwise),

- similarity in the type of work performed,

- similarities in wages, hours, and working conditions, and

- the desires of the employees.

Though the last point can be considered along with the others, the Taft-Hartley amendments make it clear that the NLRB cannot declare an appropriate unit by considering the workers' wishes alone.[40]

Often the question of what constitutes an appropriate unit is a difficult one. Very often the union will want a small unit. For instance, if a chain has five restaurants in the same city, the union will undoubtedly try to establish a unit in one or two of them because it can channel a great deal of effort into organizing a small group of employees (which can then serve as a "building block" for organizing others). Another reason for the union's desire to establish a smaller unit is its reliance upon secrecy to ward off a counterattack by the employer. Secrecy is less likely to be realized if the union tries to organize all of the chain's facilities in the city simultaneously. The employer, in such circumstances, generally wants the broader unit because of his interest in uniformity of practices and conditions of employment in all his facilities. Not only does this make administration easier, but also it tends to minimize the potential for discord and discontent among employees who might complain about differences in benefits and conditions which they perceive as putting them in an inferior position. Also, the employer generally favors a broader unit for the very same reasons that the union favors a small unit: The union will have more difficulty trying to reach a larger number of employees, and the employer's campaign to undercut the union is more likely to succeed under such circumstances. The sooner the employer finds out about the campaign, the better he is able to thwart the union's organizing efforts. As the Supreme Court has said, "virtually every Board decision concerning an appropriate bargaining unit—e.g., the proper size of the unit—favors one side or the other."[41]

Before the Taft-Hartley amendments, where the factors were roughly equal and where the union desired the smaller unit, the Board would accede to the union's wishes on the ground that, if a broader unit than that petitioned for was to be established as the appropriate unit, collective bargaining would probably not exist for the employees at all. This would be so not only because the union would be unlikely to win an election among employees in all of an employer's facilities, but also because it would be unlikely that an election would ever be held. Under the administrative rules of the NLRB, for an election to take place, 30 percent of the employees within the appropriate unit must indicate that they want an election held to determine whether collective bargaining shall exist. This is called the "showing of interest." If (to take our example) the appropriate unit is one or two of the chain's restaurants, it is likely that an election will be held because the union's organizational efforts will have reached a substantial number of the employees and will have persuaded a number of them to sign petitions or authorization cards indicating their interest in the union or in a Board-conducted election. If the unit is a larger one, it will be unlikely that an election will be held at all because less than 30 percent of the workers will support an election. Today the NLRA precludes the Board from fashioning an appropriate unit on the grounds that the union has organized the employees in that particular area. The statute says that "the extent that the employees have organized shall not be controlling." However, the extent of organization may still be taken into account along with the other factors mentioned.[42]

Although the Board has relied upon the extent of organization in conjunction with other factors to establish a unit at one location in a multilocation industry as presumptively appropriate,[43] recently it has established large units in universities[44] and hospitals.[45] The larger the unit, the more difficult a union organizational effort is likely to be.

One unit issue that has been litigated relates to whether "on-air programmers" who appear before the microphone in the broadcast industry—announcers and disc jockeys—constitute a separate unit for the purpose of bargaining. The Board has held that such employees should be within a separate unit because they "constitute a homogeneous, readily identifiable cohesive group" by virtue of their talent, which separates them from other employees — i.e., "voice, diction and personality."[46] But in a case involving a northern California radio station featuring modern jazz, *KJAZ Broadcasting Company*,[47] the

Board held that there is no "recognized distinction" where "on the air programmers do not share a substantial community of interest separate and apart from other employees of the Employer." Said the Board: "In its commitment to the jazz idiom, the Employer has historically hired only employees with an in-depth knowledge of jazz, a 'talent' shared by all its employees."[48]

Ever since the passage of the National Labor Relations Act there have been conflicts between craft and industrial unions about the unit for representation. (In the early days of the Act, such disputes arose out of the fact that management often favored craft unions because they were regarded as more conservative.) The problem is particularly troublesome in the United States because there are large numbers of both craft and industrial unions. In contrast, Britain and Australia are plagued with jurisdictional stoppages caused by proliferation of craft unions, and in Germany and Scandinavia industrial unions are dominant.

In the United States, craft unions are able to survive where the appropriate unit is fashioned on an occupational basis. Conversely, a broader unit is more to the liking of the big industrial unions. Where the question of craft or industrial unit is extremely close, the desires of the employees are to govern according to the rarely used "globe election process," which pools votes into two units when the smaller or craft group provides a majority vote for the union seeking two units.[49] If those pooled votes give that union a majority of the voters, it is certified; if there is no majority, the Board orders a runoff election between the highest vote-getters.

Another issue that arises quite frequently relates to "craft severance," the extent to which a class of skilled workers may opt out of an appropriate unit that includes semiskilled and unskilled workers. Prior to 1947, in most such cases the NLRB did not permit workers to separate themselves from the broad group. The Taft-Hartley amendments reversed this position, and the Board cannot now regard a craft as inappropriate for bargaining on the grounds that a different unit had been established previously. Today the Board determines whether craftsmen will be granted a separate unit on the basis of the following factors:

- whether the proposed unit consists of a "distinct and homogeneous group of skilled journeymen craftsmen" who are "performing the functions of their craft on a nonrepetitive basis" or are located in a functionally distinct department "where a tradition of separate representation exists,"

- the history of collective bargaining and the potential for collective bargaining if the history is continued,

- the extent to which the employees who wish to opt out have maintained a separate identity for themselves,

- the pattern of collective bargaining in the industry generally,

- the degree of integration of the employer's production processes, and

- the extent to which the union seeking to represent the skilled workers has experience in representing the particular craft involved.

The above criteria provide some notion of the kinds of problems that are involved in determining what constitutes an appropriate unit. They should also provide a bit of an appreciation of the changes that took place through the Taft-Hartley amendments, which were designed to protect employees against unions that sometimes run afoul of these interests. Most particularly, the Taft-Hartley amendments were concerned with protecting the interests of skilled tradesmen against industrial unions that (at least in the tradesmen's view) did not always adequately take their interests into account.

Holding an Election

After the appropriate unit has been found, if there is a 30 percent showing of interest the Regional Director in the NLRB field office orders an election. At a prehearing conference the Regional Director attempts to resolve the unit issue and the question of who is eligible to vote without a full hearing. If he is successful, a consent agreement is signed by all parties.

There are two kinds of consent agreements. One provides that the Regional Director's decision on all challenges to ballots and to the conduct of the election is final and binding; the other permits the parties to appeal on such matters to the Board in Washington. Sometimes all employees eligible to vote are named in the agreement.

If there is no agreement, a hearing will be held on the unit and eligibility issues. Theoretically this is not supposed to be an adversary or court-style proceeding, but sometimes the participating lawyers (as well as lay people) make it that way. Sometimes a second or third labor organization (besides the one that filed the petition) will be present and will file a motion to intervene. Any union that can show that it has signed up one employee as a supporter may be on the ballot at the election. If the second or third union (any number of unions may intervene) has a 10 percent showing of interest, it may participate fully in the hearing. If no union or the No vote has a majority, a runoff is held with the two highest vote-getters on the ballot.

Within seven days of the Regional Director's decision to order an election or his approval of the consent agreement for the election, the employer must file with the NLRB three copies of a list of the names and addresses of all employees in the unit.[50] One copy is sent to the union so that it may communicate with employees during the campaign.

Elections are generally held on the employer's premises, although if the union objects the election will be held elsewhere. A representative of the NLRB supervises the conduct of the election, and all parties are entitled to have observers. Objections to the conduct of the election by the unions or the employer or disputes about the eligibility of voters that might affect the election's outcome must be filed with the Regional Director within five days of the election. The Regional Director will investigate, but need not hold a hearing, to determine the validity of the objections. If the objections are found to be valid, the election will be set aside and another will be held.

Objections are the preferred method for resolving disputes about election conduct. The filing of an unfair-labor-practice charge "blocks" resolution of the representation issue, delaying the election and the above-described procedures until the unfair-labor-practice issue is resolved.[51] The theory is that, absent resolution of the unfair-labor-practice issues, the potential for interference with employees' freedom of choice exists.

The central theme of these procedures is the employees' freedom of choice. Employees must exercise that choice free of workplace pressures from the union or the employer. It is hoped that the choice will be an informed one. The goal is to realize majority rule in an expeditious and informal manner. Accordingly, except where the NLRB directly contradicts the language of the NLRA,[52] its decisions on representation issues are not reviewable in the federal courts. But, as a practical matter, an employer (but not a labor organization) may obtain review of the NLRB's representation decision by refusing to bargain with a union that has been certified, thus triggering an unfair-labor-practice proceeding.[53]

4

Unfair Labor Practices

As we saw in chapter 3, neither the members of the National Labor Relations Board, nor the judicial side of the Board, nor the courts can adjudicate unfair labor practices unless the General Counsel determines that a complaint should be issued. But labor-law decisions are made almost every working day of the year in unfair-labor-practice proceedings (and, to a lesser extent, in representation elections). Some of these decisions are very important and precedent-setting.

What are "unfair labor practices?" As noted above, both employers and labor organizations may engage in such practices. Employers' unfair labor practices were written into the law in 1935 and have remained unchanged. An employer is prohibited from interfering with, restraining, or coercing employees in any way in connection with their right to engage in concerted activities, to protest working conditions, and to join labor organizations for the purpose of collective bargaining (or to refrain from any of these things). The union may not restrain or coerce workers in the exercise of their rights protected under the statute (the language here is slightly less ambitious than that applied to employers). Surveillance of union activites, use of union "spies," interrogation of employees about union activities, threatening employees for being involved in the union, and promising benefits if employees desist from union activity are among the actions prohibited to employers.[1] Indeed, in 1980 the NLRB held that an employer may not lawfully "initiate questioning about employees' union sentiments even where the employees are open and known union supporters and the inquiries are unaccompanied by threats or promises."[2] However, in 1984, the Board, characterizing its earlier position as a *per se* condemnation of interrogation inconsistent with Board precedent,[3] held that such an approach "ignored the reality of the workplace" and that interrogations could be viewed as unlawful only with reference to "all of the circumstances."[4]

Although the Supreme Court has yet to resolve the interrogation issue, it has held in *NLRB* v. *Exchange Parts Co.*[5] that the bestowal of benefits during a union organizational campaign is unlawful. Said the Court: "The danger inherent in well timed increases in benefits is the suggestion of a fist inside the velvet glove. Employees are not likely to miss the inference that the source of benefits now conferred is also the source from which future benefits must flow and which may dry up if it is not obliged."[6] Similarly, an NLRB election may be set aside and a new election ordered where a union waives its initiation fees for those who sign up with the union before the election.[7]

At the same time, employers have both a constitutional and a statutory right of free speech, although they may not use it to coerce employees or to dissuade them from union affiliation through the promise of benefits. But it is frequently impossible for the NLRB to determine whether an employer's statement such as "if the union wins the election its demands will require me to close the plant" is coercive or merely an economic prophecy about which the workers should be informed before making an intelligent decision. What is an economic prophecy to a tough truck driver in Detroit may be coercive to a textile-mill worker in South Carolina.

Neither may an employer provide financial assistance to a labor organization.[8] If the NLRB finds that an employer has done so, it must issue an order to cease and desist.[9] Here, as with other unfair labor practices, the NLRB also orders the party that has acted unlawfully to post notices at its premises in conspicuous places so that the matter will be brought to the attention of the employees.[10] The notices are posted almost automatically in the United States, but in Japan this is done much less often (although that country has unfair-labor-practices provisions in its law by virtue of the 1945 American occupation). In Japan the posting of a notice seems to be more unacceptable or harmful to an employer's reputation.

An American employer may not assist in the creation of a labor organization or in its attempt to gain recognition. If the NLRB finds that an employer has done so, it may order that the employer withdraw recognition from the organization, or even that the organization be "disestablished" (completely eliminated).[11]

An employer may not discriminate in connection with working conditions against workers because of their union membership or lack thereof. However, a union may negotiate with an employer a collective bargaining agreement that includes a "union security clause" requiring that workers pay periodic dues and initiation fees as a condition of employment. If a worker refuses the union's request to pay, he may be dismissed from employment (unless the worker's objection is religious). This form of union security agreement is frequently referred to as a union shop or agency shop—as distinguished from a closed shop, which requires that a worker become a union member prior to being hired. The closed shop was outlawed by the Taft-Hartley amendments.[12] States may prohibit the negotiation of any such union security agreements, and twenty–one of them have enacted "right-to-work" legislation accomplishing this objective.[13] (Some regard "right-to-work" as a misnomer; the legislation does not provide for any right to work, but it does protect workers who do not wish to pay union dues from dismissal.)

In no situation is a union security agreement imposed by law. Where there is no right-to-work legislation, labor and management are free to enter voluntarily into such agreements. The unions have argued, with a good deal of persuasiveness, that such agreements are necessary inasmuch as the union has a duty of fair representation to bargain for all employees in the bargaining unit regardless of their union affiliation or lack thereof. Workers who do not have to pay dues receive the same benefits as those who do, and therefore have a financial advantage over dues-paying workers. The unions refer to such workers as "free riders."

Other countries have grappled with this problem. In Britain, the Trade Union and Labor Relations Act of 1976 provided that an employee could be dismissed pursuant to a closed-shop agreement unless the worker had religious objections. However, the Employment Act of 1980 broadened the grounds for objection to conscience or deeply held personal conviction. (In the United States, a 1980 amendment to the NLRA also provides for religious objections, and it seems possible that the law may be interpreted to protect personally held "religious or moral convictions."[14]) An employee may also refuse to join if he held his job classification prior to the closed shop and refused to join thereafter. Finally, 80 percent of the workers must approve a closed shop entered into after August 15, 1980. (In the United States a majority of workers may vote to "deauthorize" a union security agreement and thus prohibit its negotiation by the union.) The Employment Act of 1982 provides that where ballots are conducted for the first time on August 15, 1980, or thereafter, the dismissal of a worker under a closed-shop agreement will be unfair where support for the agreement of 80 percent of employees entitled to vote or 85 percent of those voting has not been evidenced within the past 5 years. The 1982 statute also protects employees who have been "unreasonably" excluded or expelled from membership against dismissal under a closed-shop agreement.

The closed shop is unlawful in West Germany and France—in the former country, this is due to constitutional guarantees of liberty. In Sweden, although it is lawful, most unions and employers do not appear to require membership as a condition of employment.

In the United States, other unfair-labor-practice provisions prohibit the employer from retaliating against a worker who has cooperated with the NLRB or testified in an NLRB hearing. And, finally, the employer is obliged to bargain in good faith with a union that has been designated by a majority of the employees in an appropriate unit as their exclusive bargaining agent. The difficult concept of good faith is described in more detail below.

The Taft-Hartley amendments have imposed unfair-labor-practice restrictions on unions as well as employers. As noted above, the union may not "restrain and coerce" employees. Therefore, a union may not lawfully engage in violence, disorder, or mass picketing that interferes with the movement of employees or the public into and out of the employer's property or premises. Of course, the states and localities may prosecute criminal conduct. And, to a limited extent, the federal government is the prosecutor (for example, in cases of violence committed in connection with extortion[15] and other criminal acts[16]).

A union may not cause an employer to discriminate against a worker merely because he is not a union member. (This situation generally arises in connection with a union's encouraging an employer to discriminate against workers of another rival union.)

A union is obliged to bargain with an employer in good faith. The proponents of the Taft-Hartley amendments were concerned that certain strong unions had adopted a "take it or leave it" attitude in their dealings with employers. A number of unions would simply come to the bargaining table and present the area contract (the contract negotiated with most employers in the area). Where the employer was small and without economic power, the union expected no discussion or negotiation. Sometimes a union would simply throw a proposed contract on the table and tell the employer to sign it. The obligation of unions as well as employers to bargain was intended to cure this problem.

Unions are also obliged not to engage in "secondary boycotting." A secondary boycott (frequently accompanied by picketing) is intended to force a second or secondary employer to refrain from doing business with a primary employer with whom the union has a dispute over, for instance, recognition, wages, or conditions of employment. Like the union shop–closed shop issue, the issue of secondary boycotts is deeply divisive. Free societies want to protect both solidarity and innocent third parties. In Britain, the Employment Act of 1980 made union officials and members liable to damage suits where employees engage in picketing at establishments or locations where they are not employed. The 1982 act makes unions themselves liable for injunctive relief or damages where the conduct has been authorized or endorsed by a responsible person.

Secondary economic pressure of any kind can create liability unless it is targeted at supplies going to or from the business with the dispute, or unless the struck work is transferred to a second employer. In the United States, when secondary-boycott charges are filed, the NLRB is obliged to give them investigative priority. If the regional office finds cause to believe that the statute's secondary-boycott provisions are being violated, it must immediately petition the federal district court for a temporary injunction against the violation. Additionally, a party may file suit for damages caused by a secondary boycott. In essence, then, three proceedings can take place: an administrative proceeding of the kind described above that would normally take place in an unfair-labor-practice matter, a petition for injunctive relief in federal district court, or a suit for damages.

The 1959 Landrum-Griffin amendments[17] to the National Labor Relations Act prohibit the negotiation of "hot cargo" clauses in labor contracts, which allow workers to refuse to handle goods that are "hot" (produced by an employer with whom the union has a dispute). Again, the idea is that the union ought not to involve an innocent or neutral employer in a dispute with which that employer has nothing to do. Subcontracting clauses in labor contracts that preclude an employer from contracting out work to nonunion employees are made illegal by this provision. However, labor and management may negotiate contract clauses that forbid subcontracting to employers who provide inferior conditions of employment to their employees if the object of the contractual provision is to preserve work for the bargaining unit's members,[18] and there are provisos in the statute that give the unions more strength in the clothing and construction industries because of the economic peculiarities of those industries.[19] In this situation, no provision is made for damage suits as in secondary-boycott cases. Similarly, there is no provision for temporary injunctive relief, since what is involved is not a work stoppage or picketing but only the existence of an unlawful contract clause.

Another major unfair-labor-practice protection under the Landrum-Griffin amendments outlaws organizational or reorganizational picketing to secure recognition for the union without the preferred method of selection through a secret-ballot vote—or, more specifically, without the support of a majority of workers in the appropriate unit. This procedure was enacted in reaction to the use of "blackmail" picketing to pressure an employer to recognize a union without any consultation with the workers. Congress found that some unions (particularly the International Brotherhood of Teamsters) would often picket a firm (particularly one whose work force was composed of racial minorities), force the employer's recognition, and negotiate an agreement without the workers' interests at heart. The objective was simply to get workers to authorize payroll deductions for union dues.[20] The workers would never hear from the union, and the working conditions (usually substandard) would not change.

Work stoppages arising out of jurisdictional disputes between unions over the same work are unlawful. If labor and management have not negotiated procedures to resolve such a conflict,[21] the NLRB is empowered to do so.[22] As is the case with secondary boycotts, the employer may sue the union in court without utilizing the NLRB's administrative procedures.

The Statute of Limitations

Section 10(b) of the National Labor Relations Act states that the NLRB cannot issue a complaint if the alleged unfair labor practice occurred more than six months before the filing of a charge with the Board.[23] This provision also is part of the Taft-Hartley amendments, and in 1960 the Supreme Court held that maintenance of an agreement containing a union security clause bargained by a minority union[24] was barred by the Act's statute of limitations where the agreement had been executed more than six months in advance of the charge.[25] The decision has not ended litigation on this subject. In 1984 the Board held that it will "henceforth focus on the date of the alleged unlawful act, rather than on the date its consequences become effective, in deciding whether the period for filing a charge under Section 10(b) has expired." Furthermore, "Where a final adverse employment decision is made and communicated to an employee — whether the decision is nonrenewal of an employment contract, termination, or other alleged discrimination — the employee is in a position to file an unfair labor practice charge and must do so within 6 months of that time rather than wait until the consequences of the act become most painful."[26]

Filing and Prosecution with the NLRB

Any person can file a charge alleging that a union or an employer or one of its agents has engaged in an unfair labor practice within the meaning of the National Labor Relations Act. (The diagram on p. 57 illustrates the entire procedure.) The NLRB, through its representatives of the General Counsel at regional offices throughout the United States, will generally provide such a party with a form in which to set forth the allegation of a violation of the law. A worker may fill out the form in the regional office, often with the assistance of Board officials.

Once the charge is filed, the regional director, acting under the authority of the General Counsel, will investigate to determine whether there is cause to believe that the law has been violated. If there is found to be cause, a complaint will be issued at the local level[27]; otherwise the charge will be dismissed (although generally an attempt will be made to induce the charging employee to withdraw the charge or to resolve it through some form of informal settlement). Between 80 and 90 percent of the charges filed with the NLRB are resolved through some form of settlement or withdrawal—most often at the stage when the investigation has been completed, but before anything has taken place subsequent to the deci-

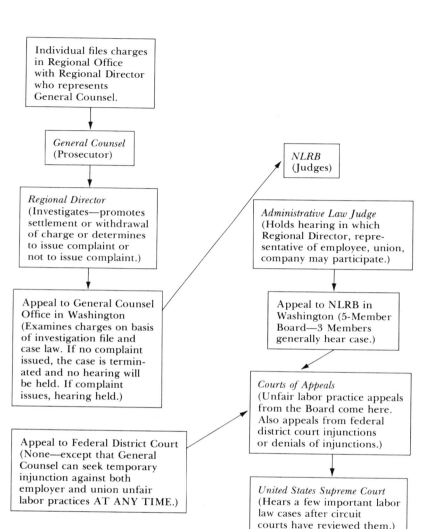

Individual files charges
in Regional Office
with Regional Director
who represents
General Counsel.

General Counsel
(Prosecutor)

NLRB
(Judges)

Regional Director
(Investigates—promotes
settlement or withdrawal
of charge or determines
to issue complaint or
not to issue complaint.)

Administrative Law Judge
(Holds hearing in which
Regional Director, repre-
sentative of employee, union,
company may participate.)

Appeal to General Counsel
Office in Washington
(Examines charges on basis
of investigation file and
case law. If no complaint
issued, the case is termin-
ated and no hearing will
be held. If complaint
issues, hearing held.)

Appeal to NLRB in
Washington (5-Member
Board—3 Members
generally hear case.)

Courts of Appeals
(Unfair labor practice appeals
from the Board come here.
Also appeals from federal
district court injunctions
or denials of injunctions.)

Appeal to Federal District Court
(None—except that General
Counsel can seek temporary
injunction against both
employer and union unfair
labor practices AT ANY TIME.)

United States Supreme Court
(Hears a few important labor
law cases after circuit
courts have reviewed them.)

sion to issue a complaint. Indeed, in 1984, 94.6 percent of all cases viewed by the Board as meritorious were settled or withdrawn. If the charge is dismissed, the charging party may appeal the decision to the General Counsel in Washington. However, it is rare for a charging party to prevail in Washington—and quite frequently Washington officials had been directly involved in the initial decision to dismiss the charge. If the charge is dismissed, normally that is the end of the matter unless the charge raises some issue on which the individual can file an action in court, such as an allegation that the union breached its duty to represent all its employees within the bargaining unit fairly, or that the employer violated the collective bargaining agreement. Such allegations frequently raise issues that are separate and apart from the question of whether a party has committed an unfair labor practice under the National Labor Relations Act.

Theoretically, if there is a conflict in testimony or a question of credibility, the General Counsel should not resolve the factual issue administratively and dismiss the charge. This kind of issue should be resolved in an open hearing subsequent to the issuance of a complaint by the General Counsel. However, in many cases private parties (particularly unions) allege that the General Counsel resolves conflicts of fact administratively and makes it impossible for the matter to be considered in a full hearing, where the examination and cross-examination of witnesses might reveal the truth more effectively.

The General Counsel, as can be seen, has broad discretion. Indeed, the courts have thus far held that the General Counsel has plenary authority to determine whether an unfair-labor-practice complaint should be issued[28]—that is to say, even arbitrary conduct by the General Counsel cannot be reversed by the courts. The Supreme Court has yet to consider this issue.

The issuance of a complaint triggers a hearing before an Administrative Law Judge (they were previously called Trial Examiners, but insisted on a more exalted title). These judges, with offices in Washington, San Francisco, New York, and Atlanta, are representatives of the judicial side of the NLRB. They are independent, although they are supposed to follow the precedent and authorities that are decided by the five-man Board.

A hearing is held before the Adminstrative Law Judge at which the General Counsel's lawyers represent the charging party, and the employer or union charged with the violation appears as a "respondent." Sometimes the charging party will be represented by his own lawyer, and it is now established that the charging party is a party to the litigation with the same rights and privileges possessed by the General Counsel and the respondent.[29] The hearing generally takes place in one of the regional NLRB offices. Although the rules of evidence used in the federal district courts apply, the hearing is often more informal than the normal courtroom proceeding. The Administrative Law Judges, like the Board members, are not really judges and do not wear robes. Although lawyers always represent the Board and usually represent the respondent as well, there is no requirement that one be a lawyer to appear and argue before the Administrative Law Judge or the Board. Very often a union that is the charging party represented by the General Counsel will send a local official or a shop steward to represent its interests, and quite frequently the union's interests are represented more than adequately by such individuals.

The hearing generally takes place on consecutive days without interruption. Generally the notice of hearing states that the hearing is to take place on a designated date and on each day thereafter until the matter is completed. After the matter is completed, the parties submit briefs to the Administrative Law Judge and he then renders a decision (which is in fact a recommended order). If there are no exceptions or appeals to be taken from the decision of the Administrative Law Judge within twenty days of its issuance, the decision is adopted by the five-member Board in Washington. If exceptions are filed, the transcript, briefs, and other relevant documents are sent to the Board in Washington for consideration and decision. Only about 4 percent of all unfair-labor-practice charges reach the Board in Washington for a decision.

Although oral argument by the lawyers and other representatives is permitted (in addition to the presentation of evidence through witnesses and exhibits), the five-member Board in Washington rarely hears oral argument. Most of its decisions are based solely on the papers submitted to it subsequent to the decision of the Adminstrative Law Judge.

Most of the cases involve factual issues relating to alleged discriminatory discharges and dismissals of workers. There is no way that the Board can evaluate these matters more effectively, from a transcript and briefs, than the Administrative Law Judge who actually saw the witnesses, observed their demeanor, and made resolutions relating to credibility. In 74 percent of the cases, the Administrative Law Judge's decisions are approved by the Board in their entirety or with only slight modification. The problem here is that a considerable amount of time is consumed by the Board at this stage.

Most cases are decided by three of the Board's five members. The record of the case is filed in the Executive Secretary's office and the case is then assigned on a rotation basis. One member is assigned the case. Three members are simultaneously designated to serve on the panel considering the case, and a legal assistant is assigned. Ultimately the Board member and his Chief Counsel will become involved in the drafting of the decision, but generally the three representatives of the Board meet first. At this meeting a decision will be made as to whether the Administrative Law Judge's decision should be affirmed, affirmed in part, or reversed. If an opinion must be drafted, it will then be put together in the office of the Board member to whom the case was assigned initially. (Often, when the Board affirms the Adminstrative Law Judge's decision, the opinion will simply state that fact; this is called a "short form" opinion.)

If any Board member thinks a case is important, it will be discussed and considered at a weekly meeting of the members. A vote is taken and an opinion (sometimes a dissenting opinion as well) is written and circulated. In recent years the language used by various Board members where there has been a disagreement on important cases has been rather biting and sharp—at least when one compares it with the language used by the courts.

The Appellate Procedure

Because the NLRB is an administrative agency and not a court, its orders are not self-enforcing. Generally, the Board issues an order that the respondent cease and desist from engaging in unlawful conduct. When workers have been discriminatorially discharged, back pay will be awarded. Sometimes respondents will be required to remedy their violations.

Once a decision by the Board has been rendered, one of two things happens. If the Board determines that the respondent is unwilling to comply with the decision, it must file a petition in the Court of Appeals for the district where the case arose.[30] This court is the appellate level immediately below the U.S. Supreme Court. Because of the increasing caseload, there are often delays at this stage of the process as well. It is often months before the Board is able to file a petition for enforcement, and in many circuits a considerable period of time will elapse before the court has an opportunity to hear the case. The respondent or the charging party, if it wishes, may file a petition for a review or an appeal. Subsequent to the decision of the Court of Appeals, a petition for a writ of certiorari or review may be filed with the United States Supreme Court. An overwhelming number of these petitions are not granted. One can readily understand why this is so; approximately 5,000 petitions are filed each year, and the Supreme Court has the time to hear only around 150 of these cases.[31]

Summary

We now have most of the general framework of the National Labor Relations Act, as amended in 1947, and we have also touched on some court rulings and later legislative amendments. Among the subjects covered have been the constitutional basis of the NLRA; the organization of the NLRB and the roles of the Board, the General Counsel, and the Regional Offices; the jurisdictions of the courts and the NLRB; the extent of the NLRA's coverage; the definition of "labor organization" and the concept of exclusivity; the definition of "appropriate bargaining unit"; the election procedure; the definition of "unfair labor practice" for employers' and unions' activities; and the handling of unfair-labor-practice charges. As we turn to the establishing of the collective bargaining relationship and to the law's application in that process and in the life of the established relationship, we will be fleshing out the skeleton. The one piece of the structure that we have not yet touched on—remedies—will be better understood afterward.

5

Establishing the Collective Bargaining Relationship: Organization and Recognition

This chapter addresses the problems that arise when a union attempts to establish itself as the exclusive bargaining agent for an appropriate unit of workers.[1] It deals with the tactics labor uses and the restraints the law places upon it. (Of course, no precise line can be drawn between the legal tactics that are available to labor and management in the organizational context and those that may be used once the collective bargaining relationship has been established. Accordingly, the reader should keep the basic concepts and principles discussed here in mind when reading the succeeding chapters.)

Recruitment and Organization

In an organizational campaign, unions and employers are concerned with union attempts to surmount obstacles to communication with workers, union efforts to protect union adherents in the workplace, the tactics that may be employed, and the circumstances under which recognition can be compelled.

Unions recruiting workers will generally make contact with a small group of potential union adherents. At the early stages of a union effort this contact may be made secretly, to make it less likely that the employer will counterattack with antiunion communications or unlawful reprisals. The names, addresses, and telephone numbers of employees in the unit are important to the union for this purpose, but the NLRB requires the employer to make them available only at a much later stage, after the Regional Director has ordered an election.[2] Often this is too late. The union needs the information early in the campaign, when secrecy is desirable—long before it seeks access to company property or files a petition. The competing interest is the privacy of the employee who does not want to be bothered by solicitation, letters, and telephone calls.

Sophisticated full-time organizers are often used,[3] and literature on other union-negotiated contracts is sometimes distributed. Sometimes the union will send the employer a list of workers who have signed cards authorizing the union to represent them or indicating the worker's support for an NLRB election. (This will be done where the union believes that management will be less likely to retaliate against union supporters if it is unable to plead ignorance of their identities.) Where union adherents at a small plant are vocal and management imposes disciplinary sanctions upon them, the NLRB will sometimes infer management's knowledge of individual workers' support for the union even though such knowledge cannot be proved. Under this "small plant" doctrine, unlawful motive can be inferred.[4]

Exclusivity and the Obligation to Bargain

Fundamental to an understanding of the rules relating to organizational disputes (and of American labor law generally) are the principles that underlie the doctrine of exclusivity as it has been defined by the Supreme Court. The essential concern of the courts has been that the collective interest should govern over individual advantages once the majority of workers in an appropriate unit have designated the union as their bargaining representative. In large part, this rule exists because individual contracts could serve as an obstacle to organization and permit employers to "divide and conquer." Accordingly, the Court held, in *J. I. Case Co.* v. *NLRB*,[5] that individual contracts of employment cannot be utilized by an employer as a basis for precluding negotiations with the union on the same subject matter. The Court held that an individual hiring contract was "subsidiary" to the terms of a collective bargaining agreement, and that therefore such a contract cannot waive any of the agreement's benefits "any more than a shipper can contract away the benefit of filed tariffs, the insurer the benefit of standard provisions, or the utility customer the benefit of legally established rates."[6] Wherever there was no obligation to bargain with a union, an individual contract could be entered into or relied upon. But, said the Court:

Individual contracts, no matter what the circumstances that justify their execution or what their terms, may not be availed of to defeat or delay the procedures prescribed by the National Labor Relations Act looking to collective bargaining, nor to exclude the contracting employee from a duly ascertained bargaining unit; nor may they be used to forestall bargaining or to limit or condition the terms of the collective agreement. . . .

We are not called upon to say that under no circumstances can an individual enforce an agreement more advantageous than a collective agreement, but we find the mere possibility that such agreements might be made no ground for holding generally that individual contracts may survive or surmount collective ones. The practice and philosophy of collective bargaining looks with suspicion on such advantages. Of course, where there is great variation in circumstances of employment or capacity of employees, it is possible for the collective bargain to prescribe only minimum rates or maximum hours or expressly to leave certain areas open to individual bargaining. But except as so provided, advantages to individuals may prove as disruptive of industrial peace as disadvantages. They are a fruitful way of interfering with organization and choice of representatives; increased compensation, if individually deserved, is often earned at the cost of breaking down some other standard thought to be for the welfare of the group, and always creates the suspicion of being paid at the long-range expense of the group as a whole. Such discriminations not infrequently amount to unfair labor practices. The workman is free, if he values his own bargaining position more than that of the group, to vote against representation; but the majority rules, and if it collectivizes the employment bargain, individual advantages or favors will generally in practice go in as a contribution to the collective result.[7]

Of course, there are special groups of employees, such as entertainers, professional athletes, and even university professors, who do not fit into the mold of the normal collective bargaining process.

Discriminatory Discipline and Dismissal

The very first problem a union confronts in an organizational campaign is how to protect employees who are dismissed or disciplined. The obvious approach for a union organizer faced with this problem is to file an unfair-labor-practice charge with the NLRB. But how does a union or an employee prove that the employer has discriminated against the worker because of union activity or other protected activity? The Supreme Court has never squarely addressed or resolved the question of what kind of evidence must be adduced in order to make out discriminatory intent.

The classic case arose in the Court of Appeals for the Third Circuit and involved the problems of one Walter Weigand. As the court said, the case of Walter Weigand was "extraordinary":

If ever a workman deserved summary discharge, it was he. He was under the influence of liquor while on duty. He came to work when he chose and he left the plant and his shift as he pleased. In fact, a foreman on one occasion was agreeably surprised to find Weigand at work and commented upon it.... He brought a woman (apparently generally known as the "Duchess") to the rear of the plant yard and introduced some of the employees to her. He took another employee to visit her and when this man got too drunk to be able to go home, punched his time card for him and put him on the table in the representatives' meeting room in the plant in order to sleep off his intoxication. Weigand's immediate superiors demanded again and again that he be discharged, but each time higher officials intervened on Weigand's behalf because as was naively stated he was a "representative" (in an organization that was unlawfully "dominated")....[8]

When Weigand joined the CIO-affiliated union, he was discharged. The NLRB and the court found that the discharge was due to union activity, despite the employer's contention that it was based on accumulated offenses. Thus, Weigand was ordered reinstated. (Some courts have awarded back pay to such individuals but refused to reinstate them.[9])

The Supreme Court has addressed the troublesome issue of mixed motives (i.e., when the employer has both valid and unlawful reasons for dismissal) in both free-speech and NLRA cases. The Court has held that an employer, once confronted with a showing that constitutionally protected conduct in the form of free speech played a "substantial" role in the decision not to rehire, could still show by a preponderance of evidence that it would have reached the same decision in the absence of the exercise of protected conduct.[10] The test is whether the employer would have dismissed or not hired "but for" the speech, where the speech was the "primary reason for the dismissal or refusal to rehire."[11] I have criticized this decision as unduly restrictive in the context of First

Amendment litigation, and my judgment is that the same is true in connection with any attempt to apply it to NLRA cases.[12] Quite frequently, the employer has more than one reason for a dismissal. The Court's recent rulings make it difficult for an employee with a less than unblemished record to succeed in such cases.

Nonetheless, the NLRB adopted the Supreme Court's test in First Amendment cases for purposes of the NLRA in *Wright Line*:[13] "... we shall require that the General Counsel make a *prima facie* showing sufficient to support the inference that protected conduct was a 'motivating factor' in the employer's decision. Once this is established, the burden will shift to the employer to demonstrate that the same action would have taken place even in the absence of the protected conduct."[14] The NLRB stressed that the General Counsel still has the burden of producing the preponderance of evidence to establish a violation—the burden that the General Counsel assumes in any unfair-labor-practice proceeding before the Board. As a practical matter, however, the slight burden that is thrust upon the General Counsel as part of the *prima facie* case and the explicit burden on the company to come forward with reasons for the action may give the General Counsel access to important information at an early point in the hearing and thus a competitive advantage that he would not otherwise enjoy.

The Supreme Court unanimously affirmed the Board's position in *NLRB* v. *Transportation Management Corp.*[15] Justice White, the author of the Court's opinion, specifically approved of the Board's burden-shifting rules relating to the employer's obligation to produce evidence subsequent to a showing that illegal conduct was a substantial or motivating factor in the treatment of the worker. Said the Court:

The employer is a wrongdoer. He has acted out of a motive that is declared illegitimate by the statute. It is fair that he bear the risk that the influence of legal and illegal motives cannot be separated, because he knowingly created the risk and because the risk was created not by innocent activity, but by his own wrongdoing.[16]

The Court stated that the proviso in section 10(c) of the Taft-Hartley Act that seems to separate (and thus put out of the law's reach) discharges "for cause" from those interdicted by the statute has no applicability to mixed-motive cases. Said the Court:

The "for cause" proviso was not meant to apply to cases in which both legitimate and illegitimate causes contributed to the discharge. . . . The amendment was sparked by a concern over the Board's perceived practice of inferring from the fact that someone was active in a union that he was fired because of anti-union animus even though the worker had been guilty of gross misconduct.[17]

Where employer conduct is "inherently destructive" of employees' self-organization rights, no proof of an anti-union discriminatory intent is necessary to establish that the law has been violated.[18] In some circumstances the focus will be on the impact of the employer's conduct on the employee.[19]

Union Access to Company Property

One of the major problems a union is confronted with in an organizational campaign is to communicate with the employees it seeks to organize. The leading case in this regard is *Republic Aviation Corp.* v. *NLRB*,[20] in which the employer had prohibited all solicitation in the factory or offices on company property. An employee who had been warned of the rule solicited union membership in the plant by passing out application cards to employees during his own free time on the lunch break. He was dismissed. Three other employees were dismissed for wearing UAW-CIO caps and union steward buttons in the plant after being requested to remove them.

The NLRB found that the dismissal of the workers, and also the rule itself, constituted unfair labor practices, and that therefore the employer's conduct had improperly interfered with the employees right to "organize mutual aid without employer interference."[21] The special problem posed in this case was that there was no evidence that the plant's location made solicitation away from company property ineffective in reaching prospective union members. Thus, the employer contended that the union could communicate elsewhere without interfering with the company's property rights. However, the Supreme Court approved the NLRB's conclusion that the employer had no business justification for precluding the activity outside of work hours and that such a rule could therefore be presumed to be an "unreasonable impediment to self organization" and unnecessary in connection with the maintenance of production or discipline.[22]

A number of basic issues involving employee activity and the promulgation of rules by the employer have plagued the Board for years. The Board had concluded that employer-promulgated rules prohibiting solicitation and distribution of literature during "working time"—even when promulgated in conjunction with prohibition against activity during "working hours"—were presumptively invalid because of their ambiguity[23]; i.e., the worker would not know of his right to engage in union activity during paid lunch breaks and rest periods. In 1984 the Board, with Member Zimmerman dissenting, overruled this decision and held that rules couched in terms of "working time" are lawful.[24] The Board's view was that the meaning of "working time" and "working hours" within the context of no-solicitation rules had "attained substantial understanding," and that "many unions and employers had fashioned their instructions, policies and rules" so as to make clear the availability of paid rest periods for union activity.[25] A majority of the Board has also held that no-solicitation rules which make an exception for charitable solicitation are not *per se* invalid.[26] Disparate enforcement of such a rule, in contrast to a "small number of isolated beneficent acts"[27] or "an employer's toleration of isolated beneficent solicitation,"[28] can run afoul of the law.

A few years after *Republic Aviation*, when the Supreme Court considered the access of nonemployee union organizers to company property, it looked at the matter quite differently—even though the employees' right to communicate, albeit with more expert outside assistance, was involved. In this context, the Court did consider the availability of alternate avenues of communication to be relevant.[29] In this case the NLRB had noted that other means of communication (such as the mail and telephones), as well as the homes of the workers, were open to the union. The Court, which found that the situation did not involve workers who were isolated from communication attempts or who lived on company property,[30] stated:

. . . when the inaccessibility of employees makes ineffective the reasonable attempts by non-employees to communicate with them through the usual channels, the right to exclude from property has been required to yield to the extent needed to permit communication of information on the right to organize.

. . . no . . . obligation [similar to that owed to the employees in connection with their right to solicit during nonworking hours on company property] is owed nonemployee organizers. Their access to company property is governed by a different consideration. The right of self-organization depends in some meaure on the ability of employees to learn the advantages of self-organization from others. Consequently, if the location of a plant and the living quarters of the employees place the employees beyond the reach of reasonable union efforts to communicate with them, the employer must allow the union to approach his employees on his property. No such conditions are shown in these records.[31]

However, as the Supreme Court noted in another context, "The place of work is a place uniquely appropriate for dissemination of views concerning the bargaining representative and the various options open to the employees."[32]

In 1978 the Supreme Court concluded that the right of workers to distribute literature on nonworking portions of the employer's property extends to disputes that involve neither organizational nor bargaining disputes.[33] The Court held that the distribution of the union newsletter expressing opposition to a state's right-to-work law and to a presidential veto of an increase in the minimum wage fell within the "right to engage in other concerted activities for the purpose of . . . mutual aid or protection" protected by section 7 of the NLRA. On the other hand, "purely political tracts" are unprotected, even though the election of political candidates, for instance, can have an effect on employment conditions.[34]

Another group of cases involving union access to company property have to do with "quasi-public" property or facilities (those open to customers or the public generally). In *Central Hardware Co.* v. *NLRB*[35] the Supreme Court was confronted with a rule prohibiting nonemployees from soliciting in the parking lots of retail establishments. The NLRB held that this prohibition was overly broad and violated the NLRA. In this case the Board relied on a Court decision that a shopping center was the functional equivalent of a business district, in which First Amendment rights can normally be asserted. But the Court, in an opinion written by Justice Powell, ruled that this decision had no applicability to the NLRA.[36] The Court characterized the principle involved in the issue of the access of nonemployee union organizers to employers' property as follows:

This principle requires a "yielding" of property rights only in the context of an organization campaign. Moreover, the allowed intrusion on property rights is limited to that necessary to facilitate the exercise of employees' [section] 7 rights. After the requisite need for access to the employer's property has been shown, the access is limited to (i) union organizers; (ii) prescribed nonworking areas of the employer's premises and (iii) the duration of organization activity. In short, the principle of accommodation . . . is limited to labor organization campaigns, and the yielding of property rights it may require is both temporary and minimal.[37]

The Court stated that precedent relative to "large" shopping centers was not applicable to every private property open to the public. Said the Court: "Such an argument could be made with respect to almost every retail and service establishment in the country, regardless of size and location."[38] Accordingly, Powell concluded that the Board and appellate court had erred in relying on the shopping-center precedent to establish protection for union access.

The next important case was *Hudgens* v. *NLRB*,[39] which concerned a group of union members who, while engaged in peaceful primary picketing within a privately owned shopping center, had been threatened with arrest for criminal trespass. Preliminarily, Justice Stewart, speaking for the Court, noted that the rights and liabilities of the parties in this case were "dependent exclusively" upon the National Labor Relations Act and not upon the First Amendment. This arbitrary determination eliminated any potential for confusion arising out of inconsistency between constitutional and statutory standards. The Court noted that early decisions involving access to company property had involved a determination of what the "proper accomodation" would be in a given case.

The Court stated that there were differences among some of the earlier decisions that involved organizational activity carried on by nonemployees on the employers' property. The Court pointed to three such differences and remanded the case to the NLRB. Said the Court: "The context of the [section] 7 activity in the present case was different in several respects which may or may not be relevant in striking the proper balance. First, it involves the lawful economic strike activity rather than organizational activity. . . . Second, the [section] 7 activity here was carried on by Butler's employees (albeit not employees of its shopping center store), not by outsiders. . . . Third, the property interests impinged upon in this case were not those of the employer against whom the [section] 7 activity was directed, but of another."[40]

Upon remand, the NLRB took the position that economic activity of the kind involved in *Hudgens* warranted "at least equal deference" as organizational picketing. Further, the Board took the position that the pickets were entitled to at least as much protection as nonemployee organizers in some of the cases that had appeared before the Court previously. But the Board noted that the messages of organizational campaigns and economic strikes were aimed at different audiences. In *Hudgens* the pickets were attempting to communicate with the public which would do business with the employer as well as the employees who had not joined the strike. Said the Board:

One difference between organizational campaigns as opposed to economic strike situations is that in the former the section 7 rights being protected are those of the intended audience (the employees sought to be organized), and in the latter the section 7 rights are those of the persons attempting to communicate with *their* intended audience, the public as well as the employees. A further distinction between organizational and economic strike activity becomes apparent when the focus shifts to the characteristics of the audience at which the section 7 activity in question is directed. In an organizational campaign, the group of employees whose support the union seeks is specific and often is accessible by means of communication other than direct entry of the union organizers onto the employer's property, such as meeting employees on the street, home visits, letters, and telephone calls.[41]

The NLRB noted that the general public was the "more important component of the audience" and that often the mass media were not "reasonable" means for publicizing a labor dispute. With regard to the Court's statement that the property rights impinged upon were not those of the employer against whom the picketing was aimed, the Board noted that the property, although privately owned, was open to the public and was the equivalent of sidewalks, which are normally public property. In this regard, the Board, which since *Hudgens* had extended those principles to property such as the interiors of private banks, seems to have been reviving a First Amendment approach that the Supreme Court had used in connection with picketing on private property in shopping centers.[42] Moreover, the Court may have given union activity on employer property more protection by concluding that the states may expand the right to distribute literature (and, presumably, to picket) at a shopping center, despite the owner's constitutional interest in his property, under circumstances where access would be denied under federal law.[43]

Hudgens has spawned litigation about union access that is bound to come back to the Supreme Court in future years. The NLRB, with the approval of the Ninth Circuit Court, has held that a union's picketing of the forty-sixth floor of a bank (in an economic dispute) was protected by the NLRA[44]; communication there was regarded as more effective by both the Board and the Ninth Circuit Court. But in another case, one involving organizational solicitation and the employer's refusal to supply employees' names and addresses, the Fourth Circuit Court reversed the Board's holding that the union had no other effective alternative. The court characterized the union's efforts as "lackadaisical."[45]

Despite the doctrine of preemption, unions may encounter other obstacles to access from state criminal-trespass statutes. Thus the role of the states is double-edged, for the Supreme Court has held (in a divided vote) that criminal-trespass statutes may be used by owners against union organizers. Generally, the American doctrine of preemption, because of the supremacy of federal law, deprives the states of authority to act in areas such as labor-management relations where Congress has legislated extensively.[46] But in cases of trespass, the owner may call on the police or other law-enforcement authorities for assistance—possibly even if the NLRB were to rule that union organizers have the right to be on the property in question.[47] Since the Board's administrative process generally moves less quickly than state courts, the employer may prevail regardless of how firmly the union activities are protected by the National Labor Relations Act.

Even though most of the prominent litigation on organizers' access involves nonemployees, there remain a considerable number of areas for dispute involving solicitation of employees by employees and the right of employees to distribute literature. As we have seen, there is a presumption of illegality when an employer bans solicitation by employees outside of their working hours. However, this presumption does not apply in the case of retail department stores. There the employer may prohibit all solicitation in the selling area during working and nonworking hours.[48] Similar broad nonsolicitation rules are permitted in restaurants and fast-food outlets.[49] After the NLRA was amended to include nonprofit health-care institutions,[50] the full NLRB ruled unanimously that a broad nonsolicitation rule was presumptively invalid "in areas other than immediate patient care areas such as lounges and cafeterias."[51] The Supreme Court approved of solicitation in hospital cafeterias and coffee shops;[52] it was not persuaded by the argument that, since the public and patients were admitted to the cafeteria of the hospital, the rule for restaurants should apply. The main function of a hospital is patient care and therapy, not the serving of cafeteria food, and the cafeteria is a natural gathering place for employees and can be used for solicitation with little interference with patient care. Thus, the balancing of employees' rights to organize and employers' rights to maintain discipline here favors allowing a presumption that a ban on solicitation in the cafeteria is illegal. However, in a later case the Supreme Court refused to extend this principle to sitting rooms and corridors, and expressed serious doubts that the presumption of illegality applied with respect to those areas.[53]

Although it appears that employees do not possess a statutory right to post union notices on bulletin boards,[54] an employer may not deny employees the right to post union notices while permitting other noncompany information to appear.[55] This practice constitutes unlawful discrimination.

Finally, it is important to note that the NLRB has held that nonemployee organizers may have access to company property to respond to an employer's speech made to a "captive audience" of workers during work hours where the employer has a legitimate but very broad nonsolicitation rule.[56] In these circumstances the Board found a glaring imbalance in opportunities for organizational communication and an interference with the right to organize.

Organizational Picketing

For the union, burdens as well as benefits attend organizational picketing. In the 1960 *Curtis Bros.* decision[57] the Supreme Court, speaking through Justice Brennan, held that an attempt by a trade union representing a minority of the workers to impose a bargaining obligation on an employer through picketing was not an unfair labor practice within the meaning of the Taft-Hartley amendments. The argument of the employer and the NLRB before the Court was that the picketing inevitably violated the free choice of employees to join or refrain from union activity, which is protected by the NLRA. The Court, referring to some of the constitutional cases that have protected picketing, noted that "in the sensitive area of peaceful picketing Congress has dealt explicitly with isolated evils which experience has established flow from such picketing."[58] Accordingly, the Court was unwilling to find a basis for statutory violation in the absence of the "clearest indication in the legislative history" of the statute.[59]

Amendments passed by Congress in 1959 purported to regulate organizational picketing in certain key respects. The idea was to permit the NLRB to enjoin picketing aimed at subverting a valid collective bargaining relationship already entered into with another union and organizational picketing aimed at reversing a union's defeat at the ballot box within twelve months of the election. The most complicated of these picketing regulations in this respect is section 8(b)(7)(C),[60] which limits picketing aimed at obtaining recognition to a "reasonable period of time" not to exceed thirty days. Informational picketing is exempted from the statutory prohibition unless it has the effect of interfering with deliveries. An expeditious election is held without the usual showing of interest prerequisite and without an administrative hearing about an appropriate unit because of the need for prompt relief. Picketing and strikes can cause irreparable harm to an employer.

The NLRB and the courts have taken the position that area-wage-standard picketing (picketing protesting wages and working conditions that are inferior to those offered by comparable employers in the geographic labor market) is not prohibited by the NLRA, and recent Board decisions have affirmatively protected employees who engage in such picketing from discipline and discharge.[61] Picketing, although it may not be engaged in for an unreasonable period of time with a view toward obtaining recognition through economic pressure rather than the ballot box, may be engaged in if it is informational in nature. Where picketing, despite unlawful recognitional intent, is simply an attempt to advertise a dispute to the public, the Board cannot find an unfair labor practice unless there is more than isolated interference with deliveries. This rule has meant that a union, with competent counsel, can easily escape the organizational-picketing provisions of the NLRA unless the picketing proves disruptive.

There are two particular difficulties with the restrictions on organizational picketing. On the one hand, Congress was deeply concerned with prohibiting "blackmail" picketing, which was often engaged in by labor. On the other hand, organizational picketing occurs in a significant number of legitimate situations, particularly in the South and in rural areas, where the union has a genuine concern with the plight of workers who need protection. Employers' counterattacks against organizational drives, sometimes involving unlawful tactics, frequently make it difficult for a union to demonstrate majority support through the ballot box. Under such circumstances, picketing to dissuade employees from working and others from doing business with the employer may be a legitimate weapon.

Moreover, the Supreme Court has attempted to establish a demarcation line between different kinds of picketing that occur in organizational efforts. The Court has seen "publicity" picketing as the kind of expression of thought that is protected by the First Amendment.[62] However, "signal" picketing, which is not only aimed at employees but also designed to produce an immediate response on the part of union members who are subject to union disciplinary sanctions, is deemed to be conduct that can be controlled and regulated by Congress and sometimes the states.[63] Specifically, the "informational picketing" proviso is meant to protect "publicity" picketing against government prohibition, even though it might be part of a union effort to secure recognition without an NLRB-approved election. The thinking of Congress was that an unduly broad prohibition against organizational picketing might not only be bad policy (because of the legitimate situation referred to above), but might also be constitutionally deficient.

Secondary Picketing

Secondary picketing is another tactic that has created legal difficulties for the trade-union movement. If the union is successful, the primary target of the boycott is more likely to settle on the union's terms or to recognize the union if the dispute has a recognitional objective. Such disputes can arise both where a union has recognitional objectives and where there is an established relationship with the primary employer and the dispute is about wages, hours, and working conditions.

As noted above, the Norris-LaGuardia Act reversed the common-law view of secondary boycotts and their illegality that had been accepted by the Supreme Court. But Congress, through the 1947 Taft-Hartley amendments, revived the secondary-boycott prohibitions both for the purposes of NLRB administrative hearings and for the purposes of damage suits in federal and state courts. The Board, as with organizational picketing, is obligated to give investigative priority to unfair-labor-practice charges involving secondary picketing and is mandated to proceed directly in a federal district court to obtain an injunction if the regional attorney in the NLRB field office has reasonable cause to believe that a violation is being committed. Additionally, secondary economic pressure undertaken by virtue of a so-called "most-favored-nation" agreement obligating the union to get the same or better terms from the secondary target than have been obtained from the primary target can still constitute a conspiracy in violation of antitrust law.[64]

The NLRA, then, is designed to protect third parties who are innocent or wholly unconcerned with the dispute in question. But who is an innocent party? Who is wholly unconcerned? In a sense, even the general public has an interest if it will pay less for an employer's goods if the union loses a strike. On the other hand, many employers who have commercial relationships with the primary target of a strike have absolutely nothing to do with the dispute, and therefore it would seem unfair to involve them.

As written, the NLRA purports to prohibit economic pressure aimed at bringing about a cessation of business between the primary employer and other employers. Literally, this might mean that a union-established picket line at the primary employer's premises that was intended to dissuade the importation of strikebreakers by another company to perform the striking workers' jobs would be unlawful because the object would be to obtain a cessation of business between the primary employer and the company importing the strikebreakers. However, the Supreme Court has not read the statute that way.[65] The first exception to the literal language of the statute is based on the "ally" doctrine, which has permitted workers to picket a secondary employer when the union is pursuing work that would have been performed by the primary employer's workers before the strike but has been farmed out to the secondary employer.[66]

Organizational disputes can affect more than one employer and thus create secondary problems in other contexts. The 1959 amendments make unlawful collective bargaining agreements containing "hot cargo" clauses (which, as mentioned above, permit employees to refuse to handle goods produced by an employer with whom the union has a dispute—e.g., one whose products do not carry a union label) or subcontracting clauses (which preclude contracting out work to a nonunion employer).[67] The reason is that such contractual provisions have a secondary objective: to influence the labor-relations policies by organizing workers through a third innocent party, the employer who has signed the contract. On the other hand, subcontracting clauses that preserve the bargaining unit's work (for example, agreements that prohibit subcontracting work to employers who provide substandard working conditions) are lawful.[68]

However, the Supreme Court held in the landmark case of *NLRB* v. *Denver Building Trades*[69] that, where an object of picketing is to interfere with the secondary employer and its employees and their relationship with the primary employer, a violation of the statute can be made out. This case arose in the context of "common situs" picketing and multiemployer construction facilities, where a picket line at the primary employer's facilities would necessarily affect the secondary employees by attempting to persuade all employees to refuse to work. This would place great pressure on the primary employer to accede to union demands, and would stand a good chance of success—particularly because employee response in the construction industry is likely to be automatic and triggered by a "signal."[70] The difficulty in reconciling *Denver Building Trades* with the ally doctrine and the Court's subsequent holding that common situs picketing at an industrial establishment where the employer maintains separate gates for outside contractors does not violate the statute[71] has created an anomaly that is inequitable for building-trades workers. On a number of occasions (most recently in 1977[72]) this has led the AFL-CIO Building Trades Department to press for legislation that would reverse *Denver Building Trades* and permit common situs picketing. The concern of the building trades in this regard has increased in recent years as nonunion construction work has spread, but every effort on their part has been unsuccessful. Even when both houses of Congress passed a common situs bill, President Ford vetoed it.[73] The prevailing view has accepted the employer's position that if *Denver Building Trades* were to be reversed unions would have considerable power to organize an entire building site by involving employers (other subcontractors) who have no interest in the dispute.

It would appear as though the construction unions have another advantage not possessed by other labor organizations: Congress exempted the construction industry, along with the clothing industry, from the secondary-boycott prohibitions contained in the statute's treatment of "hot cargo" clauses. However, the Supreme Court seems to have said that the construction-industry proviso does not immunize from the secondary-boycott prohibitions all union picketing intended to obtain an agreement under which the general contractor could subcontract work to employers who had signed contracts with the picketing union.[74] In *Woelke & Romero Framing, Inc.* v. *NLRB*,[75] the Court indicated that some kind of collective bargaining relationship between the picketing union and the contractor was a prerequisite to the protection of the construction-industry proviso, and it left open for future resolution the question of whether the union could seek a clause limiting the subcontracting of work to unionized subcontractors to one particular job site or to a geographic area, such as a county, within the union's jurisdiction. The Court unanimously held that a construction union may lawfully seek and negotiate such a clause for a geographic area.[76] The Court held that where there is a collective bargaining relationship between a union and a contractor, demonstrating the union's interest in organizing that employer's employees, a subcontracting clause is lawful under the construction-industry proviso—even though such a clause induces "top-down organizing" (organizing by pressure from other employers rather than through union recruitment), which Congress regarded as an evil when it enacted the secondary-boycott prohibitions.

The Court stated that the proviso was intended not only to avoid job-site friction between union and nonunion workers, but also to mitigate the impact of *Denver Building Trades*. Said Justice Marshall, speaking for the Court:

... we believe that Congress endorsed subcontracting agreements obtained in the context of a collective bargaining relationship—and decided to accept whatever top-down pressure such clauses might entail. Congress concluded that the community of interests on the construction jobsite justified the top-down organizational consequences that might attend the protection of legitimate collective bargaining objectives.[77]

Another part of the secondary-boycott issue relates to secondary consumer picketing (picketing to dissuade the public from patronizing retail establishments rather than to dissuade employees from working). The Supreme Court has construed the statute to permit peaceful secondary picketing that addresses the primary dispute. However, as is the case with so many secondary-picketing problems, the proposition is more easily stated in the abstract than applied to concrete situations. In the *Tree Fruits* case[78] the union had called a strike against fruit packers and warehousemen who were doing business in Yakima, Washington. The struck firms sold their apples to the Safeway chain of retail stores in and about Seattle. The union instituted a consumer boycott of the apples and placed pickets in front of a number of the stores in that city. The pickets distributed handbills and wore placards that said "To the Consumer: Non-union Washington State apples are being sold at this store. Please do not purchase such apples. Thank you. Teamsters Local 760, Yakima, Washington."[79] The Supreme Court held that not all secondary consumer picketing was prohibited by the statute, and that

Congress had legislated against "isolated evils." Conceding that the public might not read picket signs and handbills aimed explicitly at the primary employer, the Court held that where the union's appeal was "closely confined to the primary dispute" the secondary-boycott prohibitions were not violated.[80]

This Supreme Court ruling on secondary consumer picketing is difficult to apply to economically dependent or captive secondary employers who purchase only from the primary employer. Examples of this are gasoline stations and exclusive franchise dealers of major automobile companies. It is impossible for the union to confine its appeal to the primary employer in a way that will not be aimed at the entire structure of the secondary employer in this situation. At Safeway it was different, because the Yakima apples were only one of many products the company was handling. More recently a divided Court held that where the picketed secondary employer is economically dependent upon the primary employer, the union violates the statute's secondary-boycott prohibitions by engaging in consumer picketing because the secondary employer cannot shift to another product (a possibility that was open to Safeway).[81] The Court theorized that the only possible response by the secondary employer is to shut down, even though some such employers might be able to obtain new products or business relationships. Thus, the picketing would necessarily bring a neutral party into a dispute in which it is not involved—the very abuse at which the secondary-boycott prohibitions are aimed.

The Court rejected the contention that First Amendment protection was invaded by Congress inasmuch as the statute is aimed at unlawful objectives, i.e., spreading "labor discord by coercing a neutral party to join the fray."[82] Justice Stevens, in a concurring opinion, characterized the activity at issue as signal picketing: "The statutory ban in this case affects only that aspect of the union's effort to communicate its views that calls for an automatic response to a signal rather than a reasoned response to an idea."[83] Subsequently a unanimous Supreme Court spoke approvingly of Justice Stevens's characterization of consumer picketing as signal picketing.[84] The Court's simultaneous bestowal of First Amendment protection on a civil-rights boycott is puzzling and troublesome.[85]

Compulsory Recognition of a Union

In a number of relationships, the union establishes majority status and recognition without certification by presenting to the employer authorization cards indicating that a majority of the employees in an appropriate unit desire to be represented by the union. Prior to the 1947 amendments, the NLRB permitted unions to be certified for the purpose of representing employees on the basis of authorization cards and petitions as well as electoral victories. (Certification by the Board obligates the employer to bargain for specific job classifications for a unit and protects the union from challenge by rivals.) The 1947 amendments eliminated certification through any method other than an election conducted by the Board. (Unions, employees, and the employer—where a demand is made upon it—may petition the Board for an election.) But can a union obtain legally binding recognition from the employer without a Board election and certification on the basis of authorization cards or petitions? This was the issue presented to the Supreme Court in *NLRB* v. *Gissel*.[86] The Court found that legislative history relating to the Taft-Hartley amendments did not preclude union recognition on the basis of authorization cards without certification. Although the Court noted that the election process possessed an "acknowledged superiority," it held that authorization cards were not "inherently unreliable."[87] Indeed, the Court stated that cards "may be the most effective—perhaps the only—way of assuring employee choice" where unfair labor practices had made it impossible to test employees' free choice through the ballot box.[88]

But the Court left open a number of questions in *Gissel*. Does an employer have an obligation to recognize the union on the basis of authorization cards where it has not committed independent unfair labor practices that would taint the electoral process? Must the employer, if it wishes to protect itself, petition the NLRB (as it is permitted to do by the Taft-Hartley amendments[89]) for an election? In 1974 the Court held by a 5–4 vote that, even where the union presents authorization cards indicating that a majority of the employees support the union and where that support is also manifested through a refusal to cross a union picket line, the employer is not acting in "bad faith" by refusing to recognize the union.[90] It is the union that has the burden of taking the next step and invoking the electoral process.

Another unresolved issue is related to the question of when recognition may be thrust upon an employer that has engaged in extensive or egregious unfair labor practices. Under such circumstances, *Gissel* makes it clear that the union could obtain recognition on the basis of authorization cards where it has a majority. But suppose the unfair labor practices make it impossible for the union to collect a majority and (more specifically) that the union alleges that but for the employer's unfair labor practices it would have obtained a majority of the cards, or that there is a reasonable likelihood that the union would have obtained majority status. The employer in this situation would profit from his wrongdoing by engaging in more effective illegality—by nipping the union organizational drive in the bud before it is able to establish itself. Two courts of appeals have held that recognition may be imposed upon an employer under such circumstances.[91] The issue has not yet come to the Supreme Court. In one of the two aforementioned cases, *United Dairy Farmers' Cooperative Association*,[92] the Board split in three different directions on this issue. None of the Board members who participated in *United Dairy Farmers' Cooperative Association* are serving on the Board today.

Member Penello took the position that a nonmajority union could not obtain a bargaining order under *Gissel* under the NLRA.[93] Members Truesdale and Murphy held that the statute contemplated such an order, but only when there was no "reasonable likelihood of *ever* holding a [fair] election."[94] Chairman Fanning and member Jenkins took the position that a majority bargaining order could be imposed where the Board had initially attempted to determine majority status through an election and where there was a "very good probability that, had employee sentiment been allowed to emerge, it should have favored the union."

It was in this posture that the Third Circuit Court of Appeals heard the matter late in 1980 and held that the Board does have remedial authority to impose a nonmajority bargaining order where "outrageous" and "pervasive" unfair labor practices have been committed.[95] Judge Higginbotham, writing for a unanimous panel,[96] noted that the court had not squarely answered this question in *Gissel*. But careful restrictions on the employer's behavior during Board-conducted elections, said the court, were necessary, "since the employer has disproportionate economic power."[97] Said the Third Circuit Court: "The rationale for selecting bargaining representatives by certification election evaporates . . . when the employer has committed such serious unfair labor practices that the laboratory conditions of the past election, as well as any election in the immedate future, are destroyed. In these circumstances, because of the employer's attempt to undermine employee free choice, the goal of a free uninhibited certification election simply cannot be attained regardless of the reparative actions which may be attempted by the Board. Other means to protect employees must be pursued."[98]

Judge Higginbotham properly noted that *Gissel* was a remedy case and that, although both an election and evidence of majority support through authorization cards would have been preferable to the imposition of a bargaining order where no majority order had been evident, the failure to recognize remedial authority for the Board under the circumstances would have undermined the statutory goal of majority choice. Said Judge Higginbotham: "Unions which would have attained a majority in a free and uncoerced election if the employer had not committed unfair labor practices would be deprived of recognition merely because of the employer's illegal conduct. . . . The absence of such authority might create incentives for employers to engage in illegal prophylactic action with the purpose of preventing the attainment of a card majority."[99] Accordingly, the court held that the Board had the remedial authority to issue a bargaining order where the practices were so outrageous and pervasive that there was "no reasonable possibility that a free and uncoerced election could be held."[100] The court specifically avoided the question of whether the Board had the authority where there was no reasonable possibility that the union would have obtained a majority but for the action of the employer, stating that a "reasonable possibility" existed in *United Dairy* because, although the employer had committed "numerous flagrant and serious violations," the union had lost by only two votes.[101] Quite clearly the closeness of the vote will be an important factor to take into account.

Subsequently, the Board squarely accepted the propriety of minority bargaining orders and the views of Chairman Fanning and member Jenkins.[102] The Board recited a number of circumstances that prompted the fashioning of such an order: the "extreme gravity" of the violations; "mass communication" to all employees from all levels of the corporate hierarchy; and repetition and timing of unlawful conduct, which "exacerbated their long-term coercive impact." The Board also noted that 46 percent of the employees in the unit had signed authorization cards.

However, a divided Court of Appeals for the District of Columbia, with Judge Wald dissenting, refused enforcement of the Board's order[103] on the ground that Congress had not intended minority bargaining orders to be within the Board's discretion and that, where Congress had intended to sanction minority bargaining, as in the construction industry, it had done so explicitly. Meanwhile, the Board reversed itself in 1984 in *Gourmet Foods, Inc.*.[104] In reaching a conclusion opposite to the one reached two years before, the Board provided this rationale:

We seriously question . . . whether a nonmajority bargaining order, in practice, is an effective remedy. The bargaining environment established at the Board's instigation alone does not replicate that which arises from employees' impetus. What is lacking is the leverage normally possessed by exclusive bargaining representatives that derives from unions' and employers' knowledge that a majority of employees at one time, in some form, united in their support for a union and may do so again in support of bargaining demands. To gain that leverage, employees may be called on to demonstrate active support for a representative in a far more open way than a secret-ballot election. Accordingly, in imposing a representative on employees, the Board may be changing only the sphere of employees' choice. And yet the Board can be no more certain that, in this new sphere of employee choice, employees can more freely exercise their choice without regard to any lingering effects of massive unfair labor practices than it can be if a new election is directed after the Board has applied traditional as well as appropriate extraordinary remedies. The Board can be certain, however, of the possibility that it is forcing a majority of employees who do not have an interest in participating in the collective-bargaining process into that process and, potentially and consequently, into un-desired terms and conditions of employment negotiated by an unchosen representative. Given these policy considerations we do not believe we would ever be justified in granting a nonmajority bargaining order remedy.[105]

Suppose a union obtains recognition on the basis of certifi-cation through an election or authorization cards, but the ma-jority of the workers change their mind and the employer relies on this to refuse to recognize the union. The courts have held that an employer has an obligation to continue to recognize the union for a "reasonable period of time" and that where the union has been certified that reasonable pe-riod of time is for the period of the certification (one year).[106] Where the union has been recognized on the basis of authori-zation cards, petitions, or whatever, the employer also has an obligation to continue recognition for a reasonable period of time—but sometimes the Board has held that this period can elapse before the passage of one year.[107]

If a union negotiates a collective bargaining agreement with an employer after recognition, another union cannot step in and attempt to obtain recognition for itself. In the first place, if both unions are affiliated with the AFL-CIO, the union that raids the other may be held by the federation's "umpire" to have violated the AFL-CIO's No Raiding Pact.[108] In any event, a contract negotiated between the parties is a bar to such recognition, and thus, where a union files a peti-tion for representation with the Board and a valid collective bargaining agreement has been negotiated, the Board will dismiss the petition on the grounds that the contract bars it. The contract is a bar where it is signed by all parties—even if it is not embodied in a formal document.[109] Prior notification is required where the contract itself requires it.[110] The con-tract must cover workers in an appropriate unit.[111] Where there is a significant change in the identity of a contracting party, the contract is not a bar.[112] The contract bar has a duration of three years or the period of the collective bargaining agreement, whichever is shorter.[113] Between ninety and sixty days prior to the expiration of the contract a petition may be filed challenging the incumbent union's position as exclusive representative; such a petition will be regarded as timely. If it is not filed by sixty days prior to the expiration of the agreement it will not be regarded as timely. The purpose is to permit the parties to resolve their differences through collective bargaining without any distractions. This is why a petition cannot be filed at this time. During this sixty-day period, and independent of contract obligations, neither the union nor the employer may engage in strikes, lockouts, or any other form of economic pressure. Likewise, the statute, independent of any contract obligations that the parties assume, requires labor and management to give notice of their intent to modify or terminate the agreement to the mediation agencies at the beginning of the sixty-day period.

Conclusion

The law promotes the right of workers to organize, but it tempers that concern with recognition of other principles that sometimes collide with it: free choice for employees (generally expressed through the ballot box), the circumvention of such choice through economic pressure on employers, and employers' property rights.

6

Economic Pressure and Bargaining Tactics in the Established Relationship

The National Labor Relations Act has a dual purpose, and its dual concerns are often at odds with one another. On the one hand, the statute is concerned with protecting trade unions and their members against antiunion discrimination. Quite frequently, the NLRB and the courts will presume antiunion discrimination even though there is no proof that the employer was motivated in its conduct by antiunion considerations. The underlying concern is that certain tactics may have the effect of destroying the union entirely and thus destroying the collective bargaining process. Accordingly, one concern is to prop up trade unions and, by so doing, to save the collective bargaining process when it is imperiled. But simultaneously the NLRA attempts to promote the collective bargaining process as a wide-open, robust relationship in which the parties should have the widest latitude in bargaining tactics, pressure, and economic weaponry. The underlying concern is that if the NLRB and the courts try to regulate bargaining tactics, they will be regulating the substance of the collective bargaining process and ultimately the substance of the collective bargaining agreement itself. Nowhere is this concern—which is often at odds with the need to preserve free trade unions and the collective bargaining process—more clearly seen than in the landmark *Insurance Agents* decision,[1] which involved a work slowdown by the union.

In *Insurance Agents* the employer argued that the slowdown was itself an unfair labor practice—specifically, an unlawful refusal to bargain, inasmuch as the tactic tends to preclude discussion—and that the union ought to be prohibited from engaging in it. The Supreme Court rejected this argument and took the position that economic pressure that might serve as an irritant rather than as a promoter of dialogue was an essential ingredient in the collective bargaining process. Said the Court:

It must be realized that collective bagaining, under a system where the government does not attempt to control the results of negotiations, cannot be equated with an academic collective search for truth—or even with what might be thought to be the ideal of one. The parties—even granting the modification of view that may come from a realization of economic interdependence—still proceed from contrary and to an extent antagonistic viewpoints and concepts of self-interest. The system has not reached the ideal of the philosophic notion that perfect understanding among people would lead to perfect agreement among them on values. The presence of economic weapons in reserve and their actual exercise on occasion by the parties, is part and parcel of the system that the Wagner and Taft-Hartley Acts have recognized. Abstract logical analysis might find inconsistency between the command of the statute to negotiate toward an agreement in good faith and legitimacy of the use of economic weapons, frequently having the most serious effect upon individual workers and productive enterprises, to induce one party to come to the terms desired by the other. But the truth of the matter is that at the present statutory stage of our national labor relations policy, the two factors—necessity for good faith bargaining between parties, and the availability of eco-

nomic pressure devices to each to make the other party in-
cline to agree on one's terms—exist side by side.[2]

Accordingly, within limits, the success and strength of one
party ought not to matter in determining whether a statutory
violation has been committed.

Protected and Unprotected Activities

Section 7 of the NLRA affirmatively protects a wide variety of
employee pressures and protests aimed at the employer. *Insurance Agents* simply dealt with the question of whether particularly irritating slowdowns constituted a refusal to bargain.
It did not address the question of whether the activity engaged in was "protected activity" within the meaning of the
Act.

If an activity is protected, employees are immunized from
discipline or discharge for engaging in the activity. If it is
prohibited, the NLRB may obtain a cease-and-desist order
through its own administrative process against the conduct,
and may eventually enforce it through a petition to the circuit court of appeals. Activity that is neither protected nor
prohibited is in a "no man's land"; employees may be dismissed or disciplined for engaging in it.

For an activity to be protected it must be "concerted."
Though it seems clear that employees' protests must be
aimed at group concerns, the courts and the NLRB are divided on the question of whether one employee can engage
in such conduct.[3] The Court of Appeals for the Sixth Circuit
approved the Board's rule that an employee's presentation of
job-related grievances aimed at getting the employer to comply with laws or regulations is protected concerted activity.[4]
But the Board has reversed itself, concluding that "it will no
longer be sufficient for the General Counsel to set out the
subject matter that is of alleged concern to a theoretical
group and expect to establish concert of action thereby."[5]

Meanwhile, in *NLRB* v. *City Disposal System*,[6] the Supreme Court has held that a single employee — in this case, one refusing to drive an allegedly unsafe truck — is engaged in concerted activity when the worker invokes a right contained in a collective bargaining agreement. Said Justice Brennan, writing for a 5–4 majority: ". . . an honest and reasonable invocation of a collectively bargained right constitutes concerted activity, regardless of whether the employee turns out to have been correct in his belief that his right was violated."[7] Undoubtedly, the tension between *City Disposal* and the Board's most recent position on concerted activities will come to the Court for adjudication soon.[8]

The Supreme Court held in the *Weingarten* case that an employee who calls on a union representative to assist in a disciplinary interview is engaged in concerted activity.[9] However, the Board has held that reinstatement and back pay are not appropriate remedies for such statutory violations.[10] Initially, the Board extended *Weingarten* to non-unionized establishments.[11] But the courts divided on the issue,[12] and the Board subsequently reversed itself.[13]

The NLRB has relied on First Amendment cases protecting free speech against libel actions[14] as a basis for protecting employees' complaints against employers, even though such complaints may promote "discord" and "strife."[15] This is because labor-management controversy, even when it occurs within the context of an established relationship and involves collective bargaining and grievance processing,[16] may be just as "bitter and extreme" as it is in an organizational setting where union recognition is at issue.[17] The Board has invalidated employers' rules prohibiting the distribution of "scurrilous" literature[18] and has held that employees' complaints that are protected are not rendered unprotected because they involve "animal exuberance" or "impulsive behavior."[19] They are not even unprotected when the employee accuses the boss of having an affair with someone.[20]

These cases involve a balancing process. Perhaps the most controversial cases in which employee or union conduct has been found unprotected are the "disloyalty" cases. The leading one is *NLRB* v. *Local Union No. 1229, IBEW*,[21] in which the Supreme Court, over the sharp dissent of Justices Frankfurter, Douglas, and Black, held that the distribution of handbills that contained a "vitriolic attack on the quality of the company's television broadcasts" by nonstriking employees but did not refer to the labor-management controversy was unprotected. The Board subsequently extended this rule to conclude that disparagement of a company's product was unprotected even when the employees were on strike.[22] However, boycott signs in or on employees' cars on company property have been held to be protected.[23] On the other hand, employees who use "vulgar shop talk" more than others when engaged in concerted protest (especially in discussions with management officials) were held to be engaged in unprotected conduct.[24] The Court of Appeals for the Eighth Circuit has held that employees' questions and statements that interrupted a captive-audience meeting because they were a "challenge and deliberate defiance, repeatedly asserted before assembled employees"[25] were unprotected. The Board has also held that it was lawful for Michigan Bell Telephone Company to require employees—in the midst of collective bargaining—to remove sweatshirts containing the slogan "Ma Bell is a Cheap Mother."[26] That slogan is unprotected when it is displayed on company property because it is considered obscene. But when a radical trade unionist employed by the Inland Steel Company was fired for protesting company conduct while wearing a shirt emblazoned with "Inland Sucks," the Board held that his dismissal was not lawful inasmuch as the employer had not relied on the shirt as a basis for his termination.[27]

One other area of contention involves the extent to which the conduct of supervisors, who are excluded from the

NLRA's coverage, can be characterized as protected activity. The Court of Appeals for the Ninth Circuit, in reversing an NLRB order protecting supervisory activity, noted that supervisory conduct has been held protected when a supervisor is dismissed or disciplined for refusing to commit an unfair labor practice, when a supervisor is dismissed or disciplined for testifying before the NLRB, and when a supervisor is dismissed or disciplined as a pretext for dismissing pro-union employees working under him.[28] The court refused to accept the Board's position that supervisors should be reinstated with back pay when the employer's policy might have a coercive impact on the rank and file in the bargaining unit. The court reasoned that remedies for the employees are enough.

Faced with a case in which supervisors and employees had been dismissed because of a letter sent to the company president criticizing a manager, the Court of Appeals for the First Circuit held, in an opinion written by Judge Breyer, that the activity had to involve employees and their conditions of work to be protected.[29] In these cases involving the question of whether supervisors' conduct is protected, the Board's position had been that the activity must be part of the concern and needs of employees in order for the Board and the courts to respond affirmatively and to conclude that the employer has violated the statute. However, the Board has now narrowed the scope of protection afforded supervisors. In *Parker-Robb Chevrolet*[30] it said:

... although we recognize that the discharge of a supervisor for engaging in union or concerted activity almost invariably has a secondary or incidental effect on employees, we believe that, when a supervisor is discharged either because he or she engaged in union or concerted activity or because the discharge is contemporaneous with the unlawful discharge of statutory employees, or both, this incidental or secondary effect on the employees is insufficient to warrant an exception to the general statutory provision excluding supervisors from the protection of the Act. Thus, it is irrelevant that an emoyer may have hoped or even expected that its decision to terminate a supervisor for his union or concerted activity would cause employees to reconsider and perhaps abandon their own concerted or union activity. No matter what the employer's subjective hope or expectation that circumstance cannot change the character of its otherwise lawful conduct.

. . . The discharge of supervisors is unlawful when it interferes with the right of employees to exercise their rights under Section 7 of the Act, as when they give testimony adverse to the employers' interest or when they refuse to commit unfair labor practices. The discharge of supervisors as a result of their participation in union or concerted activity— either by themselves or when allied with rank and file employees—is not unlawful for the simple reason that employees, but not supervisors, have rights protected by the Act.[31]

Of course, the mere fact that the employer has the right to dismiss workers for unprotected activity (in the case of economic pressure, for instance) does not mean that it will happen. Dismissal or discipline might be counterproductive in the sense of producing more industrial warfare and not less.

What is protected economic pressure within the meaning of the NLRA? The Supreme Court has held that walkouts, with or without the presence of the union, are protected activity regardless of the judges' view about the wisdom of the action.[32] However, strikes in breach of grievance-arbitration and no-strike clauses negotiated by labor and management are unprotected.[33] Similarly, slowdowns are unprotected, because in the view of the courts such action is an attempt to require the employer to accept the employees on their own terms of employment.[34] Violent strikes and the kinds of sit-ins or plant occupations that took place in the 1930s are similarly unprotected.[35]

The Strike

Striking, in itself, is protected activity, although unauthorized or wildcat stoppages are unprotected because they derogate the status of the exclusive bargaining agent, who is supposed to speak on behalf of all employees within the apropriate unit. This includes dissident groups as well as those who are in accord with the union's policy.[36] Strikes in accord with union policy have been defined as authorized or ratified and thus protected within the meaning of the NLRA where the Board and the courts determine that the objective of the strikers is in accord with the policy of the union.[37]

Section 13 specifically states that nothing in the NLRA is intended to interfere with the right to strike. However, there are a number of limitations on the right, and one of them is set out in the Taft-Hartley amendments' prohibition of strikes during emergencies affecting the nation's safety and health.[38] In such a situation, the amendments authorize the appointment of a board of inquiry by the president to investigate the dispute but not to make recommendations. (Taft believed that the pressure to accept the recommendation would be so great that the parties would be compelled to accept it, and that this would amount to compulsory arbitration, which has traditionally been anathema to both labor and management in the United States.[39]) Subsequent to the board of inquiry's submission of a report to the president, the attorney general is authorized to seek an eighty-day injunction in federal district court, and fifteen days prior to the expiration of the eighty-day period the workers vote on the employer's last offer.

At the time of the Taft-Hartley amendments, the theory was that workers would accept offers that their militant and unreasonable union leaders were unable or unwilling to accept.[40] That theory has proved remarkably incorrect, inasmuch as every single last offer has been voted down (essentially because it is more likely to be the rank-and-file workers who are pushing the union leaders to be more aggressive and the union leaders who are urging restraint). Also, any vote conducted by an outside agency (in this case, the NLRB) is likely to become a confrontation between the union and the employer and a vote over whether the workers support their union. Invariably in these situations they do. Finally, workers know very well that there is really no such thing as a last offer—especially when it is given to the workers in public. Accordingly, this portion of the emergency strike provisions has not worked out very well. During the 1978 coal strike, when the president invoked Taft-Hartley's procedures, the district judge assigned to hear the case refused to make the injunction permanent because it had been disobeyed and because the government seemed less than enthusiastic about monitoring its enforcement. At the same time, it must be acknowledged that there are few situations where a dispute has not been resolved, when Taft-Hartley was invoked, without resort to other legislation or procedures.

Given that section 13 speaks of a right to strike that is not to be impaired by anything in the NLRA, the layman might think that the right to strike is somehow constitutional. A limited constitutional right to strike exists in France and Sweden, and some contend that the constitution of Japan, which protects the "right of workers to organize and to bargain and act collectively," accomplishes the same objective. In the United States, however, the Supreme Court has refused to hold that a right to strike can be inferred from the Constitution.[41] The difficulty with the protection afforded by statute is that ever since its 1938 decision in *NLRB* v. *Mackay Radio & Telegraph Company*[42] the Supreme Court has held that, although striking is protected conduct, employers may permanently replace striking employees with strikebreakers. In other words, even though an employer may not discharge or discipline workers for engaging in a strike, the employer, in order to keep production going and the plant open, has a business justification for permanently ousting strikers through the recruitment of strikebreakers, and thus may just as effectively deprive employees of their job security as would be the case if they were dismissed or disciplined for striking.

One particularly pernicious consequence of *Mackay* is that it provides employers with an opportunity to rid themselves not only of workers and pension obligations but also of the union itself. The employer, it must be remembered, is entitled by the Taft-Hartley amendments to file a petition for an NLRB election when there is a question about whether there should be union representation. When a number of workers are replaced, the employer's petition is filed on the ground that the workers involved in the decision to select the union are no longer in the work force. For twelve years after the Taft-Hartley amendments the Board refused to permit permanently replaced economic strikers to vote in the election, but the 1959 amendments to the statute permit such strikers to vote until twelve months after their replacement.[43] To a limited extent, this has mitigated some effects of the harsh *Mackay* doctrine.

In fairness, it must be said that a growing number of limitations have been imposed upon the *Mackay* doctrine. Where the strike is caused in part by an employer's unfair labor practices, the employees are entitled to reinstatement. If after the commission of the unfair labor practices and the strike the employees offer unconditionally to return to work, they may be entitled to back pay as well.[44] And even in an economic strike, such as that which occurred in *Mackay*, the Supreme Court has held (in a decision that is difficult to reconcile with *Mackay*) that an employer may not offer extra seniority to strikebreakers—even if the employer can show that such an offer was necessary to keep production going.[45]

The Court's conclusion is based on the fact that the use of such "superseniority" as a vehicle to counterattack against the strike would greatly diminish, if not destroy, the strike weapon itself. Though the Court refused to reassess its *Mackay* decision that replacements may be hired, it was hard put to distinguish the two cases. Nevertheless, it did so on the following grounds: that superseniority affects the tenure of all strikers, whereas replacements only affect those workers who are actually replaced; that superseniority necessarily operates to the detriment of those who engage in the strike as opposed to nonstrikers; that superseniority is an offer of an individual benefit to induce employees to abandon the strike, and promises of benefits by employers are generally viewed as unlawful; that the use of new replacements with superseniority would deal a crippling blow to the strike effort; and that future bargaining would become difficult for the union because of the built-in tension between those employees who had superseniority and those who did not.

Though the Supreme Court has frequently used the National Labor Relations Act as a basis for interpreting the Railway Labor Act,[46] the 1985 United Airlines strike, in which the company bestowed superseniority on strikebreaking pilots, highlights the fact that the statutes have been interpreted differently.[47] The Supreme Court has yet to resolve this issue. Deregulation seems to have promoted the growth of unfair-labor-practice litigation in the airline industry.

Further limitations were placed on the *Mackay* doctrine by the Supreme Court's subsequent holding that an employer is required to offer reemployment to strikers who have been replaced when new jobs are made available by expansion or turnover.[48] The Court has noted that section 2(3) of the NLRA provides that an individual whose work has ceased as a consequence of a labor dispute continues to be an employee within the meaning of the Act until he has obtained regular and substantially equivalent employment.[49] The strikers who have been replaced have preferential access to jobs when their replacements depart,[50] and the NLRB has held that no time limit may be placed on the obligation of the employer to reinstate such workers[51]—although the Court of Appeals for the Seventh Circuit held that strikers may not displace replacements who have been laid off.[52]

A new dimension has been added to the issue of strikes by the institution of wrongful-discharge actions—predicated upon breach of contract or misrepresentation—by replacements who have been dismissed to make way for employees returning from strikes. In *Belknap, Inc.* v. *Hale*,[53] the Court held by a 6–3 vote that such damage actions may be maintained in state court where an NLRB settlement necessitated termination of replacements because of its provision for the reinstatement of strikers. Justice White, speaking for five members of the Court,[54] rejected the argument that such actions are preempted because they interfere with the "free play of economic forces"[55] on the settlement of labor disputes that is promoted by federal labor policy. Justice Brennan, dissenting with Justice Marshall and Justice Powell, was of the view that the employer's right to replace, fashioned in *Mackay*, was "burdened" by such actions, and that the Court, by stating that strikers could be permanently replaced by replacements given "conditional" offers of employment, was shaping the balance of power between labor and management—a matter left to federal labor law.[56] The decision would seem to make the resolution of strikes over alleged unfair labor practices far more difficult.

The Lockout

What of the employer's rights? What may the employer do to utilize its own economic weaponry and protect its bargaining position? In *American Shipbuilding Company* v. *NLRB*[57] the Supreme Court held that, under certain circumstances, lockouts by employers are lawful under the NLRA. Until the *American Shipbuilding* decision it had been generally assumed that a lockout was unlawful unless an employer, confronted with a stoppage at a time when it would have perishable goods and thus would suffer irreparable harm, used the lockout at an earlier period so as to shift the economic burden to the strikers and make it less likely that a cessation of work would occur at a time that would be disastrous to the employer[58] or unless a company that was part of an employer association locked out its employees in response to an attempt by the union to divide and conquer the association by striking against one employer at a time (called "whipsawing").

In a way, *American Shipbuilding* is consistent with the same general theme. The employer was confronted with a bargaining history in which the union had struck on a number of occasions in the past and appeared to be deliberately delaying negotiations during a slack period so that it could bring economic pressure to bear at a time when the employer needed to deliver goods and was thus weak and vulnerable. Said the Court: "Although the unions had given assurances that there would be no strike, past bargaining history was thought to justify continuing apprehension that the unions would fail to make good their assurances. It was further found that the employer's primary purpose in locking out its employees was to avert peculiarly harmful economic consequences which would be imposed upon it and its customers if a strike were called either while a ship was in the yard during the shipping season or later when the yard was fully occupied."[59] Accordingly, the Court took the position that the lockout may be utilized by management to protect its collective bargaining position. In *American Shipbuilding*, there was no evidence that the employer was hostile to the employees' interest in organizing for the purpose of collective bargaining or that the lockout was used to "discipline" them for engaging in the bargaining process. Thus, the Court noted that it could not be said that the employer's intention was to "destroy or frustrate the process of collective bargaining" or that there was no indication that the union would be diminished in its capacity to represent the employees in the unit.

The Court, in *American Shipbuilding*, spoke of the lockout and the strike as "correlative" in terms of statutory usage. But it seems questionable whether *American Shipbuilding* and the right of employers to lock out can apply where the bargaining relationship is not so well established as it was in that case—particularly in a first-contract situation where the parties are dealing with one another for the first time and the relationship is not as mature as the one in *American Shipbuilding*. Moreover, the employer had a legitimate apprehension based on the union's previous behavior. It would have been placed in a very difficult position if it had been confronted with a strike during its boom period. In effect, it was transferring the economic burden of the dispute to the employees. As in *Insurance Agents*, the Court took what might be characterized as a "freedom of contract" position, permitting the collective bargaining process to operate in a robust and open-ended fashion and allowing both parties to use economic pressure to resolve their differences.

But how far can the scales be tipped in favor of the employer? May the employer buttress its right to lock out through the use of temporary or permanent replacements? Where a group of employers in a multiemployer association are "whipsawed" by one union, all employers not struck have the right to lock out, for some of the same considerations present in *American Shipbuilding*. They have the right to shift the economic burden to the strikers at a time propitious to the employers.[60] Rather than permit the union to establish a pattern through a minimal economic burden imposed upon its own members who continue to work in most of the plants and to pick the employers off by pressuring them one by one, a substantial burden is thrust upon the resources of the union and the employees because of employer unity. The Court has held that, in the multiemployer lockout situation, temporary replacements may be utilized to keep production going.[61]

The appellate courts have not been sympathetic to the view that temporary replacements may be utilized in the *American Shipbuilding* context where the union has not officially struck any employer.[62] Apparently, the theory is that there is no substantial and legitimate business justification. But it is difficult to distinguish this sort of case—and indeed even that of permanent replacements in a lockout context—from the basic theme of *American Shipbuilding* and *Insurance Agents*. The idea in those cases was that the collective bargaining process can be used by both sides so long as it is not used in a manner that appears to be intended to or to have the effect of destroying the process. The test in all of these cases should be whether the union in the collective bargaining process continues to function despite the employer's tactics. This carries a certain risk, and it is difficult to articulate with precision the parameters of union and employer economic pressure under such a test. But, given the Court's concern with minimum interference with bargaining tactics on the theory that therein lies the road to regulation of the substance of the collective bargaining agreement, there is little choice. Accordingly, it would seem appropriate in all of these cases involving strikes and lockouts to see whether the union is able to function as a collective bargaining representative in the wake of employer tactics: Does it collect dues? Is it able to negotiate a union security agreement requiring collection of dues as a condition of employment, and thereby to establish a relatively secure position for itself? Does it continue to process grievances? Is it able to exert economic pressure subsequent to the lockout or the replacement of strikers? All of these factors would appear to be valid for the Court and the Board to look to in future litigation.[63] But the case law is so confused that it becomes impossible to determine how far the balance may be tipped or how extreme the economic tactic may be before the statute can be said to have been violated.

The Duty to Bargain in Good Faith

Thus far, we have dealt with the economic weaponry each party may bring to bear during the collective bargaining process. Labor and management employ such tactics on behalf of their demands. But what demands may be made by each side, and under what circumstances? All of this goes to the question of whether the union or the employer is lawfully bargaining in "good faith" as the statute requires. What is good-faith bargaining?

When the Wagner Act was being debated in 1935, Senator Walsh, the chairman of the Senate Labor Committee, stated that the question of how a party (at the time of the Wagner Act only an employer) would discharge its obligations to bargain under the statute was a relatively simple one. The Board would take the parties by the hand to the conference room in which negotiations were to take place. It would see that the parties were properly seated and would close the door so that negotiations could commence.[64] The difficulty is that this relatively simple picture painted by Senator Walsh in 1935 has become far more complicated.

The Board has increasingly found itself pushing open the door and becoming involved in the discussions and the tactics of the parties while the process moves forward. Although the Board has been careful to state that a proposal by one side does not necessitate a counterproposal by the other, some response is required as a test of good faith. Neither side may engage in discussion that is simply "surface bargaining."[65] Neither party is required to enter into a contract. Good-faith bargaining is an attempt to consummate an agreement. However, the other party may be so obstinate or its demands may be so unacceptable that it becomes impossible to negotiate a contract.

In *NLRB* v. *American National Insurance Company*[66] the Supreme Court had held that management could insist on bargaining on the basis of a "management prerogatives" clause under which the union was ousted from involvement with important conditions of employment and under which such matters as discipline and work schedules were nonarbitrable—that is, management's position with regard to these areas would always prevail. The Court stated that the Board could not "directly or indirectly compel concessions or otherwise sit in judgment upon the substantive terms of collective bargaining agreements."[67] The Court rejected the Board's position that an employer was obligated to establish ongoing bargaining during the term of the collective agreement on these subjects.

American National Insurance dramatizes the fundamental difference between the American and German systems. In Germany, involvement by the *Betriebsrat* in a whole range of employer decisions affecting employment conditions is explicitly provided for by law. The statutory approach does not contemplate the idea that such rights as the right to veto hiring and firing decisions pending Labor Court or conciliation determinations or the right to have worker directors will be waived. The weakest *Betriebsrat* cannot be induced or required to relinquish any statutory right that it chooses to assert. The American approach contains an antithetical assumption; the weak must fend for themselves in obtaining some little portion of the lion's share. Generally, the American statute guarantees little to the weak.

Mandatory Subjects of Bargaining

The above generalization must be qualified, for there are other cases that cut in a direction opposite to the freedom-of-contract line of authority in *Insurance Agents* and *American Shipbuilding* (which promotes a wide-open use of economic pressure) and that involve the NLRB and the courts in extensive regulation of subject matter at the bargaining table. To repeat, the Supreme Court—within limits—has permitted the parties to "take their gloves off" and to exert whatever economic pressure is at their disposal. Yet there is a concern that either side could completely subvert the collective bargaining process through a refusal to discuss subject matter that is important to both workers and employers.

This is why the statute prohibits the termination or modification of an agreement[68] (although the Supreme Court permitted the bankruptcy law to override this obligation for financially beleaguered employers[69]—a holding that was later modified by statute[70]).

The Supreme Court, in the landmark *Borg-Warner* case,[71] held that there are three categories of subject matter that might be raised by the representatives of the union or the employer at the bargaining table: mandatory, nonmandatory, and illegal subjects of bargaining. Until an impasse is reached, the employer may not unilaterally change conditions of employment,[72] because this would preclude or limit both sides in negotiations about unresolved items and thus is inconsistent with the concept of good-faith bargaining. (It is the permanence of the change that precludes good-faith bargaining.)

With regard to mandatory subjects, both sides have an obligation to bargain to the point of impasse. This does not mean that the parties must be deadlocked on all issues or items, but rather that they must be deadlocked in the negotiations generally.[73] Under the NLRA, the party that refuses to bargain on mandatory subjects to the point of impasse is unlawfully refusing to bargain. The significance of such an unlawful refusal, in this context and others, is not merely that the Board will issue a "cease and desist" order aimed at remedying the parties' bargaining behavior. Rather, it lies in the possibility that a strike ensuing as a result of such bargaining behavior would be an unfair-labor-practice strike, and that therefore, in contrast to economic strikers who may be replaced, the workers would be entitled to reinstatement and possibly to back pay.[74] Accordingly, the *Borg-Warner* rule can alter considerably the balance of power in a strike deemed to have been caused by the employer's posture at the bargaining table.

A nonmandatory subject is "permissive." That is to say, either party may raise the subject at the bargaining table for the purpose of discussion. It is perfectly lawful to discuss such an issue. However, when a party insists upon a position in such an area to the point of impasse, an unlawful refusal takes place under the Act. The purpose of the rule—which is extremely difficult to implement—is to exclude frivolous subjects from the bargaining table and to infer bad faith on the part of the party that clogs the table with such subjects. (Illegal subjects may not be discussed at all.) For instance, a union's insistence upon the employer's attendance at the annual union picnic to the point of impasse might be said to have little if anything to do with conditions of employment within the meaning of the Act. If, for instance, the employer insisted to the point of impasse that the union not hold a picnic, or that the union elect its officers in a particular way, one would assume that the subject matter was so remote from labor-management problems as to be in bad faith.

Some mandatory subjects of bargaining are layoffs and recalls, sick leave, incentive pay, paid holidays, vacation schedules, hours of work, and such fringe benefits as cost-of-living adjustments and profit-sharing plans. Interest arbitration providing for arbitral resolution of future contract terms is a nonmandatory subject of bargaining because it substitutes a third party for labor and management, the appropriate parties in the collective bargaining process.[75] But the issues are not always so simple. The facts of *Borg-Warner*, and other decisions in its wake, make this clear. In *Borg-Warner* the employer had insisted upon a "ballot" clause calling for a secret prestrike vote by all union and nonunion employees within the bargaining unit on the employer's last offer. The employer also insisted upon a "recognition" clause that excluded as a party to the contract the international union, which had been certified by the Board as the employees' exclusive bargaining agent. The Supreme Court found the employer's bargaining position with regard to both matters unlawful, inasmuch as it had insisted upon what the Court characterized as nonmandatory or permissive subjects of bargaining to the point of impasse.

It might be said that the Borg-Warner Corporation was subverting one of the basic statutory procedures and the role of the Board in designating an exclusive bargaining agent. Accordingly, the Court's holding that the recognition clause was a nonmandatory subject of bargaining is somewhat understandable. But the ballot clause is a little more difficult. Suppose an employer is concerned about the extent to which his production has been interrupted by a union he regards as strike-happy, and that he believes there is some basis for assuming that employees are out of sympathy with the union's behavior. Quite clearly, the employer could insist upon a clause that would preclude employees from striking altogether, at least during the term of the agreement. Why can he not insist upon a ballot-box clause to achieve the same purpose?

The answer is by no means clear. The Court's rationale rests upon the notion that the prestrike ballot is an attempt to interfere with the union's internal political process and, as such, substantially modifies the collective bargaining system provided for in the NLRA by weakening the independence of the representative chosen by the employees.[76] Said the Court: "It enables the employer, in effect, to deal with its employees rather than with their statutory representative."[77]

The difficulties here are enormous. First, although the Board and the courts have taken the position that the parties need not be deadlocked on all issues in order for there to be an impasse, the fact is that it is sometimes powerless to make the assessment—and, as we have already seen, the consequences for either the union or the employer can be significant.

Second, it could be argued that involvement in the determination as to what constitutes a mandatory or nonmandatory subject of bargaining within the meaning of the Act is an indirect method of regulating the substance of the collective bargaining agreement. This is contrary to the statutory philosophy. But the counterargument is that the substance of the agreement is not being regulated—only the extent to which the subject matter may be discussed or negotiated.

A third area of contention relates to the way in which collective bargaining is to be conducted. *Borg-Warner* involves the Board in establishing the details of the parties' ground rules. This is less important in the United States than in Japan, where litigation can arise out of management's insistence that is not obligated to bargain because of provocative union conduct such as abusive name-calling, imprisonment of the boss in his own office or factory, or the wearing of armbands.[78] The closest American analog is a refusal by management to bargain with a union because of the violent behavior of a union leader.[79] However, the Board and the courts have disagreed on whether an employer is obliged to bargain with a lawfully recognized union that is seeking new affiliation without taking a vote among the nonunion employees as well as the union members in the bargaining unit.[80] The need for unions to merge in order to redress the imbalance between conglomerates and unions makes this an important issue in labor law. Generally, the employees are entitled to select as a union representative anyone they would like to have represent them.[81] Closely related to this kind of issue is the demand by one side that a court stenographer be present at bargaining sessions. The Board and the courts have rejected this view and held that the subject is nonmandatory in that a stenographer's presence might inhibit the free flow of discussion.[82] The goal of retaining a completely accurate record, as in an adjudicative proceeding, is a subordinate one.

The fourth major problem in this area is the difficulty of defining what is mandatory and what is nonmandatory. In a case involving an employer's subcontracting of maintenance work previously performed by employees in the bargaining unit, the Supreme Court attempted to come to grips with this issue.[83] The Court identified three governing considerations in its conclusion that the subject was mandatory. The first was whether the subject matter was within the "literal definition" of "conditions of employment." Since workers' jobs were affected by the subcontracting, it was not difficult to reach the conclusion that their conditions of employment were being affected. The second consideration was whether industrial peace was likely to be promoted through the negotiation of the issue. Of course, one might say that, since the party proposing a particular subject is likely to feel less aggrieved in the event that it is able to discuss it thoroughly, it is more likely that a peaceable settlement would be reached. But this would permit any party to put any subject on the table. Third, the Court stated that the practice in the industry was important. Since many unions and employers had negotiated clauses and collective bargaining agreements providing for limitations or prohibitions on subcontracting, it was thought that this factor weighed in favor of making subcontracting a mandatory subject of bargaining. But the Court was doing what it had said in some of its "freedom of contract" cases it would never do: impose upon union and employers a procrustean rule based on practices that might well have evolved in different industries under totally different circumstances. It might be said that if some unions and some employers wished to bargain seriously about subcontracting and to incorporate clauses in their collective bargaining agreement they should be free to do so, and that those who did not wish to do so would be allowed to go their own way. The response of the Court and the Board to this idea was that, whatever is dictated by the refusal-to-bargain cases, it is not a requirement to include a particular subject within the collective bargaining agreement.

There are many problems with the last of the three criteria explained in the preceding paragraph, but some of the language in the subcontracting case and in its progeny indicates how difficult the first criterion is in actual application. The Supreme Court, and Justice Stewart in a special concurring opinion, were at pains to emphasize that the Board cannot modify the free-enterprise economy through its interpretation of labor legislation in defining what constitutes a mandatory subject of bargaining. As Stewart said: "This kind of subcontracting falls short of such larger entrepreneurial questions as what shall be produced, how capital shall be invested in fixed assets, or what the basic scope of the enterprise shall be. In my view, the Court's decision in this case has nothing to do with whether any aspects of those larger issues could under any circumstances be considered subjects of compulsory collective bargaining under the present law."[84]

Justice Stewart's concurring opinion is not very clear about the demarcation line between mandatory and nonmandatory subjects of bargaining, but the Court has relied on his thinking in attempting to draw lines. Said Justice Blackmun in an opinion issued in 1981:

Some management decisions, such as choice of advertising and promotion, product type and design, and financing arrangements, have only an indirect and attenuated impact on the employment relationship. See *Fibreboard*, 379 U.S. at 223 (Stewart, J., concurring). Other management decisions, such as the order of succession of layoffs and recalls, production quotas, and work rules, are almost exclusively "an aspect of the relationship" between employer and employee. . . . The present case concerns a third type of management decision, one that had a direct impact on employment, since jobs were inexorably eliminated by the termination, but had as its focus only the economic profitability of the contract [between a maintenance company and a nursing home] . . . a concern under these facts wholly apart from the employment relationship. This decision, involving a change in the scope and direction of the enterprise, is akin to the decision whether to be in business at all, "not in [itself] primarily about conditions of employment, though the effect of the decision may be necessarily to terminate employment." . . . At the same time, this decision touches on a matter of central and pressing concern to the union and its member employees: the possibility of continued employment and the retention of the employees' very jobs.[85]

It seems clear that any complete closing of a business is a managerial prerogative that is beyond the scope of any portion of the NLRA[86]—at least where the business is not sold as a going concern. The appellate courts have generally held that partial closings were similarly outside the reach of refusal-to-bargain charges by unions.[87] However, both the Second and Third Circuit Courts of Appeals began to fashion limitations on managerial freedom in this area.[88]

In an opinion authored by Judge Morris Lasker for the Second Circuit, that court stated the following:

We believe that the determination whether to impose a duty to bargain should not depend on the relative injury to the employer and the employees, but rather on the relative merits of the arguments put forth as to those classic considerations of whether the purposes of the statute are furthered by the decision to impose a duty to bargain in a particular case.

Accordingly, the presumption that the employer has an obligation to bargain over a decision partially to close the business may be rebutted by showing that the purposes of the statute will not be furthered by imposition of a duty to bargain. Without an attempt to enumerate all those instances in which the presumption may be rebutted, a few examples may be noted for purposes of illustration. The employer might overcome the presumption by demonstrating that bargaining over the decision would be futile, since the purposes of the statute would not be served by ordering the parties to bargain when it is clear that the employer's decision cannot be changed. Other relevant considerations would be that the closing was due to emergency financial circumstances, or that the custom of the industry, shown by the absence of such an obligation from typical collective bargaining agreements, is not to bargain over such decisions. The presumption might also be rebutted if it could be demonstrated that forcing the employer to bargain would endanger the vitality of the entire business, so that the purposes of the statute would not be furthered by mandating bargaining to benefit some employees to the potential detriment of the remainder. This might be a particularly significant point if the number to be laid off was small and the number of the remainder was large.[89]

The Supreme Court categorically rejected this position by a vote of 7–2. In an opinion authored by Justice Blackmun the Court, expressing concern that the Second Circuit's standards were not sufficiently precise and would unnecessarily expose employers to back-pay liability, concluded that "the harm likely to be done to an employer's need to operate freely in deciding whether to shut down part of its business purely for economic reasons outweighs the incremental benefit that might be gained through the union's participation in making the decision."[90] The Court reasoned that it was unlikely that the union could induce the employer to change its mind, and that delay would harm management's interests in speed, flexibility, and secrecy. The decision to partially close, therefore, is not itself a mandatory subject of bargaining, but the "effects" of the decision (severance payments, relocation allowances, retraining, and the like) are. The Court has left open the question of whether management decisions on plant relocations, plant sales, automation, and types of subcontracting not covered by the previous Supreme Court decision referred to above are mandatory subjects. The Board, while sometimes limiting the thrust of *First National Maintenance*,[91] has generally interpreted it so as to require the union to show that labor costs are the reason for the employer's decision.[92]

Meanwhile, in *Milwaukee Spring I*[93] the Board seemed to fashion a route by which the potential implications of *First National Maintenance* could be circumvented, holding that layoffs due to the relocation of a plant constituted a repudiation of the contract provision that sets forth the wage rates. This important decision was reversed by a new Board majority in 1984.[94]

"Take It or Leave It" Bargaining: Boulwarism

Other difficult refusal-to-bargain charges involve Boulwarism (a term derived from the name of General Electric's vice-president for labor relations). In essence, this was a policy that required the employer to announce its final position at the outset of bargaining. The employer's idea here is that a tortured process of give and take in which the employer is excoriated for its obstinacy and unreasonableness and gradually brought down to a modified position only enhances the prestige of the union and diminishes that of the employer. The position of the General Electric Company—which created and refined Boulwarism—was that it would provide a firm and fair offer to its workers, and that it would announce to the employees what was going on in the collective bargaining so that the workers would not have to rely on the union's characterization of the discussions.[95] In some respects this resembles the union conduct that prompted the Taft-Hartley Congress to impose the duty to bargain on unions. Unions, it is to be recalled, often threw the contract on the table and told small employers to "take it or leave it." Here, however, General Electric took the position that external factors, such as a change in the economy, could alter the company's position.

The prevailing view is that the mere announcement of the employer's final offer at the commencement of negotiations is not *per se* an unfair labor practice. Good-faith bargaining does not require the parties to make proposals and counterproposals; it merely requires good-faith intent to consummate an agreement. However, the courts have said that it is appropriate to take into account other conduct of the employer which, along with tactics such as Boulwarism, may be considered as a basis for inferring bad faith under the totality of circumstances.

Again, freedom-of-contract cases such as *Insurance Agents* and *American Shipbuilding*, which are consistent with the *General Electric* "totality of conduct" approach, provide for the use of tactics that (at least in the short run) seem to discourage genuine dialogue. On the other hand, the Supreme Court has held that employers have an obligation to open their books and disclose financial data when they plead an inability to pay in collective bargaining,[96] in the interest of genuine dialogue between parties truly concerned with reaching a settlement. This decision, which regulates conduct and tactics, is aimed at establishing collective bargaining that will concentrate on the economic conditions confronting the employer. However, it has been circumvented by managements not asserting an inability to pay, even if that is the basis for their negotiating posture. Only employers lacking competent labor counsel fail to rely upon other considerations, such as wage comparability. The inclination to rely on the totality of circumstances (in these cases, on whether management pleads poverty) shows the courts' unwillingness to regulate too much. Only employers in unusual industries, such as baseball, have difficulty with the NLRA's disclosure requirements. Because there are no comparable wage scales to be cited in baseball, it was difficult for the owners to say that their position in the 1981 negotiations was based on anything other than their view that the industry was imperiled economically.

Two comments are in order here about the duty-to-bargain concept generally and the *General Electric* case in particular. The first is that again the schizoid tendencies in the National Labor Relations Act come to the forefront. On the one hand there is a reluctance to interfere with tactics— again, the concern is that this will lead to regulation of the substance of the collective bargaining agreement. At the same time, it is quite obvious that the General Electric Company was attempting to denigrate the union, to make it an ineffective bargaining agent, and perhaps ultimately to eliminate it altogether as a bargaining agent. The employees would get the message that the union could not alter the employer's basic view of what constituted a fair and firm offer, and would soon begin to ask themselves why they had joined the union at all. Surely this was the basic objective of GE's strategy. The law tries to ride two difficult horses: preservation of the collective bargaining process (which argues for condemnation of Boulwarism) and freedom of contract (which eschews regulation).

Another basic problem with Boulwarism is the elusiveness of the remedy. The courts, unwilling to condemn the tactic itself, elect to rely on totality of conduct. The next time around in the bargaining process, the employer simply changes one tactic and the question of whether the totality of circumstances warrants a finding of bad faith requires another round of adjudication. To put it another way, the likelihood of a contempt sanction for misconduct is extremely remote given the lack of precision involved in any order. All of this leads to the next chapter, which is concerned with remedies.

7

Remedies and the Labor Reform Bill of 1978

The principal reasons for the considerable focus on remedies and the emergence of proposals for labor-law reform in the Labor Reform Bill of 1978 are the increased caseload of the National Labor Relations Board and the strain that caseload has placed on an administrative statutory scheme that was already convoluted and tortuous. As Chairman John Fanning of the NLRB said in testimony before the House Committee on Education and Labor: "In 1957, when I was first appointed to the Board, the agency processed a total of 16,000 cases and the Board issued 353 decisions in contested unfair labor practice cases. In the current fiscal year (1972) we will receive more than 52,000 cases and we expect to issue 1,121 such decisions. In fiscal year 1978 we estimate that 57,000 cases will be filed with the agency and we expect to issue 1,242 decisions. In fiscal year 1979 the number of cases will amount to 61,000, and our published decisions will number 1,400."[1] This has delayed the administrative process. A worker dismissed for union activity during an organizational campaign may not obtain the remedies provided by the statute until long after they are meaningful. The worker's losses in the interim can never be adequately remedied by the law. As the

House Committee on Education and Labor said: "The committee heard testimony about workers who had their homes foreclosed and cars repossessed while waiting an ultimately favorable disposition of their case. Clearly, in addition to failing to deter violations of the act, remedies under existing law also fail to compensate the victims of such illegal conduct."[2]

Remedies Mean Compensation

One reason for the difficulties with the NLRA is the Supreme Court's holding that the Act is designed to perform a remedial function and that punitive sanctions may not be imposed for violations.[3] This translates into the proposition that if an employee receives more than he had lost, the remedy is punitive rather than remedial.[4] In line with this approach, the Act provides that interim earnings or those which would have been obtained with "reasonable diligence" be deducted from any back pay the employee receives from the employer (unemployment compensation and social-welfare benefits are not deducted, for public-policy reasons).[5] This means that back-pay hearings often take place after an unfair-labor-practice proceeding, and in such hearings detailed testimony is taken about the kinds of work at which the worker was employed after the commission of the unfair labor practice, or whether the worker was available in the relevant labor market. Often, litigation over the question of what is the relevant labor market adds to the delay.

The problem here is that the worker is exasperated with the mere award of back pay and in future situations will be unlikely to engage in protected activity. A dismissed worker may not even make use of the remedies the Board provides. As one study has noted, the number of employees accepting reinstatement was found to equal only 5 percent of all persons discriminatorily discharged where reinstatement was not offered until six months after the violation.[6] As the conservative journal *Business Week* noted, when an appeal is taken to the court subsequent to an NLRB proceeding the process can stretch for so long that the "worker is financially and emotionally exhausted."[7]

The Collective Interest

Even more troublesome is the impact that all of this can have on a union's general organizational activity. Union adherents who have not been disciplined for union activity will quickly get the message. If they are found out or retaliated against for their union activity, they will suffer similar consequences and will wait a considerable period of time before obtaining a remedy even if they are able to prove unlawful employer conduct. If the remedy is reinstatement, it may simply put them back to work in an uncongenial environment. Back pay will come only after litigation about what work they actually held or (even more vexatious) what work they could have obtained with reasonable diligence. The effect of all of this will be to encourage workers to eschew union activity and to thus kill an organizational campaign. Under such circumstances the employer is perceived as merely paying a license fee for dismissing workers unlawfully, and pays out considerably less than would have been provided in wages, fringe benefits, and other improved conditions of employment by a collective bargaining agreement—benefits that might have been negotiated had a union come on the scene.

Delays

A dramatic example of the legal abuses here concerns J. P. Stevens & Co., which according to NLRB data supplied during Representative Frank Thompson's Oversight Hearings in 1975 had at that time 96 different unfair-labor-practice cases pending before the Board, in addition to having violated the NLRA on many occasions.[8] The same hearings showed similar management misbehavior in San Francisco, a union stronghold, where some corporation attorneys have attained new levels of sophistication in achieving delay.[9]

A decade later, the problem remained; in some respects things were worse. In 1983 the median time from the filing of an unfair-labor-practice charge to the issuance of a complaint by the Board was 45 days. Another 75–94 days were consumed from the issuance of the complaint to the close of the hearing before the Administrative Law Judge. From the close of the hearing to the time of the Administrative Law Judge's decision the period was 116 days. From the Administrative Law Judge's decision to the decision by the Board the period was 194 days (versus 120 and 143 in 1976 and 1977). The interval between the filing of the charge and the Board's decision was 627 days (versus 358 and 410 in 1976 and 1977)—and this without any appeal to the courts. The problem became worse because of a shortage of Adminstrative Law Judges.

In 1976 and 1977, resorting to the judicial process after an NLRB decision often took even longer than the Board's own administrative process. For instance, 37–50 days were consumed from the date of decision until referral of the matter for enforcement in the court of appeals. Another 38–43 days elapsed before a petition was filed. The agency no longer keeps such statistics, but in 1976 between 317 and 350 days elapsed from the filing of the petition until the court of appeals reached a decision. In addition, quite frequently a petition for certiorari, or review, is filed with the United States Supreme Court. Each year more than 5,000 such petitions are filed and only approximately 150 are granted.[10] The chances of success are remote. Again, more time goes by until the litigation is finished.

Another delay comes in connection with representation proceedings before the Board after the filing of an election petition. From 1980 through 1984, half of all elections took place within 50 days of the filing of a petition. Where the parties had agreed to a so-called consent election, in which case there is no litigation about such issues as the appropriate unit, the median delay in 1984 was 41 days. But litigious parties do not generally agree to such a procedure, and there are about half as many Regional Director and Board consent elections as those which take place subsequent to litigation and a hearing.

Subversion of Election Outcomes by Employers

A third variation on the same basic theme are cases where a majority of employees voting have cast their ballots for the union as their exclusive representative but the employer refuses to bargain with the union on the ground that the unit is inappropriate or that ineligible employees had voted. When an employer refuses to bargain with a union that has been certified by the Board as exclusive representative, the union files an unfair-labor-practice charge, the General Counsel issues a complaint, and a hearing is held before an Administrative Law Judge. The record in the representation hearing is incorporated in the unfair-labor-practice record. The Administrative Law Judge, relying upon what had already been decided by the Board, finds that the employer has unlawfully refused to bargain with the union, and this is affirmed by the Board. Then the employer appeals to the circuit court of appeals and, in some instances, petitions for certiorari to the Supreme Court. Between three and five years later, subsequent to the certification, the employer is ordered to bargain with the union. But meanwhile the improved wages, fringe benefits, and other conditions of employment that might have been negotiated have been lost to the employees. Moreover, the employees, frustrated by the lack of collective bargaining and confronted with the employer's legally defensible position[11] that it cannot bargain with the union while the representation issue is pending in the courts, have achieved nothing, while unorganized employees have forged ahead. The lesson for the employees is that a vote for the union has made life more difficult for them.

In the *Ex-Cell-O* decision[12] the NLRB held that a remedy providing the employees with benefits lost during the interim period (a "make whole" remedy) would have been an impermissible imposition of contract terms upon the parties and thus was beyond the Board's remedial authority. The Board, however, has fashioned remedies including litigation expenses in cases where the violation was "clear and flagrant."[13]

Expediting the Administrative Process

The Labor Reform Bill of 1978 attempted to cope with many of the problems described above. Inasmuch as the principal problem is delay, it provided for "summary affirmance" of Administrative Law Judges' decisions by the National Labor Relations Board. Since most issues are ones of fact (that is, of whether the management representative or the employee is telling the truth about the basis for discipline or discharge), the Administrative Law Judge is presumably in the best position to make such a decision; the Board could never assess credibility or demeanor on the basis of a dry transcript. Approximately 74 percent of all contested cases taken to the Board subsequent to the Administrative Law Judge's decision are adopted without any modification or minor clarification—a "short form" adoption. More than 80 percent of Administrative Law Judges' positions are affirmed by the Board. Accordingly, the Labor Reform Bill would have provided that one party could petition for summary affirmance on the ground that the issue was essentially fact and not law or a novel issue of law.

The Board now has the authority to seek relief from the federal district court where a delay would produce irreparable harm to the charging party. Section 10(j) of the NLRA authorizes the Board to obtain temporary injunctive relief to preserve the status quo as it was prior to the unfair labor practice pending hearings before the agency.[14] In the case of a discharge, this would require reinstatement of the worker pending appeal. However, the Board has not been particularly successful in convincing the federal courts that such relief is appropriate—indeed, it has been argued, sometimes with a good deal of merit, that the Board has been excessively cautious in seeking such relief. (In fairness to the Board, it should be pointed out that delay is built into its own internal process by the statute; concurrence of the five-member board must be sought subsequent to a decision by the General Counsel to seek such relief. This stands in sharp contrast to Section 10(l) of the Act,[15] which *mandates* the Regional Attorney—without the involvement of the General Counsel in Washington or the full Board—to seek injunctive relief in connection with certain kinds of union unfair labor practices.[16])

The Labor Reform Bill would have encouraged both the Board and the courts to seek and fashion temporary injunctive relief, by providing criteria under which the courts could issue injunctions. For instance, the bill was intended to make possible injunctions against discharges where the union had not negotiated its first contract. Accordingly, the desire was to promote collective bargaining when it was most vulnerable to complete undermining through unlawful management conduct. Another useful proposal here would have been to allow the Board to seek injunctive relief at the regional level so as to expedite the Board's own internal process, just as the regional office has such authority in connection with certain unfair union practices referred to above.

All these proposals were attempts to cope with delays in the administrative process that dimmed the prospect of collective bargaining even where the union had the allegiance of a majority of the workers. But there still remained the problem of effective remedies. The Labor Reform Bill would have provided for the awarding of more than back pay to dismissed workers. The House favored double back pay and no deduction for interim earnings; the Senate, more modestly, would have provided for one and a half times the amount of back pay. Similar remedies are available in different forms in the antitrust and equal-employment-opportunity fields. (The provision in some of the reform proposals for compensation to be awarded automatically, rather than only where employer conduct had been malicious or deliberate, may have been a flaw.)

Another concern over the Labor Reform Bill was that more comprehensive relief in the form of double or one-and-one-half damages would not deter wrongdoing, but would simply represent a more expensive "license." Accordingly, it was proposed that any party found by the Board to have willfully violated Board orders would be barred, upon authorization by the Secretary of Labor, from participating in federal contracts for three years. This weapon is currently available in connection with equal employment opportunity, but the record of law enforcement in that area has not been particularly good.[17] Government, which wants to have its contracts with private employers fulfilled, generally seems able to find a basis for moving ahead with the future contracts rather than canceling, debarring, or whatever.

Finally, the Labor Reform Bill would have reversed the *Ex-Cell-O* decision, in which the NLRB refused to provide "make whole" relief for employees where employers refused to bargain with a certified union and utilized the appellate process. As noted above, the only remedy is a court order obligating the employer to bargain—years after the initial obligation. The bill provided that in cases where the employer had unlawfully refused to bargain for an initial contract, employees would be awarded compensation for the delay in bargaining. The workers would receive an amount based on the average wage settlements negotiated by workers at plants where collective bargaining had proceeded lawfully, and would receive wages and fringe benefits retroactively from the time of the unlawful refusal to bargain until bargaining was commenced.

Still, a recidivist employer might well not be affected by any of these remedies where a union was attempting to obtain a first contract. In the final analysis, the only effective remedy for a union is one that puts it in a position to obtain a collective bargaining agreement. It is the inability to get a first contract that, more than anything else, has stimulated demands for reform of the present laws. In hearings before the House Subcommittee on Labor-Management Relations, Jack Crowley, president of the San Francisco Labor Council, concurred in this view: "If the union wins an election, then there should be some sanction imposed upon the employer, if the employer has delayed the case at any stage of the proceeding. Such a sanction could include the awarding by the Board of benefits to the employees represented by the union which are consistent with the contracts that the union has in the geographical area in the identical or similar industry in which the individual employer is involved."[18] One difficulty with this kind of approach is that both unions and employers are less than enthusiastic about anything that smacks of compulsory arbitration in the wage or economic area—even though some unions recognize that this is the only effective remedy in many cases. In British Columbia, such objections have not been allowed to override the province's experiment with first-contract arbitration as a remedy for unfair labor practices.

The Labor Reform Bill was defeated in 1978. (More accurately, it was not voted upon on its merits because of a filibuster in the Senate.) Of course, there were considerable arguments put forward by the employers on the merits. The most formidable of these was that severe remedies would be counterproductive in that they would create fewer settlements and more numerous and longer delays. There would be more of an incentive to litigate because the cost of settlement would be greater, and thus there would be more cases, hearings, and delays.

The problem of delay and ineffective remedies remains an important one in labor-relations law. It is sure to be addressed in the years to come. In the meantime, however, the labor movement's failure to obtain reform and its frustration with the Reagan Board have prompted AFL-CIO president Lane Kirkland to promote the idea that the National Labor Relations Act ought to be repealed.[19]

8

Dispute Resolution in the Established Relationship

Dispute-resolution machinery, whether it is devised by private parties or imposed by legislation, generally focuses on two quite different problems. The first relates to disputes that arise during the term of the collective bargaining agreement, usually involving its interpretation. These are called "rights" disputes; the question is what resolution shall be made where the parties disagree as to the application or interpretation of the agreement. The second area is "interest" disputes; that is, disputes that arise over the terms of the new collective bargaining agreement (generally after the expiration of the old one). These disputes, frequently resolved under guidelines or criteria established by the parties or by legislation, generally concern wages and other economic issues that go right to the core of the bargaining relationship.

The mode of dispute resolution can vary. In the United States we have generally utilized mediation, fact finding, or arbitration. Mediation involves the intervention of a third party, appointed by labor and management or by government, whose role it is to attempt to get the parties to resolve their differences amicably. The mediator has no authority to do anything—even to make recommendations to the parties as to how the matter should be resolved. Mediators often play innovative and important roles in the resolution of disputes, although sometimes they simply carry coffee from the labor side to the management side. But the third party's function is to clarify the issues, appeal to the parties' reasoning processes by using the arts of persuasion, and (when specifically authorized by the parties) to make recommendations to them. The mediator must have the parties' confidence. They must be able to entrust their secrets and confidences to him, without fear that this information will be leaked to the other side. A skillful mediator is able to make use of such information in making suggestions, structuring the dialogue, or formulating proposals.

Fact finding differs from mediation in the sense that fact finders not only may investigate the dispute, but may make public recommendations for its resolution. The theory is that pressure is placed upon the party who resists the recommendations to come to terms because the public or those interested in the dispute will exert pressure upon whichever side is more obstinate. Usually, we tend to associate the use of mediation and fact finding with interest disputes relating to the terms of a new contract, but this is not always the case. Both mediation and fact finding can be and are used in connection with grievance or rights disputes.

When we speak of arbitration in the United States we generally mean private, voluntary negotiations conducted with the mutual consent of the parties—a pattern that contradicts the general impression that foreigners have of the American system as written into and governed by law. (The Railway Labor Act, which covers airline and railway workers, and some state laws relating to public-sector disputes mandate arbitration, and interest disputes in the public sector have assumed great importance in recent years.) Arbitration in the United States is encouraged by the National Labor Relations

Act and by Supreme Court decisions handed down since the early 1960s. However, the practice of arbitration developed prior to and in some circumstances in spite of the law, since in some jurisdictions arbitration agreements were considered void as against public policy. Jealous courts did not wish to have their jurisdictions undermined.

Arbitration began in the United States before the turn of the century, appeared in 1903 in the form of the "umpire" system of the Anthracite Coal Commission, was accepted by the hosiery and clothing industries in the form of the "impartial chairman" system in the 1920s, and was well on its way even prior to the Wagner Act of 1935. It gained greater impetus through the War Labor Board, which, operating under the emergency conditions of World War II, encouraged, nurtured, and in some instances imposed no-strike obligations and arbitration machinery. All of this was well in advance of Taft-Hartley, which merely ratified a trend the parties had evolved for themselves.

Arbitration Defined

Arbitration is quite different from mediation, which also involves third-party intervention. In the United States and in other countries it means a decision-making process, although many arbitrators rely upon mediatory skills as well. Indeed, the use of mediation was a prominent characteristic of both the "impartial chairman" system and some of the permanent umpireships that existed during the 1940s. In the final analysis, however, a decision or award can be issued by the third party. This is the significance of arbitration as opposed to other modes of dispute resolution.

Interest arbitration is a relatively rare phenomenon in the United States.[1] However, as collective bargaining has extended itself into the public sector, where striking has been considered less acceptable, interest arbitration has become popular as a substitute for strikes. The Postal Reorganization Act's provision for interest arbitration in the Postal Service was utilized in 1984 when a Board of Arbitrators, chaired by Dr. Clark Kerr, rendered the first arbitration award ever rendered at the federal level.[2]

Moreover, an increasing number of jurisdictions have begun to use "final-offer" arbitration, under which the arbitrator is required to select one of the two parties' last offers. (Nine states provide for final-offer arbitration for firefighters under some circumstances.[3]) Some of these states make the same provision for police, and some for municipal employees or even public employees generally. Twenty–nine jurisdictions have passed statutes providing for some form of binding interest arbitration.[4] Final-offer arbitration is designed to force both sides to be reasonable and thus to avoid one of the major objections to interest arbitration (particularly when it is compulsory): that it will erode the collective bargaining process and keep both sides from compromising out of fear that the arbitrator will "cut the baby in half." This fear inhibits the give and take and the flexibility that are prerequisites to collective bargaining, because anyone who compromised would feel that he had sacrificed his position with the arbitrator. Because of the uncertainty about whose offer will be selected, both sides are induced to be reasonable and compromise. Final-offer arbitration has been used in salary disputes in baseball. It also has been suggested as the procedure to be used in Taft-Hartley and Railway Labor Act emergency disputes.[5]

By 1976 the steel industry seemed to have adopted interest arbitration through its negotiation of the Experimental Steel Negotiating Agreement,[6] but it appears as though the parties have now discarded this approach. The theory in an industry such as steel is that the prospect of a strike prompts present and potential customers to buy from foreign producers, particularly the Germans and the Japanese. Once customers are motivated to buy elsewhere they often become permanent customers. The assurance that a dispute will be resolved through arbitration and not a strike is likely to hold customers who would otherwise be lost.

But it is grievance or rights arbitration involving disputes during the term of the agreement that is the most important aspect of the American experience. Some 95 percent of collective bargaining agreements negotiated between labor and management in the United States contain arbitration clauses, and all but 1 percent permit one of the two sides to obtain arbitration during the term of the contract without obtaining an agreement from the other side to arbitrate the particular dispute in question. To be sure, there are exceptions to this pattern. In the National Trucking Agreement there is no provision for arbitration. In the construction industry only 70 percent of the agreements contain arbitration clauses and it appears that arbitration is used less than in manufacturing, even where it is provided for by contract.

At this point it is important to distinguish between different modes of arbitration. Most arbitration in the United States is *ad hoc*; that is, an arbitrator is selected to hear a particular dispute during the term of the contract. At one time it was thought that permanent umpireships, with one individual or a rotating list of individuals chosen for the term of the agreement to resolve disputes, were going to be the wave of the future. However, despite the apparent desirability of an arbitrator who is not a stranger to the industry or company and is therefore presumably more expert, only 12 percent of arbitration clauses provide for permanent umpireship today.

Where there is *ad hoc* arbitration, the arbitrators are often chosen from lists prepared by the Federal Mediation and Conciliation Service (an autonomous governmental mediation unit) and the American Arbitration Association (a nonprofit organization that provides arbitration services to private parties throughout the country). Sometimes state mediation agencies that are analogs or counterparts to the Federal Mediation and Conciliation Service perform the same function. No one really knows how much arbitration takes place in the United States, since most arbitrations appear to arise out of private communications between the parties and the individual arbitrators.

Most of the more experienced arbitrators are among the 600-odd members of a professional association called the National Academy of Arbitrators, who are chosen on the basis of the number of cases they have heard and the reports of the parties who have appeared before them or heard about them. Since the early 1970s, there have existed programs for the recruiting and training of new arbitrators who will be acceptable to both labor and management. These programs have been promoted by universities, the American Arbitration Association, and the American Bar Association.

The Advantages of Arbitration

Why do Americans use arbitration rather than the courts to resolve their disputes? There are five principal reasons. The first is that the system, for the most part, has been a voluntary one, devised by the parties to deal with their own problems. The American system is intended to fit the parties' own peculiar needs; this is the reason for its rich diversity and the difficulty of making generalizations about it. When one understands this, some of the difficulties of determining what constitutes a mandatory subject of bargaining under the *Borg-Warner* line of cases become more apparent. The system is by no means uniform, although the parties are interested in what their counterparts are doing in other industries and often appear to emulate what is done elsewhere.

Second, in most relationships, grievance-arbitration machinery resolves problems before arbitration has to be invoked as a last resort. Most contracts provide for three to five steps in which discussions take place between increasingly high-ranking labor and management representatives without outside involvement. At these steps attempts are made to resolve differences on an informal basis (in the first instance, between an employee and/or a union steward and the foreman) and to clarify what is in dispute. This aspect of the process is not always informal and free of trouble. In litigation arising under the National Labor Relations Act's unfair-labor-practice machinery, the Supreme Court held that an employer's denial of an employee's request that her union representative be present at an investigation interview violated the statute.[7] However, the NLRB has limited the scope of the Court's decision through its holding that there is no statutory right to union representation where the employer has already reached "a final, binding decision to impose certain discipline on the employee prior to the interview."[8] Of course, the parties may handle this matter differently under the provisions in their collective bargaining agreement if they wish to do so.

A third reason for the acceptance of arbitration is its relative informality. The principle of *stare decisis,* which American courts use to bind the court to legal doctrines established in the past, is not applicable to arbitration proceedings.[9] In other words, what another arbitrator has previously decided where the same facts are in evidence may be persuasive authority, but a second arbitrator has discretion to consider the matter anew. At the same time, arbitrators will often adhere to the "law of the shop" in the form of past practices, settlements, or arbitration awards in the plant in which the dispute arose. Lawyers are present in an increasing number of instances, and each party is always represented; exhibits are generally introduced; and generally there are witnesses (who need not be sworn but are in more and more instances, and who may be examined and cross-examined). However, arbitrators do not follow judicial rules on the admissibility of testimony and other evidence. Greater formality may be a sign of a less mature relationship, but not always. Transcription by a court stenographer generally implies formality, but it may well be worthwhile—particularly if many facts are in dispute, if many witnesses contradict one another, or if complex contract interpretations are involved.

Fourth, the principal attraction of arbitration for both sides is that it is more expeditious than litigation (although the American system has recently developed some deficiencies: delay, expense, and difficulty in coping with employment discrimination).

Finally, arbitration, to some extent, serves as a substitute for the right to strike for a period of time. This is a major part of the legal theory that has developed in the area. Although the American system has by no means eliminated unauthorized stoppages in breach of contract, it has reduced the inclination to strike—particularly in discipline and discharge disputes, where workers know that an impartial arbitrator will determine cases on merit. Unions with negotiated peace machinery rarely make the strike weapon the mode of dispute resolution in the first resort, even when no-strike clauses permit them to strike after an exhaustion of procedures over certain subject matters.

Other Attractions of Arbitration

For the union, two of the main attractions of the arbitration process are the ability to have a built-in planned dismissal machinery which protects workers against arbitrary actions by the employer and the removal of the union from the inevitable political crossfire in disputes over who should be promoted or transferred to a particular job. Since seniority is all-important and promotion is at the heart of a good number of grievances, the union is removed from the political battle by defending a relatively objective standard before the employer and, if necessary, the arbitrator.

For the employer, it is particularly significant that arbitration usually guarantees an uninterrupted period of industrial peace. Moreover, although employers are required in many instances to consult with the union under the duty-to-bargain provision of the National Labor Relations Act before engaging in unilateral changes in working conditions,[10] the assumption behind the arbitration process is that management decides first and that the union challenges the employer's authority through the grievance machinery.

The Arbitration Process

The hearing is usually held on the company's premises, since that is where the parties are and where most of the witnesses will be found. If the union wants neutral ground, usually that can be arranged. Quite frequently the hearing takes place in a motel or hotel of the parties' choosing. I have sometimes held hearings at the Stanford Law School and other institutions where I have taught.

The hearing usually begins with each side summarizing its position and with the formulation of a submission to indicate what issue is in dispute. Sometimes the parties can take the better part of a day or even more on this submission, and it becomes necessary to move on to the evidence in the hope that the issue will become clearer as more is learned about the case. Most arbitrators will suggest that the parties allow the arbitrator to define the dispute in the event that they are unable to define it themselves; invariably they will agree to this.

As mentioned above, there are exhibits, examinations, and cross-examinations. Often a transcript is not taken, and the arbitrator takes his own notes on the testimony. A stenographer makes it easier for the arbitrator; on the other hand, nothing can boost the financial cost of arbitration more quickly for the parties than the presence of a court stenographer to take down and transcribe the proceedings.

When the hearing is concluded, the parties sometimes submit briefs and the arbitrator retires to his office to write an opinion and make an award. Although an opinion is not required under American law, the practice is to write one, and the parties would be deeply concerned if the arbitrator issued an award without an opinion.

On the West Coast docks, among other places, labor and management rely on bench awards (awards that must be rendered orally or in a short period of time, and are sometimes limited in length) in walkouts over safety disputes. When notified by "beeper" that a dispute is in progress, the arbitrator goes to the docks, listens to the arguments, and issues an award. Though the parties on the docks are entitled to get an opinion in writing, they generally do not ask for one. Bench awards are becoming more common beyond the West Coast docks, and their use is sometimes specified in contracts.

The arbitration process has been satisfactory to most of the parties that have used it. Although appeals may be taken to the courts, generally the parties adhere to the arbitrator's award without recourse to the judicial process. In this atmosphere, it is not the least bit surprising that the arbitrator is paid by the parties. The fee and the costs are usually split equally, although sometimes the loser pays all, sometimes the company pays all (regardless of the outcome), and sometimes a different allocation is agreed upon (usually with the company paying the greater percentage). These obligations are covered by the contract.

The Subject Matter of Disputes

The kinds of disputes likely to come before arbitrators in grievance matters involve a wide variety of issues. Most prominent are dismissals, discipline, and questions relating seniority to promotions or layoffs. Disputes over job classifications, what kind of work is to be performed, and whether employers can contract out work previously performed by the bargaining unit's employees are all grist for the arbitrator's mill. Contrary to foreign belief, the process is not excessively legalistic, although it has had tendencies in that direction in recent years. Contract interpretation is usually involved, but there is much more than that. Great scope is left to the arbitrator, who must determine whether a worker has been dismissed for "just cause" within the meaning of the collective agreement. A good deal of common sense, rather than a technical knowledge of labor law, is a prerequisite for functioning as a competent arbitrator.

The Limitations of Arbitration

There are considerable problems with grievance arbitration in the United States. William J. Usery, former Federal Mediation and Conciliation Director and Secretary of Labor, has noted that one out of three strikes takes place during the term of an agreement[11]—although it is not clear to what extent these stoppages are in fact in defiance of arbitration and no-strike machinery or to what extent the machinery is deficient.

Moreover, the arbitration process has had considerable difficulty in coping with employment discrimination.[12] This is not altogether surprising, since unions and employers— who control grievance arbitration—are often the parties accused of discrimination. The courts have not treated employment-discrimination arbitration in the same manner as other types of arbitration. This is important because an increasing number of arbitrations involve allegations of race, sex, national-origin, and religious discrimination.

Quite frequently, the arbitrators who are identified with a position favoring fair employment practices are civil-rights activists not chosen by the parties. In addition, very few arbitrators are members of minorities, or women. The National Academy of Arbitrators, whose membership is involved in important and prestigious arbitrations (but by no means a significant percentage of all the hearings that take place in this country), has a very small number of minority and women members. In important employment-discrimination arbitrations, as well as other kinds of cases that go to third-party neutrals, unions and employers may not be willing to select an arbitrator who is not a member of the Academy. Of course, this statistical absence is by no means dispositive of the question of whether arbitration can cope with employment discrimination. The federal judiciary, in the early years of the Civil Rights Act of 1964,[13] was of considerable assistance in providing an expansive interpretation of the statute, which benefited minorities and women, yet until 1977 there were very few minority members or women on the federal bench. (The number is still small.)

But the problem is that arbitrators, whatever their race or sex, must necessarily be responsive to the interests of those who appoint them—labor and management—and not necessarily to those of third parties who have no direct involvement in either the selection of or word-of-mouth recommendations for future cases. Arbitrators, like other people, are not often likely to bite the hand that feeds them, and can be counted on to respond to the parties' conscious and subconscious expectations about standards to be applied in finding contract violations and in fashioning remedies.[14]

An additional problem is that arbitrators are often unaware of the requirements of employment-discrimination law, which is usually made relevant to the arbitration by virtue of the fact that the no-discrimination clause obligates the parties not to violate the law.

Finally, because unions and employers control the arbitration process, they are not generally sympathetic to third-party representation when it is demanded by minority members and women who feel that the union would not be vigorous enough in pursuing their interests. Invariably, third-party representation or a representative or counsel of the employees' choosing has been rejected where it has been inconsistent with the position of labor and management.[15]

The Role of the Courts

Although the law is on the periphery of some aspects of the labor arbitration process, it nevertheless is important. Except under the Railway Labor Act and in states with legislation requiring arbitration in public-sector disputes, the law becomes involved only where the parties voluntarily negotiate agreements. In the former situation arbitration is sometimes mandated, but generally it is for the parties to decide.

The landmark decisions relating to the law of arbitration are *Textile Workers Union* v. *Lincoln Mills*[16] and the *Steelworkers Trilogy*.[17] What is particularly ironic about the *Lincoln Mills* decision and some of the Taft-Hartley amendments, which have promoted the arbitration process (a process the unions were generally interested in achieving), is that those amendments were passed out of a concern for the disciplining of unruly and troublesome trade unions that were thought to be unfaithful to no-strike clauses they had negotiated. Because unions are voluntary unincorporated associations at common law, many state jurisdictions held that a union could be sued only in the names of its individual members—a considerable task. This was made even more difficult when a union had mbers outside of the state jurisdiction in which it was being sued. Traditionally, the problems involved with "serving" out-of-state defendants (putting them on notice of the suit, a requirement of due process) have given rise to a good deal of litigation.[18]

Section 301 of the National Labor Relations Act was designed to change this. It made collective bargaining agreements enforceable in the federal courts. After disposing of some constitutional problems with the statute,[19] Justice Douglas, speaking for a majority of the Court in *Lincoln Mills*, concluded that arbitration clauses were enforceable in the federal courts inasmuch as they were the *quid pro quo* for no-strike agreements. The Norris-LaGuardia Act, which barred injunctions in labor disputes, was held to be inapplicable because arbitration did not involve problems that were "part and parcel" of the abuses that had given rise to the Norris-LaGuardia Act.[20] Congress, said the Court, had intended to promote the arbitration process, and had done so through Taft-Hartley.

But *Lincoln Mills* raised more questions than it answered. What was to be the role of the judiciary with respect to arbitration; would the courts interject themselves into the arbitration process and thus usurp the role accorded to arbitrators by labor and management? Would state courts still preserve their jurisdiction in breach-of-labor cases, and thus in arbitration disputes, even though Taft-Hartley gave to the federal courts jurisdiction—that is, would the state courts be ousted by the doctrine of preemption? Would employers be able to sue for violations of collectively negotiated no-strike clauses despite the bar against injunctions in labor disputes contained in Norris-LaGuardia, or were such violations again "part and parcel" of the abuses at which Norris-LaGuardia was aimed? Could individuals maintain suits for violations of collective bargaining agreements, and to what extent could they bypass the union in so doing?

The Court answered the first of these questions in the landmark *Steelworkers Trilogy* cases. The issue confronted in those cases related to the circumstances under which the judiciary would order the parties to go to arbitration and the extent to which the Courts could review the arbitrator's award. The Court, again with Justice Douglas speaking for a substantial majority, concluded that Taft-Hartley's public policy promoting arbitration[21] required that all doubts about whether the dispute was arbitrable should be resolved by the courts in favor of arbitrability. Moreover, the Court concluded that an arbitrator's award could not be reversed by the Court unless it manifested clear infidelity to the contract. And though most arbitrators write opinions, as the parties expect, the Court stated that an opinion is not necessary as a matter of federal labor law.

The Court's reasoning drew upon the judicial experience with arbitration—best represented by the New York Court of Appeals decision in the *Cutler-Hammer* case,[22] which had involved the judiciary in the interpretation of collective bargaining agreements (the very function the arbitrator was commissioned by the parties to perform). The Supreme Court noted that courts, under the guise of determining arbitrability issues, had become involved in interpretations of collective bargaining agreements or the merits of the underlying grievance. For instance, in the first of the *Steelworkers Trilogy* cases[23] the issue was whether the company had properly subcontracted work outside the bargaining unit under the collective bargaining agreement. But an examination of the question of whether or not a subcontracting dispute was arbitrable necessarily focused on a number of considerations that an arbitrator would consider in determining the merits of the underlying grievance issue of whether the company had the right to contract out work under the agreement: bargaining history, past practice between the parties, and the like. A detailed examination of the merits of the arbitrability issue would send the courts down a slippery slope at whose bottom they might become ensnared in the merits of the dispute itself; by so doing they would deprive the parties of their bargain that the arbitrator would have jurisdiction over such matters.

The Court concluded that all doubts should be resolved in favor of arbitrability, and that a detailed examination of the arbitrability issue should be avoided for the reasons stated. The Court also noted that the processing of frivolous grievances has a therapeutic effect on the relationship between labor and management and gives each employee his "day in court." Additionally, Justice Douglas noted that the parties, through negotiating an arbitration clause in their contract, had bargained for the arbitrator's expertise. (Some arbitrators would hardly recognize themselves from Douglas's glowing characterization of their abilities; however, the arbitrator's expertise is an important theme in the *Steelworkers Trilogy* rationale.) As Jusice Douglas wrote:

The labor arbitrator's source of law is not confined to the express provisions of the contract, as the industrial common law—the practices of the industry and the shop—is equally a part of the collective bargaining agreement although not expressed in it. The labor arbitrator is usually chosen because of the parties' confidence in his knowledge of the common law of the shop and their trust in his personal judgment to bring to bear considerations which are not expressed in the contract as criteria for judgment. The parties expect that his judgment of a particular grievance will reflect not only what the contract says but, insofar as the collective bargaining agreement permits, such factors as the effect upon productivity of a particular result, its consequence to the morale of the shop, his judgment whether tensions will be heightened or diminished. For the parties' objective in using the arbitration process is primarily to further their goal of uninterrupted production under the agreement, to make the agreement serve their specialized needs. The ablest judge cannot be expected to bring the same experience and competence to bear upon the determination of a grievance, because he cannot be similarly informed.[24]

The Court was also influenced by the argument that arbitration of labor disputes is essentially different from commercial arbitration involving business relationships and other matters. The Court stated that the collective bargaining agreement is "more than a contract"; it is a "generalized code to govern a myriad of cases which the draftsman cannot wholly anticipate."[25] The Court's view was that the mature labor agreement contained manifold ambiguities and gaps because of the nature of the agreement. In essence, since the law compels the parties to bargain with one another and imposes a relationship (if not the contract itself) upon the parties, it can be called a "shotgun marriage" dictated by economic force or law. In such a situation, more than the usual number of unforeseen contingencies and ambiguities remain to plague the parties. Sometimes the parties will be aware of the problem and yet recognize that it makes more sense to submit a dispute to an effective resolution process because of the cost of disagreement at a particular time.

The Court said that collective bargaining is an effort to "erect a system of industrial self government"[26]; that the compulsion to reach agreement and the "breadth of the matters covered, as well as the need for a fairly concise and reliable instrument" produce a relatively peculiar contract for which the arbitration process is available to the parties in the event of the disagreement about interpretation.

Thus, all doubts about arbitrability, said the Court, should be resolved in favor of arbitration. Arbitration awards fashioned by arbitrators are enforceable in federal or state court in the absence of manifest infidelity to the contract itself or to some "explicit public policy," which "must be well defined and dominant, and is to be ascertained by reference to the laws and legal precedents, not from general considerations of supposed public interests."[27] But what of the other problems? For instance, could the employer obtain injunctive relief for violation of the no-strike clause despite the broad prohibitions of the Norris-LaGuardia Act?

The No-Strike Clause

The Supreme Court first answered the preceding question negatively in the *Sinclair* decision in 1962. Justice Black, a strong proponent of the literal use of language in the constitutional area of First Amendment litigation, noted that Norris-LaGuardia was a bar to the issuance of injunctions for employers—even though unions could obtain injunctions in the form of motions to compel arbitration clauses. Eight years later, however, the Supreme Court reversed *Sinclair* in the landmark *Boys Market* decision.[28]

In *Boys Market* a 5–2 majority concluded that injunctions against violations of no-strike clauses could be issued by the federal courts where the underlying grievance that had given rise to the controversy over which the strike was taking place was itself arbitrable under the collective bargaining agreement. The Court's rationale rested upon a number of considerations. The first was that state court jurisdictions still remained available to parties seeking enforcement of labor contracts, and that in states where there were no "baby Norris-LaGuardia Acts" employers were free to sue for injunctive relief in state courts. The problem insofar as injunctive relief against no-strike violations was that employers had an incentive to proceed in state courts even though federal labor law applied there as well as in the federal courts. In other words, in the interest of uniformity it seemed undesirable to have an employer-initiated action moved from state to federal court. This created, said the Court in *Boys Market*, "an anomalous situation which, in our view, makes urgent the reconsideration of *Sinclair*."[29] With the removal from the state to the federal courts, the states were ousted from jurisdiction they had possessed in breach-of-contract cases prior to the enactment of the Taft-Hartley amendments—even though Supreme Court authority had said that state-court jurisdiction should supplement that of the federal courts. As the Supreme

Court said in *Boys Market*: "It is ironic indeed that the very provision that Congress clearly intended to provide additional remedies for breach of collective bargaining agreements has been employed to displace previously existing state remedies. We are not at liberty thus to depart from the clearly expressed congressional policy to the contrary."[30]

The Court, as it said in commenting on *Sinclair*, was confronted with a dilemma. On the one hand, the availability of state-court jurisdiction in labor-injunction cases involving violations of no-strike clauses made the state judiciary the preferred forum for labor-contract interpretation where federal law was to apply. On the other hand, the availability of removal from the state court subsequent to the exercise of jurisdiction deprived the states of preexisting remedies for breach of contract by unions—even though the statute had been aimed, in particular, at union behavior that was inconsistent with its no-strike obligations.

A second reason the Court found *Sinclair* less than satisfactory was because it was inconsistent with the basic federal labor policy recognized in both *Lincoln Mills* and *Steelworkers Trilogy*: that the no-strike obligation was the *quid pro quo* for an undertaking by the employer to submit grievances to the process of arbitration. Said the Court:

Any incentive for employers to enter into such an arrangement is necessarily dissipated if the principal and the most expeditious method by which the no-strike obligation can be enforced is eliminated. While it is of course true, as respondent contends, that other avenues of redress, such as action for damages, would remain open to an aggrieved employer, an award of damages after a dispute has been settled is no substitute for an immediate halt to an illegal strike. Furthermore, an action for damages prosecuted during or after a labor dispute would only tend to aggravate industrial strife and delay an early resolution of the difficulties between employer and union.[31]

Third, the Court rejected the argument that Norris-LaGuardia was a bar to an injunction because it and Taft-Hartley were aimed at a different problem. The Court noted that a considerable number of union strikes and picketing activities were enjoined and that a substantial number of abuses were being committed by the federal courts in this connection. But the Court noted that the labor organizations had grown in strength and "developed toward maturity" and that therefore Congress, in fashioning a national labor policy under Taft-Hartley, had shifted from "protection of the nascent labor movement to the encouragement of collective bargaining and to administrative techniques for the peaceful resolution of industrial disputes."[32] An appropriate accommodation between the competing policies of Taft-Hartley (which reflected the new approach) and Norris-LaGuardia (which barred injunctions in labor disputes) was to permit injunctions for violations of no-strike clauses where the underlying grievance was arbitrable. Said the Court: "The Norris-LaGuardia Act was responsive to a situation totally different from that which exists today."[33]

After the *Boys Market* decision, the Court concluded in a controversial opinion by Justice White that injunctive relief was not available in the context of sympathy strikes where it was claimed that such strikes violated the no-strike provision. The dubious reasoning[34] was that there was no underlying grievance that was susceptible to the arbitration process. However, the question of whether a sympathy strike itself violates the no-strike clause can under many collective bargaining agreements be resolved in the arbitration process. Accordingly, the issuance of an injunction pending the outcome of this matter is, as Justice Stevens's dissent in this subsequent case makes clear, just as vital as it is in the *Boys Market* context.

Finally, as the Court noted in *Boys Market*, damages awards may be obtained against the union for a no-strike violation—

even on the basis of a broad arbitration clause from which a no-strike obligation may be inferred.[35] However, damage actions in courts often are stayed pending arbitration of the issue, and employers do not consider arbitrators as sympathetic on this issue as the judiciary.[36] And the Court has held that, in the case of wildcat strikes in which the contract is violated and in which the union is not involved, there is no affirmative obligation (unless the contract provides otherwise) for an international union to urge the local to comply with the agreement.[37] Moreover, the Court has held that union representatives may not be sued as individuals when they have intitiated or authorized a strike,[38] and that individual rank-and-file employees may not be sued for violating a contract when they engage in a wildcat strike.[39] But the question of what responsibility the local union had to urge its members to return to work and the question as to whether the local union can be held liable on a "mass action" theory that imputes liability to the union on the basis that the rank and file will not act spontaneously without some kind of encouragement from the leadership have not been addressed by the Court.[40] The Supreme Court did rule (unanimously) that employers may not selectively impose harsher discipline upon union officials than upon rank-and-file employees for a violation of a no-strike clause,[41] but the Court did not rule on the question of whether selective sanctions may be imposed upon union officials where they have played a "leadership" role in the strike.[42]

The NLRB and Arbitration

The National Labor Relations Board has also facilitated the arbitration process through careful use of its own jurisdiction. For instance, it has held that in unfair-labor-practice proceedings it will not reverse an arbitrator's award where the arbitration proceedings were fair and regular on their face, where the issues raised before the Board were raised before the arbitrator, where the arbitrator's award was not "repugnant" to the public policy of the National Labor Relations Act, and where the unfair-labor-practice issue had been addressed by the arbitrator in some form.[43] The Board has held that the arbitrator will be deemed to have "adequately considered the unfair labor practice if (1) the contractual issue is factually parallel to the unfair labor practice issue, and (2) the arbitrator was presented generally with the facts relevant to resolving the unfair labor practice."[44] Said the Board:

. . . we would not require an arbitrator's award to be totally consistent with Board precedent. Unless the award is "palpably wrong," i.e., unless the arbitrator's decision is not susceptible to an interpretation consistent with the Act, we will defer.[45]

Under certain circumstances, the Board has held that it will stay its hand and refuse to process an unfair-labor-practice charge while it is pending before the arbitrator.[46] Numerous exceptions to the latter proposition have developed.[47] Meanwhile, the Board has reverted to a policy of more pristine deferral.[48]

Successor Employers

In *Wiley* v. *Livingston* the Supreme Court held that "the disappearance by merger of a corporate employer which has entered into a collective bargaining agreement with a union does not automatically terminate all rights of the employees covered by the agreement, and that, in appropriate circumstances . . . the successor employer may be required to arbitrate with the union under the agreement."[49] However, the Court has held that, although a successor employer has a duty to recognize the union of the predecessor, the NLRB cannot impose the labor contract upon the successor employer[50] because to do so would contradict the Court's instruction to the Board to eschew the imposition of contract terms upon labor and management.[51] In a third case, the Court limited the thrust of *Wiley* by holding that it applies only where there is "substantial continuity" in the work force.[52]

The Individual Employee

Shortly after the *Steelworkers Trilogy*, the Supreme Court held that individuals may sue in federal and state court for violations of collective bargaining agreements; however, the rule has been carefully circumscribed in a number of respects. In the first place, the grievance-arbitration machinery must be exhausted prior to the initiation of a lawsuit.[53] But even more formidable are the barriers that exist by virtue of the Court's decision in *Vaca* v. *Sipes*,[54] a leading duty-of-fair-representation case. Since many of the issues in *Vaca* dramatize the tensions between individual and collective interests, they are more properly described in the next chapter. But the question of union and company liability where the union declines to take the grievance to arbitration and where the employee shows—as he must if he is to prevail—that the union has violated its duty-of-fair-representation obligation and that the employer has breached the collective bargaining agreement is more appropriately addressed here.

In *Bowen* v. *U.S. Postal Service*,[55] a 5–4 majority of the Court held that the union is liable in damages to a discharged employee where the failure to take the grievance to arbitration has increased the employer's liability to the employee for breach of contract. Because of the considerable period of time between the potential date of reinstatement in the event of an arbitration and the court trial of a case involving duty of fair representation and breach of contract, the practical impact of *Bowen* is to impose most of the damage liability upon unions rather than employers. This is what prompted Justice White to state in his dissent that:

The union's breach, even if totally unrelated to the employer's decision to terminate the employee, now serves to insulate the employer from further backpay liability, as of the hypothetical arbitration date, even though the employer, unlike the union, can stop backpay accretion at any moment it desires, simply by reinstating the discharged employee.[56]

Arbitration and Employment Discrimination

To what extent have the rules evolved in the *Steelworkers Trilogy* litigation been applied to employment-discrimination cases? In *Alexander* v. *Gardner-Denver* the Supreme Court held that a final arbitration award did not preclude an individual from suing to redress employment discrimination. The Court, speaking through Justice Powell, stated that since such a lawsuit in the courts was filed under the Civil Rights Act of 1964, the individual employee was relying on independent statutory rights accorded by Congress and not on contractual rights contained in the collective bargaining agreement that would be at issue in an arbitration proceeding. The Court nevertheless stressed the importance of voluntary conciliation as well as arbitration as a means to resolve such matters—a particularly important consideration, given the substantial backlog of employment discrimination cases before administrative agencies and the courts. The Supreme Court, while rejecting a policy of deference to arbitration awards, concluded that the award could be "admitted as evidence and accorded such weight as the Court deems appropriate."[57] The Court added the following in a footnote:

We adopt no standards as to the weight to be accorded an arbitral decision, since this must be determined in the court's discretion with regard to the facts and circumstances of each case. Relevant factors include the existence of provisions in the collective-bargaining agreement that conform substantially with Title VII, the degree of procedural fairness in the arbitral forum, adequacy of the record with respect to the issue of discrimination, and the special competence of particular arbitrators. Where an arbitral determination gives full consideration to an employee's Title VII rights, a court may accord it great weight. This is especially true where the issue is solely one of fact, specifically addressed by the parties, and decided by the arbitrator on the basis of an adequate record.[58]

This footnote has prompted some parties to negotiate special arbitration procedures addressed to particular problems of employment discrimination,[59] which are considerably different from the ordinary grievance that comes to arbitration.

Arbitration and Welfare or Minimum-Standards Legislation

In 1981 the Supreme Court, in a 7–2 opinion authored by Justice Brennan, extended the *Gardner-Denver* holding to the Fair-Labor Standards Act of 1938.[60] The Court held that arbitration awards should not be deferred to where the statute in question provides minimum substantive guarantees to individual workers. The Court expressed concern that individual rights might be sacrificed by the union, which acts in the collective interest under legislation promoting collective bargaining and majority rule.

This approach has produced the same result in a case where a public employer unsuccessfully relied on an employee's defeat in an arbitration proceeding where the employee alleged that there was "no proper cause" for his discharge and that the discharge had been instituted because of his exercise of the constitutionally protected rights of freedom of speech, freedom of association, and freedom to petition the government for redress of grievances.[61] The Court's reasoning applies to statutes such as the Employee Retirement Income Security Act of 1974 and the Occupational Health and Safety Act of 1970, and it means that courts will not defer to arbitration awards rendered where the plaintiffs sue under those statutes—although the awards might be given "great weight," as in *Gardner-Denver*.

Arbitration in the Public Sector

Finally, there is the matter of public-sector arbitration. In the grievance-arbitration area it appears as though the *Steelworkers Trilogy* has not been followed by state courts in a number of jurisdictions.[62] But what is particularly interesting is the use of arbitration in the public sector as a means to resolve interest disputes. There has been a decline in interest on the part of some public-employee unions in the right to strike and an increased emphasis on arbitration. Most of the states with public-employee labor legislation have adopted some form of arbitration procedures for police and fire unions, and Iowa, Wisconsin, Connecticut, and the City of New York have extended arbitration to other municipal employees as well. (In Iowa all state employees are covered.[63]) Although a number of states have passed "experimental" statutes, no jurisdiction has repealed an arbitration law and returned to another procedure such as fact finding.

The critical question with regard to arbitration statutes is whether the procedures tend to stultify or chill the collective bargaining process and induce the parties to rely on arbitration rather than negotiations. Thomas Kochan has found that during the first decade of public-sector bargaining "a higher percentage of cases have reached impasse under both conventional arbitration and final offer arbitration than under fact-finding procedures," that there was overdependence on arbitration "in a number of jurisdictions operating under both fact-finding and arbitration," and that in general "large jurisdictions tend to rely heavily on whatever dispute resolution is available."[64] This last observation should come as no surprise; although interest arbitration in the United States may be in its formative stage, and although there are problems with grievance arbitration, the institution, its rules, and its practice are well established.

9

The Individual Employee and the Collective Interest

The Duty of Fair Representation

The duty of fair representation, under which a union as exclusive bargaining agent has an obligation to deal fairly on behalf of all of a bargaining unit's employees (union and non-union), has been inferred from the NLRA's grant of authority to the union to negotiate on behalf of all workers. That other nations do not have the exclusivity concept and all its consequences makes this kind of litigation peculiar to the United States.

In 1944 the Supreme Court held that the failure of a union to meet its duty of fair representation constituted a violation of federal labor law, and the NLRB subsequently held that it constituted an unfair labor practice as well.[1] In *Vaca* v. *Sipes* the Court held that the federal courts as well as the Board had jurisdiction over duty-of-fair-representation cases. However, unless the collective bargaining agreement authorizes the individual to take his grievance to arbitration, the union maintains control of the grievance and may determine whether to initiate arbitration. The Court held that the individual employee had no "absolute right" to initiate arbitration, and that the industrial self-government that had been created by the parties would be harmed by a contrary rule. At the same time, the Court concluded that an employee could attack the union's failure to process the grievance if its actions toward an employee in the bargaining unit were "arbitrary, discriminatory, or in bad faith."[2] It is difficult to determine what the Court meant by these words. Whether a union's simple failure to process a grievance because it was lost or forgotten constitutes a failure to meet the duty of fair representation is unresolved,[3] but it certainly presents a difficulty for the employee whose grievance is meritorious. In *Vaca* the Court gave the union some discretion because a contrary rule would involve the courts in second-guessing union decisions. Just as the courts do not want to be second-guessing arbitrators, they wish to apply the same policy to the manner in which matters are dealt with at lower levels of the grievance machinery, which are even more important in industrial self-government.

However, the Court held by a 5–4 vote that an individual union member does not have an obligation to utilize internal union procedures and remedies prior to filing suit where the union cannot contractually reactivate the grievance in the event that it was in error in not processing it.[4] It is not entirely clear whether the individual has a right to participate in the arbitration hearing. Thus far it appears as though the union may exclude the employee without violating its duty of fair representation,[5] although recent authority casts some doubt on this.[6] Some judges appear to accept the view that a union has a duty to fairly represent the claims of junior workers competing against their more senior colleagues for the same jobs where the contract contemplates selection of employees for job vacancies on the basis of both seniority and qualifications. Unions generally support the concept of seniority as a basis for determining preference in promotions, transfers, and layoffs, and sometimes the collective bargaining agreement reflects this philosophy. In the steel industry, a junior employee must be "head and shoulders" above a senior worker in qualifications in order to be selected. But more often there is a more complex interplay between seniority and qualifications set forth in the labor contract. If the view that unions have a duty to present the claims of the junior employee under such circumstances carries the day, the effect will be burdensome for the unions and revolutionary for industrial relations.

If the union has breached its duty of fair representation in handling the grievance at the arbitration, the employer may be liable to relitigation of an arbitration award despite the preference expressed in the *Steelworkers Trilogy* for the finality of arbitration awards. For instance, in dealing with an arbitration case in which employees dismissed for dishonesty had brought to the tribunal's attention evidence that the union had failed to present, the Court noted that the employer had intitiated the discharges. Even though the employer was not responsible for the failure to present evidence, an award tainted by the union's failure to represent fairly was invalid.[7] Said Justice White, speaking for the Court: ". . . enforcement of the finality provision where the arbitrator has erred is conditioned upon the union's having satisfied its statutory duty fairly to represent the employee in connection with the arbitration proceedings. Wrongfully discharged employees would be left without jobs and without a fair opportunity to secure an adequate remedy."[8] For awhile, the Court's 1981 holding that a relatively short statute of limitations would apply to duty-of-fair-representation suits attacking arbitration awards[9] seemed sure to bar many otherwise valid claims. Now the statute of limitations is 6 months—the Court rejected a briefer period, partly because of the time it takes an employee "unsophisticated in collective-bargaining matters" to "evaluate the adequacy of the union's representation, to retain counsel, to investigate substantial matters that were not at issue in the arbitration proceeding, and to frame his suit."[10]

Union Security Agreements and Union Discipline

The issue of union security agreements and an employee's obligations to the union with respect to union membership has broad implications in American labor law. In *NLRB* v. *The General Motors Corp.*[11] the Court held that, except for religious objectors (who may pay an equivalent sum elsewhere by virtue of a 1980 amendment to the statute), the worker's only obligation is to pay dues and initiation fees—although many lawyers, trade unionists, corporate officials, and workers believe that more is required under the law. The obligation to pay arises thirty days after employment (seven days in the construction industry, because of the temporary nature of the work). This rule bears directly on the extent to which unions may discipline members under the National Labor Relations Act.

The leading case on this question is *NLRB* v. *Allis-Chalmers Mfg. Co.*,[12] in which the Court held by 5–4 vote that a union may fine strikebreakers who cross picket lines by virtue of its role as exclusive bargaining agent. The Court has taken the position that "reasonable discipline" of members who violate union rules is necessary to protect the union against erosion of its status as exclusive agent. However, the Court indicated that the extent of a union's disciplinary authority could vary depending upon the extent to which workers had voluntarily assumed membership obligations beyond those requiring the payment of dues and initiation fees. The Court noted that in *Allis-Chalmers* the workers who had been fined had attended union meetings at which a secret strike vote was taken, pledged allegiance to the union's constitution, taken the oath of full membership, and fully participated in the proceedings leading to the strike. The Court indicated that if such voluntary union activity were not present the union might well have run afoul of the law by imposing fines upon the workers. The difficulty here is that few if any workers know that they are not obligated to do more in a union than pay initiation fees and dues. So, quite frequently, collective bargaining agreements obligate them to assume membership obligations as a condition of employment, without reference to the fact that this is limited by law. The rule established in *Allis-Chalmers* seems unfair to individual employees, at least in this respect.

Subsequent to the *Allis-Chalmers* decision, the Court held that a union may not fine a worker for something he did after resigning from the union. Although the Court initially hinted that unions might lawfully impose obligations and limitations upon the right to resign,[13] in 1985 it held by a 5–4 vote that the Board's conclusion that a union could lawfully prohibit a member from resigning was appropriate.[14] Specifically, the Court held that a union's fining employees who had resigned from the union during a strike could be regarded as an unfair labor practice and that this conclusion was a reasonable interpretation of the statute. Said the Court: "Because the closed shop was outlawed by the Taft-Hartley Act . . . it is not surprising that Congress thought it unnecessary explicitly to preserve the right to resign. . . . The Board reasonably has concluded [that the union fine] 'restrains or coerces' employees . . . and is inconsistent with the congressional policy of voluntary unionism."[15]

Finally, who decides on the reasonableness of the amount of a fine levied by a union? Although for a while there was considerable debate about whether or not the Board had jurisdiction to invalidate "unreasonable" fines, the Supreme Court has made it clear that this question is to be resolved by the state courts and not by the NLRB.[16]

Exclusion from Union Membership and Responsibilities

There is no right under American labor law to be admitted to a union. However, exclusion from membership or activities on the basis of race, sex, color, religion, or national origin is violative of title VII of the Civil Rights Act of 1964.

Although members of a union must pay dues where a union security agreement has been negotiated, they may not be compelled to pay dues that would be used for political purposes if they believe that such payment would violate their First Amendment right to free speech.[17] (This is discussed below in the section entitled "Unions and the Political Process.")

The Landrum-Griffin Bill of Rights

The Labor Management Reporting and Disclosure Act of 1959 (often referred to as the Landrum-Griffin Act) contains a bill of rights for union members,[18] largely procedural in nature, which emerged from the McClellan hearings in which considerable union corruption and other forms of abuse were exposed. Title I of the Landrum-Griffin Act declared the right of every union member to equal protection, freedom of speech and assembly, reasonable and uniform dues, and freedom to sue unions and their officers.

In *United Steelworkers* v. *Sadlowski*,[19] which involved a hard-fought campaign for the presidency of the Steelworkers, the Supreme Court, in a 5–4 decision, held that a union constitution's "outsider rule" prohibiting solicitation of or financial assistance from nonmembers for election campaigns or election-related litigation did not violate Landrum-Griffin's provisions for free speech and the right to sue. Said Justice Marshall, speaking for the majority: " . . . we do not believe that [the Landrum-Griffin Act] should be read as incorporating the entire body of First Amendment law, so that the scope of protections afforded by the statute coincides with the protections afforded by the Constitution."[20] Justice White, in a sharply worded dissent, stressed the imbalance in strength between union incumbents and challengers: " . . . leadership is not only determined to discourage opposition; it also has at its disposal all of the advantages for doing so, including the facilities of the union. Those leaders have normally appointed the union staff, the bureaucracy that makes the union run."[21] Concluding that the outsider rule was inconsistent with the Act's legislative history, the dissenters noted that "Congress intended to help the members help solve these very difficulties by guaranteeing them the right to run for office and to have free and open elections in the American tradition."[22]

The other shoe dropped in *Finnegan* v. *Lau*,[23] where the Court held that "rank and file union members—not union officers or employees"[22] are protected by the Act against a retaliatory discharge by the union for the exercise of free speech. The Court's assessment of legislative history led it to the conclusion that Congress did not intend to regulate union patronage. The Court left open the question "whether a different result might obtain in a case involving nonpolicymaking and nonconfidential employees,"[25] but it seemed to ignore the difficulties for dissidents engendered by a decision that makes the bureaucracy more subordinate to the leadership.

Even where a union may discipline an employee in connection with a reasonable rule in the union's constitution, procedural due process as required by section 101(a)(5) of Landrum-Griffin obligates the union to provide the member with adequate notice of charges, reasonable time to prepare his defense, and a full and fair hearing. In this connection and in others, the 1959 statute guarantees the rights only to union members, not to all employees represented by the union.

Contrary to public impression, the Landrum-Griffin Act does not guarantee members the right to ratify a union contract. However, union members have a right to equal protection, which can be modified only by reasonable rules and regulations. A union may limit eligibility to vote in contract ratifications to members in good standing.[26] Similarly, "moonlighters" have been denied the right to vote because they have no "vital interest" in the outcome.[27] But in *Local 6885* v. *American Postal Workers*,[28] Judge Mikva, speaking for the Court of Appeals for the District of Columbia, concluded that it was denial of equal protection to preclude ratification of the contract by a non-mail-processing local union when other members of mail-processing locals had been accorded such rights. And where a vote is conducted, the members have the right to a "meaningful vote" in the sense that they are entitled to "adequate notice and information regarding the subject matter and nature of the vote."[29] Thus, for instance, the 1984 ratification of the Teamsters–United Parcel Agreement was deemed unlawful because emergency membership meetings had been called on short notice, members had not known that a new contract was being negotiated, and many members had been away on summer vacation.[30]

Trusteeships

The Landrum-Griffin Act is also aimed at limiting the circumstances under which the unions may impose trusteeships, an administrative device whereby dissident local unions could be controlled and their treasuries raided by national and international union officials. Careful standards are established relating to circumstances under which the imposition of administration of trusteeships may be established, and information must be filed with the Secretary of Labor.[31]

Union Elections

The Landrum-Griffin Act provides that members have the right to elect their officials and guarantees the right to an election every three years.[32] Some trade unions use the ballot box and some use conventions to elect their national officials. Those unions that have relied on the direct vote seem to have had the greatest amount of internal debate and controversy—for example, there have been hard-fought elections in the United Steelworkers of America and the International Union of Electrical Radio and Machine Workers. On the other hand, the United Auto Workers, a democratic union that has established a Public Review Board to review charges by union members against officialdom, elects its national officers at a convention, and there has never been a substantial vote against the incumbents.

Much of the litigation over union elections relates to unions' eligibility requirements for candidates. The Supreme Court had struck down union by-laws limiting the right to run for major elective offices to union members who hold or previously held elective office under circumstances where the effect was to disqualify 93 percent of members for office. Similarly, attendance rules requiring that a member who seeks local union office must have attended at least half of the regular meetings for three years previous to the election have been held unlawful where only 23 of 600 members would have been eligible. The Court has held that the anti-democratic effect of such rules is inconsistent with the Landrum-Griffin provision that "every member in good standing shall be eligible to be a candidate and to hold office . . . subject . . . to reasonable qualifications uniformly imposed."[33]

Although the Secretary of Labor is the only party who may file suit challenging an intraunion election that has already been held, the Supreme Court held in *Trbovich* v. *United Mine Workers*[34] that an aggrieved member may intervene in the suit. Although the Secretary of Labor assumes the mantle of the union member's lawyer, the Court acknowledged that the member might have "a valid complaint" about the performance of his lawyer and therefore ought to be able to intervene to present evidence and arguments in support of the Secretary's complaint.

The Court has held that union members may not institute actions where the remedy sought is the invalidation of an election already conducted.[35] Only the Secretary of Labor may bring such actions. But where the relief sought is "less intrusive" the individual may bring the action without the Secretary.

Not only must members have a fair opportunity to run for office as a prerequisite to an appropriate election, they must also have an opportunity to reach the members. This means that the union must honor a reasonable request to distribute campaign literature at a candidate's expense and that no monies received from dues or similiar kinds of levies may be used to promote any person's candidacy. Employers are precluded from contributing financial support to candidates for union office. Literature, if distributed at a reduced rate for one candidate, must be distributed at a reduced rate for all. If one candidate is allowed to copy membership lists, all candidates must have the same opportunity. These privileges must be extended equally.

Unions and the Political Process

Political activity is another area of tension between unions and individual union members. One must recall Gompers's statement that labor would reward its friends and punish its enemies. Though the unions are not attached to a political party, they are very much involved in the political process. Unions have established special political arms to support those who are friendly to organized labor's position on a wide variety of issues.

It is, however, a crime for any labor organization to "make a contribution or expenditure in connection with any election at which Presidential and Vice-Presidential electors or a Senator or Representative in . . . Congress ought to be voted for" or in connection with a related primary convention. Such activity is prohibited by section 304 of the Taft-Hartley Act.

Under the Federal Election Campaign Act of 1971, as amended, unions and corporations may use their monies in connection with the election of federal candidates for the purpose of sending political messages to their own members or shareholders, for conducting nonpartisan registration and get-out-the-vote campaigns directed at such groups, and as seed money to solicit contributions to a union or corporate political action committee. Any direct contribution by labor unions to the treasuries of federal political candidates is prohibited. However, the Supreme Court has held that a union may use funds contributed voluntarily outside the normal dues structure by union members as contributions to federal candidates. None of the above-described prohibitions has any bearing on union contributions to state campaigns.

A union member may object to having his dues money used on behalf of certain candidates or political programs, but a union may spend dues as it wishes for puposes germane to collective bargaining. What is relevant to collective bargaining and what is relevant to the political process has been a subject of considerable debate.[36] Unions have been encouraged by the Supreme Court to devise their own internal rebate procedures in connection with this problem, and the United Auto Workers and the Brotherhood of Railway Clerks have done so. The UAW has provided that a dissenting member may allocate a portion of his dues to be used in support of "nonpartisan ideological community groups."

In a unanimous opinion outlined by Justice White, the Court held that a rebate procedure is legally inadequate.[37] Said the Court: " . . . there are readily available alternatives, such as advance reduction of dues and/or interest-bearing escrow accounts, that place only the slightest additional burden, if any, on the union. Given the existence of acceptable alternatives, the union cannot be allowed to commit dissenters' funds to improper uses even temporarily. A rebate scheme reduces but does not eliminate the statutory violation."[38]

In the same case, the Court also held that the spending of dues money on litigation or on organizational campaigns not related to the bargaining unit was not "germane" to collective bargaining.

10

The Public Sector

In recent years, state and local legislation on the subjects of
collective bargaining and labor in the public sector have
grown considerably.[1] Forty-one of the states have some form
of fairly comprehensive legislation protecting the right of
public employees to organize and bargain collectively. (Some
states provide that the public employer need only "meet and
confer" with the union, but the practical result is often similiar to that under the duty to bargain.[2]) The same trend is
present at the federal level for federal employees, although
federal employees still may not negotiate wages. Congress replaced an executive order originally promulgated by President John F. Kennedy with the Civil Service Reform Act of
1970.[3] The Postal Reorganization Act of 1970[4] created an independent establishment within the executive branch. Postal
employees are subject to the National Labor Relations Act
and the Landrum-Griffin Act, but prohibitions against federal
strikes apply to them, and therefore the Postal Reorganization
Act contains its own dispute-resolution procedures. Striking
federal employees can be punished with felony charges and
dismissal.

Public employees have a right to union membership that is protected by the right of freedom of association under the First Amendment.[5] However, the Supreme Court has balanced this right against the government's interest in regulating the speech and conduct of its employees, an interest that differs significantly from any interest in regulating the speech of all citizens.[6] The means used to advance an important governmental interest must be those least restrictive of constitutional rights.[7] The balance between the constitutional right to union membership and various important government interests is not always clear. For example, police and firefighters share in the right to join unions,[8] but whether they may be restricted in the kind of labor organization with which they may affiliate has not been definitively resolved.[9] Moreover, the right of public employees to bargain collectively, let alone the right to strike,[10] is not protected by the Constitution. But a majority of the Supreme Court of California has supported the view that the right to strike enjoys some degree of constitutional protection in that state.[11]

The Supreme Court has held that a state may constitutionally prohibit union representation of workers in the processing of their grievances[12]—a less ambitious objective than that of constitutional protection for the collective bargaining process itself. Moreover, exclusivity is limited. The Court has also held that teachers other than union representatives have a constitutional right to speak at open school-board meetings.[13] The Supreme Court has held that a minority union can be constitutionally denied access to teachers' mailboxes and the interschool delivery system[14] because of the Constitution's free-speech and equal-protection guarantees, despite the statutory right of minority unions or dissident employees not to be denied the right to communicate in the private sector under the NLRA.[15] Justice White, writing for a 5–4 majority, reasoned that the state has a legitimate interest in furthering the effectiveness of representation. Since the Court also noted the absence of a showing that "permission has been granted as a matter of course to all who seek to distribute material" as a basis for its decision, the Court of Appeals for the Fifth Circuit has concluded that the minority union has a right to access when the mail system is open to all employee organizations "without distinction."[16] In 1984 the Court, again deferring to the state's interest in providing the exclusive bargaining representative with communication opportunities, held that the exclusion of nonmembers from "meet and confer" sessions on employment-related matters, which are not subject to mandatory collective bargaining, was constitutional.[17]

Another line of cases involving constitutional rights for public employees arises out of wrongful discharge.[18] In 1985 the Court, speaking through Justice White, held that the Due Process Clause of the Constitution mandates that some pretermination process must be accorded public employees, who can be dismissed only for cause. The Court noted that the need for "some form of pretermination hearing" was evident from a balancing of the competing interests at stake, i.e., "the private interest in retaining employment, the government interest in the expeditious removal of unsatisfactory employees and the avoidance of administrative burdens, and the risk of an erroneous communication."[19]

Public-employee unionism has grown by leaps and bounds since the mid 1960s. Before that time, the organization of public employees into unions lagged behind organization in the private sector for a number of reasons.

First, the legal concept of sovereignty translated itself into the idea that government was supreme and that public employees had no rights that could be asserted against their employer.

A second idea, very much related to the first, was that elected officials could not delegate their responsibility to others. Collective bargaining and arbitration therefore were considered inconsistent with the democratic process and with the idea that officials were responsible to the voters and not to trade unionists. Moreover, some of the benefits associated with labor organizations in the private sector, such as grievance-arbitration machinery, were not apparent until the 1950s and 1960s, and public employees were not dissatisfied with their position. But the turmoil of the 1960s, a perceived gap between benefits in the public and private sectors, and increased attention to the public sector by a trade-union movement in search of arenas in which it could recoup its membership losses among private employees contributed to substantial changes. A surge of unionization has taken place in the public sector. Between 1966 and 1976 the American Federation of Teachers and the American Federation of State, County, and Municipal Employees increased their membership by 257 and 167 percent, respectively. (Their memberships are approximately 500,000 and 1,000,000.) The National Education Association, which like the Teamsters is not affiliated with the AFL-CIO, has a membership of 1,800,000.

Despite all this, there continues to be controversy about collective bargaining in the public sector and about whether the growth of such bargaining ought to be protected by a labor law similiar in content to the National Labor Relations Act. One major argument against the applicability of private-sector labor law to the public sector is that the economics are different. It has been contended that the private sector is based on a market economy that has no applicability to the public sector (the Taylor Report,[20] which was written in advance of New York's labor legislation, expounded this theme). Proponents of this theory have stated that the constraints in the public sector are political; as noted above, the argument is that those who make the decisions to levy taxes and raise revenues are penalized or rewarded through the democratic process. Very much related to this argument is the fact that the employment-benefit relationship or tradeoff that exists in the private sector is not present in the public sector. In the private sector, trade unions are restrained from making wage demands because of the discipline of the market (the loss of jobs that would be attributable to increased benefits and to the flow of work to nonunionized employers). Also, as employers are confronted with higher labor costs they have a greater inducement to automate. Third, it is contended that public employers have less of a monopsony power than private employers because employees (particularly in cities) are able to compete effectively for employment in both public and private sectors.[21] Accordingly, proceeds this argument, public employees have more strength than their private-sector counterparts in dealing with employers. Fourth, it is argued that public employees are in a superior position because of Civil Service legislation, which traditionally has provided a much greater measure of job security than was available with unionized or nonunionized private employers. However, the security enjoyed by the public sector has been undermined recently by two factors. One is the emergence of arbitration clauses, which protect private employees against dismissal and discipline except where the employer has just cause for imposing the penalty. The second is that since the early 1970s public employers have been all too willing to respond as most private employers do when confronted with increased economic demands: by laying off workers to reduce the budget. To some extent this undercuts the argument that market forces do not come into play in the public sector. Moreover, the tendency of many employers to contract out work previously performed by public employees resembles the behavior in the private sector. Many public employers have begun to contract out garbage collection, just as private employers have contracted out janitorial services.[22]

In the public sector, those who bargain with the unions—the executive branch of the government—must rely on appropriations committees in the legislative branch to implement any arrangements that are made. (This problem does not exist at the federal level, because federal public-employee unions still may not bargain about wages.) In collective bargaining it is generally desirable, if not vital, for the parties representing each side to be able to speak with authority for their constituents. Inasmuch as the public employers are fragmented, this poses practical problems in connection with collective bargaining in the public sector and makes the process more difficult.

Another difference between the public and private sectors is that the line between supervisory and other employees is more confused than it is in the private sector. One of the direct results of this confusion is that there is more of a demand for supervisory unions and sometimes for unions that include supervisory and other employees under the same umbrella.[23] This causes problems for employers relating to the loyalty of employees who in the private sector might be regarded as management or lower-level management.

The most frequently cited difference between private and public sectors is that unions in the public sector can bring pressure on their employers through the political process. It is certainly true that in recent years some unions (particularly in New York state, where 13 of 39 bills sponsored by public sector unions in 1977 were attempts by labor to gain what it has failed to obtain at the bargaining table) have frequently used legislatures to obtain, for instance, increases in pension benefits that were under negotiation at the bargaining table. The argument is that the public employer is put at a disadvantage with respect to the public employees' union in a way that does not exist in the private sector. However, it must be said that private employees' unions also may (and often try to) improve their economic benefits through legislative activity. Private-sector unions are also deeply involved in the American political process.

Many of the issues raised at the bargaining table by public employees' unions affect the public as well as the workers. A union's demand that police officers confronted with discipline or discharge be exempted from appearing before a public review board might be viewed very differently by union leaders and by black and Hispanic leaders in New York, Chicago, or San Francisco. The same is true of demands made by teachers' unions about curriculum content. This is not to suggest that such matters are inappropriate for the bargaining table. But matters such as these and whether Detroit police should be required to live in that city,[24] and whether San Jose police can wear firearms,[25] raise issues that obviously affect the public directly and therefore must be considered away from the negotiating table. At the same time, however, traditional issues such as the entitlement of federal employees to expenses incurred in negotiations under the Civil Service Reform Act have prompted the Court to note that, although "Congress unquestionably intended to strengthen the position of federal unions and to make the collective bargaining process a more effective instrument of the public interest than it had been under the Executive Order regime,"[26] the basic assumption about an adversarial relationship applies to the public sector as well as the private sector.

The most difficult public-sector issue in the United States relates to whether public employees should have the right to strike. The federal government and most of the states prohibit striking by common law or statute. However, an increasing minority of jurisdictions (Hawaii, Pennsylvania, Vermont, Alaska, and Minnesota have been the leaders) have permitted a limited right to strike to be incorporated into statute.[27] These statutes generally permit workers other than police, firefighters, and prison guards to strike, sometimes only after the utilization of impasse procedures designed to resolve disputes over new contract terms. And the Supreme Court of California has articulated the following standard: ". . . strikes by public employees are not unlawful at common law unless or until it is clearly demonstrated that such a strike creates a substantial and imminent threat to the health and safety of the public." "This standard," said the Court "allows exceptions in certain essential areas of public employment (e.g. the prohibitions against firefighters and law enforcement personnel) and also requires the courts to determine on a case-by-case basis whether the public interest overrides the basic right to strike."[28]

The argument on behalf of public-sector striking is that it is impossible for the collective bargaining process to operate without the possibility of strikes. Unless the employer faces the prospect of inconvenience or injury, there is no inducement to compromise or negotiate seriously about wages, hours, and working conditions. Moreover, it is pointed out that the line between the private and the public sector is a difficult one to draw sharply. For instance, during the 1966 transit strike in New York, public employees on one bus line were prohibited from striking by state labor legislation but employees on another line, operating on nearby streets, were protected in their right to strike because they were employed by private operators or public utilities covered by the NLRA. It is anomalous and inequitable to impose different rules on employees performing the same tasks in connection with an issue so vital to employees and the employer.

One argument that cuts in the other direction is that the line between the industries that are essential (where strikes should be prohibited) and those that are not (where strikes should be allowed) is difficult to draw. Most observers seem to accept the view that police and firefighters should not have the right to strike, but there is little consensus about other jobs. There is considerable controversy about the propriety of strikes in public education. Does it affect the health and security of the community for teachers to strike? Most would say that a few days lost from school would not matter much, but what if a strike goes on longer? Generally, the longer children are home from school, the more parents begin to perceive school services as essential, independent of the value of education. The fact that often both parents are working would seem to increase their concern about teachers' strikes.

Another problem is that where one group of workers has another process by which to resolve a dispute, such as compulsory arbitration, a generous award may have the effect of eating up all revenues available for wage increases for others. Indeed, there are many instances where a generous arbitration award has encouraged strikes by workers forbidden to strike.

The opponents of the right to strike for public employees often state that when one draws a line between essential and nonessential services, one is basically granting the right to strike where it would not hurt the employer and prohibiting it where it would. For example, since lawn care is a nonessential service, the gardener who mows the governor's lawn should be able to assert the right to strike.[29] But doesn't this simply give the worker the strike weapon when he has no muscle and therefore cannot make adequate use of it?

Opponents of the right to strike for public employees have also focused on the fact that public-sector labor relations, particularly at the municipal level, involve a number of different unions. Generally, multiunion industries are "sick" industries in terms of industrial relations. Classic examples of this proposition outside the public sector are the newspaper, printing, and maritime industries. If a right to strike is granted to one union, how will other unions that are prohibited from striking react to picket lines in front of a municipal government's facilities? In the United States there is a long-standing tradition for workers to refuse to cross a picket line. Will not the right to strike for certain employees produce, at least under certain circumstances, general strikes?

The biggest argument for the right to strike in the public sector is that strikes are taking place. Hardly a month passes without a strike or another form of economic pressure in the public sector in some state. In effect, granting the right to strike on a limited basis would bring the law into accord with reality. The right to strike exists on a *de facto* basis. Under the present circumstances the imposition of fines and contempt penalties on strikers may produce a lack of respect for law and the judiciary. There is already considerable evidence of judicial reluctance to declare strikes unlawful, even where statute or common law makes them so. Even decertification, employed against the air traffic controllers as a penalty for their unlawful strike in 1981, does not always work.

The debate has shifted to substitutes for striking. Foremost among these is fact finding. The supposed virtue of fact finding is that a judicial-type proceeding is established that issues a formal report with recommendations. The theory is that the unreasonable party will have the weight of public pressure against it and will yield or modify its position. This is said to be especially true in the public sector, where parties are presumably more sensitive to those who pay taxes and cast votes.

A substantial number of jurisdictions provide for fact finding, and indeed this is now one of the options made available in the federal sector.[30] But fact finding has not always worked out as well as anticipated. Even though the resolution of public-employee disputes is the public's business and one could therefore assume that the public would be interested in the report, it is often said that little attention is given to the report by the news media. Thus, the opportunity to galvanize support for the recommendations and place pressure on the resisting party is minimized. Moreover, rather than moving one of the parties to a different position, the report often hardens the parties' positions and makes it less likely that they will be able to resolve their dispute. (This seems to run contrary to the concerns that Senator Taft expressed in the Taft-Hartley amendments.) Once the report has been issued, the party that perceives itself as the winning one will take no less than what the report provides for. Quite frequently, the party that has lost and is excoriated by the fact finders simply hardens its own position. As the debate becomes more public, the parties begin to posture for their respective audiences and constituencies.[31]

Finally, fact finding does not provide for finality. A binding arbitration award permits a dispute to go on after the procedures have been exhausted. This, as well as other factors, has induced an increasing number of jurisdictions to adopt compulsory-arbitration provisions in the public sector.

11

Public-Interest Labor Law

Three developments since the advent of modern labor legislation that are important to workers, unions, and employers, although they do not directly involve the balance of power between unions and their members, are the Employee Retirement Income Security Act (ERISA), the Occupational Safety and Health Act of 1970, and employment-discrimination law (especially title VII of the Civil Rights Act of 1964).

The Employee Retirement Income Security Act

ERISA is the first comprehensive pension labor law enacted by Congress, although section 302(c)(5) of the National Labor Relations Act provides for the establishment of financial trust funds for the benefit of employees.[1] ERISA does not require the establishment of a pension plan, but it does require disclosure and reporting of financial and other information through the establishment of standards of "conduct, responsibility, and obligation for fiduciaries of employee benefit plans."[2] It is administered by the Department of Labor and the Internal Revenue Service. The full extent of coverage and protection under the statute is beyond the scope of this chapter, but some of its elements should be mentioned.

ERISA established mandatory vesting requirements for workers so that they receive some entitlement to pension funds before they reach retirement age. Additionally, it restricts a plan's power to deprive a union member of all prior service that may be unvested. ERISA does not provide for the transferability of pensions from one company to another (often referred to as "portability"). This is a particularly important deficiency, given the mobility of the American worker. However, in the Multiemployer Pension Plan Amendment Act of 1980, amending ERISA, Congress strengthened the solvency and stability of multiemployer pension funds by circumscribing employers' withdrawals from them.[3]

ERISA provides that all "nonforfeitable" benefits must be paid. In *Nachman* v. *Pension Benefit Guaranty Corp.*[4] a majority of the Supreme Court held that a plan that imposed no condition on the benefits to be paid created vested benefits in the event of a plant closure. However, the Court has held that the level of benefit offsets attributable to an employee's receipt of a worker's compensation award is "forfeitable."[5] In the same case, the Court held that state law that is inconsistent with ERISA on the issue of level of benefit and offset is preempted by the federal statute.

The Occupational Safety and Health Act

The Occupational Safety and Health Act of 1970 was enacted, as the Supreme Court has said, "for the purpose of ensuring safe and healthful working conditions for every working man and woman in the nation."[6] The Supreme Court has held that the Secretary of Labor, in fashioning regulations dealing with particular toxic materials or harmful physical agents, must show that an exposure limit is "reasonably necessary or appropriate to provide safe and healthful employment."[7] But a major problem to be hammered out in the courts during the coming years is how significant a risk must be to warrant regulation under this act. The Court has stated that the statute does not guarantee a risk-free workplace,[8] but the Occupational Safety and Health Administration (OSHA) has not taken that position. Even though the risks are often uncertain because of lack of scientific evidence, OSHA must provide some explanation for its determination that regulation is necessary.

A critical issue involved in the interpretation of the statute is whether "the Secretary of Labor is required to balance the benefits to the workers against the cost of the required charges to the employer."[9] OSHA has always taken the position that costs must be taken into account as regulations are formulated. But although OSHA has appropriately regarded the requirements of economic feasibility as a barrier to the imposition of a cost burden that would cripple or eliminate an industry, the disproportionate burden on particular plants that may be older, smaller, or less competitive cannot be equated with infeasibility. The Court of Appeals for the District of Columbia has said that "even if a few firms are forced to shut down, the standard is not necessarily economically infeasible."[10] On another occasion the same court said the following: "It would appear to be consistent with the purpose of the Act to envisage the economic demise of an employer who has lagged behind the rest of the industry in protecting the health and safety of employees and is consequently financially unable to comply with new standards as quickly as other employers."[11] And in 1981 the Supreme Court, by a 5–3 vote, held in the "Brown lung" case[12] that a cost-benefit analysis is not contemplated by the statute. Said Justice Brennan, writing for the majority: "Congress itself defined the basic relationship between costs and benefits by placing the 'benefit' of worker health above all other considerations save those making attainment of this 'benefit' unachievable. Any standard based on a balancing of costs and benefits by the

Secretary that strikes a different balance than that struck by Congress would be inconsistent with the command set forth [in statutory provisions]. Thus, cost-benefit analysis by OSHA is not required by the statute because feasibility analysis is."[13]

The problems of enforcing the Occupational Safety and Health Act are considerable. The Secretary of Labor cannot unilaterally shut down a plant when the operations are unsafe or hazardous to workers.[14] Where an employer resists on-site inspection, the Supreme Court has held that the Constitution requires the Secretary of Labor to obtain a warrant before an inspection;[15] this provides the opportunity for a coverup. The Secretary of Labor has argued unsuccessfully that a worker has the implied right to enforce the statute through a lawsuit because the government cannot cope with the large number of complaints that have been filed.[16]

Ordinarily the penalty for a violation of the statute is $1,000, but in the case of "nonserious" violations a penalty is discretionary. In the case of willful or repeated violations the penalty can go up to $10,000, but the courts are divided on the question of what number of infractions constitutes repetition and on whether a serious infraction must be both repeated and willful.[17]

What can workers do for themselves with regard to health and safety? Under the National Labor Relations Act, workers have the right to engage in walkouts aimed at protesting conditions they deem unsafe.[18] A walkout triggered by conditions that can be objectively characterized as abnormally dangerous cannot violate a union-negotiated no-strike clause in a labor contract.[19] And the Court approved interpretive regulations put forth by Secretary of Labor Ray Marshall that permit workers to refuse to work where the employee is ordered by his employer to work under conditions that the employee reasonably believes pose an imminent risk of death or serious bodily injury and where the employee has reason to believe that there is not sufficient time or opportunity either to seek effective redress from his employer or to apprise OSHA of the danger.[20] A proposal that pay be provided to employees on strike under such circumstances was rejected by Congress.[21]

Employment-Discrimination Law

Probably the most litigated area of "public-interest labor law" is employment discrimination. The most comprehensive legislation is title VII of the Civil Rights Act of 1964, which established the Equal Employment Opportunity Commission and which prohibits discrimination in employment on account of race, color, sex, national origin, or religion.

The EEOC, initially provided with authority to investigate and to attempt to conciliate allegations of discrimination, has since 1972 had the power to sue defendants in federal district court for alleged discrimination subsequent to resort to the administrative process.[22] It now has jurisdiction and authority over virtually every kind of discrimination in employment.[23]

Although the EEOC (and the Justice Department for the public sector) has responsibility for most employment-discrimination problems arising under title VII and related civil-rights legislation, private plaintiffs have carried the primary burden of law enforcement—particularly in the early days of litigation, before the EEOC had authority to sue in the courts to establish violations and provide for relief.

Proving Discrimination

The courts have held that statistics showing the absence or disproportionate exclusion of minority members or women from a plant or a job classification establish a *prima facie* case of discrimination.[24] This puts the burden on the other side to explain why there are so few of a group that alleges discrimination. Statistics may be used in class actions, in which a liability is established for large numbers of people throughout the plant or enterprise, or in individual suits, where one or a relatively small number of workers seeks to show discrimination.[25]

Probably the most important case in this field is *Griggs* v. *Duke Power Co.*,[26] in which a unanimous Supreme Court held that it is not necessary to show an intent to discriminate in order to prove a violation of employment-discrimination law. In *Griggs*, the employer's written examinations and educational requirements had the effect of making it impossible for the blacks in a plant to have upward mobility. A disproportionate exclusion, unless justified by a business necessity for the procedure, was found to establish a violation of law.[27] This decision, which had not been fully applied to the employment-discrimination disputes in the public sector[28] (or, indeed, to other anti-discrimination statutes in the private sector[29]), has had enormous implications for the development of law in this area. For instance, although title VII allows employers to apply "bona fide occupational qualifications" in denying one sex access to a job, the Supreme Court has held height and weight qualifications that disproportionately exclude women from being prison guards invalid on the ground that this allowance was meant to be "an extremely narrow exception to" the statute's broad prohibitions against sex discrimination.[30] In age-discrimination cases, where the bona fide occupational qualification process is also applicable, the Court has said the following:

The restrictive language of the statute, and the consistent interpretation of the administrative agencies charged with enforcing the statute convince us that, like its Title VII counterpart, the BFOQ exception was in fact meant to be an extremely narrow exception to the general prohibition of age discrimination. . . ."[31]

In individual cases in which allegations of intentionally disparate treatment are made, a *prima facie* for discrimination is relatively easy to establish[32] but the burden of rebuttal for the defendant is far less burdensome than for the defendant in a *Griggs* case, who must prove business necessity.[33] The Court of Appeals for the Eleventh Circuit has held that an employer rebuttal based upon subjective evidence imposed a burden more substantial than would otherwise be applicable.[34] The same holds true where the *prima facie* case of discrimination consists of direct evidence of discrimination, not an inference.[35] Thus, in individual cases of discrimination the ultimate burden is on the plaintiff to show that the employer-defendant's conduct was a "pretext" for discrimination. The courts have been divided as to whether defense evidence that the employer would have taken the same action against the employee for legitimate reasons despite the fact that discrimination was a factor permits the employer to escape liability.[36] The Eighth Circuit Court has held that, where unlawful motive "played some part in the employment decision or decisional process,"

the plaintiff is entitled to some relief, including, as appropriate, a declaratory judgment, partial attorney's fees, and injunctive relief against future or continued discrimination. However, even after a finding of unlawful discrimination is made ... the defendant may avoid an award of reinstatement or promotion and back pay if it can prove by a preponderance of the evidence that the plaintiff would not have been hired or promoted even in the absence of the proven discrimination."[36a]

Bona Fide Seniority Systems

Another defense against discriminatory conduct relates to the existence of bona fide seniority systems, which if negotiated by an employer and a union are not rendered violative of the anti-discrimination provisions of title VII. But what constitutes a bona fide seniority system? Initially, the appellate courts (at the level immediately below the U.S. Supreme Court) held that the seniority systems that were neutral and nondiscriminatory on their face violated the statute when they carried forward the effects of past discrimination—even discrimination that antedated the effective date of the statute, July 2, 1965. That is, where blacks, Mexican-Americans, or women had been locked into low-level jobs through discriminatory hiring patterns, or through departmental seniority systems that have made it impossible for employees to bid for available high-level jobs on the basis of seniority accumulated in low-level jobs, past discrimination embodied within the present system had effectively thwarted their upward mobility.

However, in a 7–2 vote the Supreme Court held in *International Brotherhood of Teamsters* v. *The United States*[37] that pre-July 2, 1965 conduct could not be remedied under any circumstances and that seniority credits based on time spent in low-level jobs during that period could not be accorded to minorities or women. More significantly, employees who have been frozen into low-level jobs must establish that they have been discriminated against as individuals even subsequent to a finding of liability against the employer or the labor organization for a pattern of across-the-board discrimination. Although employees who have filed applications for vacant jobs under such circumstances are presumed to have been discriminated against, and the defendant carries the burden of establishing that there was no discrimination, proceedings to determine whether individuals are entitled to seniority and back pay before either a judge or a specially appointed master can consume a considerable amount of time. Hundreds and sometimes thousands of employees or applicants may be involved.[38] As a practical matter, once liability is established in a pattern- or practice-of-discrimination case, there is a tremendous incentive for the plaintiff to settle. Plaintiffs in employment-discrimination cases do not generally have the resources (financial and otherwise) possessed by the defendants, and settlements all too often provide them with less than they would be entitled to in adjudicated proceedings.

Sex Discrimination

Although the pressure for the passage of fair-employment-practices legislation emerged from the struggle for the rights of blacks, concern with sex discrimination (which almost inadvertently found its way into the language of title VII[39]) has increased considerably since the late 1970s. Except in cases involving a failure to provide equal pay for equal work—a practice prohibited by the Equal Pay Act of 1963[40]—women are exclusively reliant on title VII, on state fair-employment-practices statutes (which often mirror the federal statute), and on an Executive Order that not only prohibits discrimination by government contractors but explicitly requires affirmative action in recruitment and promotion without the necessity of finding discrimination.[41] Reconstruction legislation, the most prominent of which is the Civil Rights Act of 1866,[42] prohibits discrimination on the basis of race in addition to title VII. The significance of this is that women, unlike blacks, must meet some of the procedural statutory requirements contained in title VII (such as the finding that the employer-defendant is involved in interstate commerce, or the filing of an administrative charge within 180 days) if they do not choose to rely exclusively on an executive order or a state statute.[43]

Sex-discrimination cases present other problems not posed by racial cases. For instance, the Supreme Court was called upon to determine whether an all-inclusive disability benefits plan that failed to include pregnancy-related disabilities violated the statute. A majority of the Court answered in the negative,[44] but Congress reversed this judgment through new legislation in 1978.[45] Subsequent to the 1978 statute, the Court held that an employer's health-insurance plan that covered medical expenses of employees' spouses but limited pregnancy-related expenses of male employees' spouses discriminated against male workers, in violation of title VII.[46] The Court has held that requiring women to make larger pension contributions because actuarily as a group they live longer is violative of title VII. The Court conceded that women as a group may be subsidized without such a requirement,[47] but emphasized that with one many women would be discriminated against. Using the same reasoning, the Court has held that retirement benefits offered employees from one of a number of insurance companies requiring sex-based differentials in contributions are unlawful when they too are based on actuarial tables.[48] However, the Court also concluded that benefits derived from contributions made prior to the date of the decision (July 6, 1983) could be calculated on the basis of the previous sex-discriminatory insurance terms.

Another major issue is that raised by "sex plus" cases (cases involving issues associated with sex). The most prominent of these is *Martin-Marietta*,[49] in which an employer had refused to employ women who had pre-school-age children but had not imposed the same condition on men. In *Martin-Marietta* the Supreme Court held that the imposition of a dual standard for men and women is discriminatory under title VII. However, disparate standards for men and women based on other considerations, such as grooming or length of hair, have generally not been viewed as unlawful.[50] The Court of Appeals for the Fifth Circuit held that an employer may properly require English-speaking Mexican-Americans not to speak Spanish in front of customers whose primary language is English, even though there is testimony that this policy reflected the societal discrimination against Mexican-Americans in this country.[51] This case is similiar to the "sex plus" cases in that it tends to make possible harm or ostracism of one group although the policy is not based on immutable characteristics such as race, sex, and national origin.

Two developing areas in sex-discrimination law are sexual harassment and comparable worth. Sexual-harassment cases involve situations where supervisors or superiors (generally male) require sexual favors as a condition of employment or maintain a work environment in which women are made to feel ostracized for reasons having to do with sex. A number of courts have found this (generally the former conduct) to be unlawful sex discrimination.[52] The comparable-worth cases are the sleeping giant of sex discrimination. Plaintiffs seek to impose liability on the basis of discriminatory wage differentials where the work is not equal or similiar but where the wage gap between male and female employees is discriminatory. The Supreme Court, by a 5–4 vote, has taken a tentative step in this direction by interdicting intentional wage discrimination.[53] Noting that plaintiffs alleged that women were not paid in accordance with their job evaluations whereas men were, Justice Brennan, writing for the majority, stated the following:

[The suit] does not require a court to make its own subjective assessment of the value of male and female guard jobs, to attempt by statistical technique or other methods to quantify the effect of sex discrimination on the wage rates.

We do not decide in this case the precise contours of lawsuits challenging sex discrimination in compensation under title VII. It is sufficient to note that [the] claims of discriminatory undercompensation are not barred . . . merely because [the women] do not perform work equal to that of the male jail guards.[54]

Accommodations of Handicaps and Religious Observances

Another question arising under title VII relates to religious discrimination and the extent to which employees can be required to work during a period of time when their religion forbids work. A majority of the Supreme Court has held that the imposition of more than a *de minimus* cost upon an employer under such circumstances does not make out a violation of title VII.[55] Specifically, it found that the proviso in the 1972 amendments to title VII that requires an employer to accommodate employees' religious observances or practices "without undue hardship on the conduct of the employer's business" is not violated under such circumstances.

Similarly, accommodations must be made to physical and mental handicaps under the government's contract-compliance program, which is administered (as are all such efforts) by the Department of Labor's Office of Federal Contract Compliance Programs and is pursuant to the Rehabilitation Act of 1973.[56] The difficulty here is how to balance the plight of the handicapped against the very considerable costs of wheelchair ramps and the like.

Age Discrimination

The Age Discrimination in Employment Act of 1967,[57] over which the EEOC also has jurisdiction now, prohibits discrimination against workers between 40 and 70 on account of age. Either the EEOC or private plaintiffs may bring an action for damages suffered, and for additional monies if the violation was "willful." Except for executives in high policy positions and university faculty members, retirement programs that force retirement before 70 are unlawful.[58] Nineteen states have banned mandatory retirement altogether, and there is debate about the desirability of federal legislation of a similar nature. A difficulty here is that age, like handicaps, affects the ability of some people to function. But according to *Business Week*, "few [employees] complained about incompetent old workers, and only a small fraction of older people have opted to keep working anyway."[59]

The most formidable problem in employment-discrimination cases is that of remedies. The Supreme Court held in *Albe-marle Paper Co.* v. *Moody*[60] that once liability is established by virtue of a class action or government-initiated pattern-of-practice employment-discrimination case, the presumption is that back pay and other forms of equitable relief are to be awarded.[61] The courts have held that punitive and apparently compensatory damages cannot be awarded under title VII,[62] but the Supreme Court has stated *in dicta* that punitive damages are awardable under the Civil Rights Act of 1866,[63] and a number of circuit courts have so held.[64]

The rationale for damage awards is not simply compensation but also the fact that they have a prophylactic effect on illegal conduct and wrongdoing. Employers and labor organizations confronted with employment-discrimination litigation began to have a very serious incentive to remedy the problem once federal courts held that class actions on this issue involving large numbers of workers could be maintained in federal courts and that back pay was to be awarded. At that point, defendants became quite interested in settling litigation and obtaining waivers against future damage claims. (The latter practice has given rise to considerable litigation to determine whether the individuals solicited have knowingly and voluntarily waived their right to sue.[65])

The appellate courts have held uniformly that quotas or goals for the hiring and promotion of minority and female employees—perhaps the most controversial of employment-discrimination remedies—are appropriate under the litigation in this area.[66] The federal and state governments have imposed such requirements on government contracts.[67] The Supreme Court's important *Bakke* decision indicated that some forms of race-conscious remedies for past discrimination are appropriate, but did not say much more.[68] The Court held in the *Weber* case[69] that voluntarily negotiated affirmative-action programs in the private sector[70] that include quotas are compatible with civil-rights legislation. It has yet to pass on the question of whether courts and the government may impose such quotas. The Court has invalidated a consent decree, agreed upon by parties to litigation, that modified a bona fide seniority system[71]:

> Here, the District Court itself found that the layoff proposal [last hired, first fired] was not adopted with the purpose or intent to discriminate on the basis of race, nor had the [employer] . . . in agreeing to the decree admitted in any way that it had engaged in intentional discrimination.[72]

If the Supreme Court were to expand its ruling and distinguish between judicially and governmentally imposed programs and voluntarily negotiated ones, like those in *Weber*, the latter would soon disappear, inasmuch as he main incentive for voluntary plans has been the prospect of litigation, damages, and the imposition of quotas.

The precise scope of the Court's holding is unclear at this writing, although it can be said that the Court stressed the existence of a bona fide seniority system, the absence of proof of discrimination, and the fact that the consent decree did not identify any specific employee entitled to "particular relief."

Wrongful Discharge

American common law has traditionally recognized that employment relationships are terminable at the will of either party, absent a contractual commitment to the contrary.[73] Several federal and state statutes referred to earlier have limited the applicability of this doctrine, protecting employees from discharge because of race, religion, sex, national origin, age, or union activity.

Despite these protections, employers, until very recently, had considerable freedom in deciding whether or not to discharge a nonunion employee. Since the late 1970s, however, an increasing number of jurisdictions have recognized a cause of action for wrongful discharge or termination. The state courts, rather than the legislatures, are responsible for this development. Representative of the reasoning that has imposed implied contractual obligations upon employers in their dealings with individual employees is that of the New Jersey Supreme Court in 1985:

Our courts will not allow an employer to offer attractive inducements and benefits to the workforce and then withdraw them when it chooses, no matter how sincere its belief that they are not enforceable. . . . Job security is the assurance that one's livelihood, one's family future will not be destroyed arbitrarily; it can be cut off only "for good cause," fairly determined. Hoffman–La Roche's commitment here was to what working men and women engaged as their most basic advance. It was a commitment that gave workers protection against arbitrary termination.[74]

A cause of action for wrongful termination does not rest only on contractual theories. It is based on any of three exceptions to the doctrine of employment at will:

• discharges that are contrary to public policy—i.e., dismissals instituted because the employee refuses to act unlawfully, or because the employee performs a public obligation (such as serving on a jury), or in retaliation for the exercises of statutory right (such as free speech),[75]
• discharges that breach implied contract of employment arising from a handbook, a policy, or some other representation,[76] and
• discharges that breach an implied covenant of good faith and fair dealing.[77]

Through 1984, some 26 states have adopted the public-policy exception to the doctrine of employment at will,[78] 26 have held that binding contracts of employment are implied by handbooks and other representations,[79] and 7 have recognized an implied covenant of good faith and fair dealing.[80]

California courts have been the most active in applying these exceptions. In *Tameny* v. *Atlantic Richfield* [81] the California Supreme Court held that an employer "contravene[d] the dictates of public policy" when he discharged an employee for refusing to take part in a price-fixing conspiracy. In *Pugh* v. *See's Candies*,[82] an appellate court found that an employer had made an implied promise not to terminate an employee, based on the duration of the employee's employment, his promotions and commendations, assurances he received from the employer, and the employer's acknowledged personnel policies. Finally, in *Cleary* v. *American Airlines*,[83] an appellate court found that an employee was protected by a covenant of good faith and fair dealing implied by his longevity of service, and that the employer had failed to adhere to specific procedures for adjudicating employment disputes.

Another development in this area relates to the relationship between wrongful-discharge litigation and grievance-arbitration machinery in collective bargaining agreements. The Court of Appeals for the Ninth Circuit in San Francisco and at least three state supreme courts have held that such actions may be initiated despite the availability of procedures in a collective agreement.[84] This is an area of law in which there will be disputes and litigation.

Finally, there has been much discussion about legislation that would provide the employee with more access to a tribunal and, since punitive as well as compensatory damages are available in the public policy and some of the contract cases, would limit the employer's liability. Some states have enacted legislation protecting "whistle blowers,"[85] but no state has enacted comprehensive legislation dealing with unfair dismissal[86].

Conclusion

Pensions, health and safety, employment discrimination, and wrongful-discharge litigation have become the new frontier of labor law. Unlike the law relating to labor-management relations (principally the National Labor Relations Act), they directly affect the substantive terms of the employment relationship. More legislation and case law in this area promises to be with us in the future. It is possible that it will dwarf more traditional labor law before the turn of the century.

12

Conclusion

The system of American labor law and industrial relations
has strengths and deficiencies. Because American society is litigious and dynamic, and because labor law will evolve and
change in the coming years, the deficiencies may receive
greater attention. The area of public-interest labor law will
continue to grow rapidly. It may be that the legal struggle
against discrimination will convince the courts and legislatures
that protection against arbitrary treatment by employers for
all workers is good policy and good law.[1] The difficulty thus
far has been that neither labor nor business has had an adequate incentive to promote legal safeguards for unorganized
workers who are not protected by union-negotiated collective
bargaining agreements.

More changes may result from the willingness of unions to
accept seats on corporate boards, as has been done in the
automobile industry. This is bound to promote reexamination
of the adversary-relationship model so uncritically accepted
by both labor and management in this country—the view expressed by the Supreme Court in *Insurance Agents* that collective bargaining is not some "academic search for truth."[2] The
current economic climate, inextricably linked as it is to the

scarcity of and uncertainty about critical resources, may focus American attention on means of achieving cooperation as an adjunct to, if not a substitute for, conflict. The success of West Germany and Japan in this area may be of interest to Americans.

The search for cooperation will bring attempts to apply the experience gained in grievance arbitration to interest disputes about new contract terms. The controversy about public-sector striking has encouraged such efforts. It is quite possible that the developments in the public sector will have substantial impact on the private sector.

Finally, one must take note of an important matter that has not been discussed in this book at all: incomes policy. The decentralized nature of the American system makes any incomes policy, voluntary or otherwise, difficult to administer. It would be particularly arduous to implement such policies through national legislation, for local unions are in the cockpit in most wage negotiations. Although a number of industrial unions negotiate national pacts, decentralization places incomes policy in a totally different perspective than in the European countries, which suffer from "wage drift" (the increase of payments above nationally negotiated norms). It is difficult enough for the international unions of the United States (let alone the AFL-CIO, which has been the principal party to debates and discussions on the subject since the early 1970s) to deliver any bargain or social contract, because of their remoteness from wage negotiations. Moreover, the decline of unions means that a wage explosion is not an issue as of this writing. But this is an issue that will not go away. Productivity problems, increased unit labor costs, inflation, and the need to be competitive internationally mean that proposals to deescalate leapfrogging wage demands—particularly in declining industries—will continue to be made.[3]

The purpose here has been to describe the labor-law system briefly and clearly, with some reference to the pattern of industrial relations. One hopes that this will further understanding among workers, unions, business, and government, and that this, in turn, will promote—in the spirit of the law—a working environment in which the standard of living will be improved and industrial peace fostered.

Notes

Preface

1. W. Gould, "Mistaken Opposition to the NLRB," *New York Times*, June 20, 1985, p. 31, col. 2

2. This took the form of an AFL-CIO report, "The Changing Situation of Workers and Their Unions: A Report by the AFL-CIO Committee on the Evolution of Work" (February, 1985). See W. Gould, "Labor Takes Look at Itself, Finds Unsettling Things," *Los Angeles Times*, March 29, 1985, part II, p. 7, col. 1.

Chapter 1

1. *American Can Co.*, 13 NLRB 1252 (1939).

2. Edw. 7, c. 47.

3. Norris-LaGuardia Act, Mar. 23, 1932, c. 90, 47 Stat. 70 (1932), 29 U.S.C. §§ 101-15 (1970).

4. T. C. Johnston, *Collective Bargaining in Sweden* (1962).

5. Works Constitution Act of 1952, Bundesgesetzblatt, Teil I, 681.

6. The 1974 percentage of union members in the nonagricultural work force was 27.6 in the United States and 50.4 in Great Britain. In Japan the percentage of union members was 34.5 in 1975 but declined to 30.5 in 1982. See generally J. Dunlop and W. Galenson, *Labor in the Twentieth Century* (1978). As of 1978, the American percentage had declined to 23.6 (U.S. Bureau of Labor Statistics, Directory of National Unions and Employee Associations, 1971, 1977, and 1979). In 1980, the American percentage declined

again to 20.9. William Serrin, "Union Membership Falls Sharply; Decline Expected to Be Permanent," *New York Times*, May 31, 1983, p. 1, col. 1.

7. L. Sayles and G. Strauss, *The Local Union* (1953).

8. See "After 13 Years, Auto Union Joins AFL-CIO Again," *New York Times*, July 2, 1981, p. 8.

9. S. Perlman, *A Theory of Labor Movement* (1928).

10. *Tameny* v. *The Atlantic Richfield Co.*, 27 Cal. 3d 167 (1980).

11. See generally "Protecting At Will Employees Against Wrongful Discharge: The Duty to Terminate Only in Good Faith" (comment), 93 Harv. L. Rev. 1816 (1980); "Implied Contract Rights to Job Security" (note), 26 Stan. L. Rev. 335 (1974); C. Summers, "Individual Protection Against Unjust Dismissal: Time For A Statute," 62 Va. L. Rev. 481 (1976).

12. Four states have plant-closing legislation: Connecticut Gen. Stat. Annot. Title 31, Sec. 31-51(n)(o) enacted 1983 eff. 7-1-83; Maine Rev. Stat. Annot. Title 26, Sec. 625-B (1979) as last amended eff. 1981; Massachusetts Annot. Law. Ch. 151A, Sec. 71A enacted 1984 eff. 1-1-85; Wisconsin Stat. Annot. Sec. 109.07(1)(2)(1975) as last amended eff. 3-14-84. Bureau of National Affairs, State Labor Laws (1984).

13. See generally W. Gould, *Japan's Reshaping of American Labor Law* (1984), pp. 94–116.

14. See Forty-sixth Annual Report of NLRB, Fiscal Year 1979, in *Labor Relations Yearbook* (BNA) (1983). Figures for the years 1960–1976 are collected in H.R. Rep. No. 95-637, 95th Cong., 1st Sess. 26 (1977) (chart 3). A four-year decline in the case load now appears to have reversed. See Shinoff, "The NLRB Tests Labor and Vice Versa: Union Organizing and Federal Board's Case Load Both Increasing," *San Francisco Examiner*, December 12, 1985, p. A-7.

Chapter 2

1. See J. Commons, *Documentary History of American Society* (1910), vol. 3, p. 59.

2. 45 Mass. (4 Metc.) 111 (1942).

3. *Id.* at 129.

4. A. Cox, D. Bok, and R. Gorman, *Cases and Materials on Labor Law*, eighth edition (1976), p. 19.

5. *Vegelahn* v. *Gunter*, 167 Mass. 92, 44 N.E. 1077 (1896).

6. 44 N.E. at 1080.

7. *Id.*

8. *Id.* at 1081.

9. A. Rees, *The Economics of Trade Unions*, second edition (1977).

10. 26 Stat. 209 (1890), as amended 15 USC §§1–7 (1976).

11. 208 U.S. 274 (1908).

12. *Id.* at 301.

13. A. Mason, *Organized Labor and the Law* (1969), p. 170.

14. Clayton Antitrust Act §6, 38 Stat. 730 (1914), as amended 15 USC §§15, 17, 26 (1970), 29 USC §52 (1979).

15. S. Gompers, "The Charter of Industrial Freedom—Labor Provisions of the Clayton Anti-trust Law," 21 Federationist 971 (1914).

16. 254 U.S. 443 (1921).

17. *Id.* at 469.

18. *Id.* at 470.

19. *Id.*

20. *Id.* at 471.

21. *Id.* at 477, 478.

22. *Id.* at 481 (Brandeis, J. dissenting).

23. *Id.* at 482 (Brandeis, J. dissenting).

24. *Id.* at 484 (Brandeis, J. dissenting).

25. *Id.* at 488 (Brandeis, J. dissenting).

26. *Id.* (Brandeis, J. dissenting).

27. 268 U.S. 295 (1925).

28. F. Frankfurter and N. Greene, *The Labor Injunction* (1930), p. 201.

29. Norris-LaGuardia Act, 47 Stat. 70 (1932), 29 USC §101–15 (1970).

30. Norris-LaGuardia §13(c): "The term 'labor dispute' includes any controversy concerning terms or conditions of employment, or concerning the association or representation of persons in negotiating, fixing, maintaining, changing, or seeking to arrange terms or conditions of employment, regardless of whether or not the disputants stand in the proximate relation of employer and employee."

31. 312 U.S. 219, 231 (1941).

32. *Id.* at 235.

33. *Id.* at 232.

Chapter 3

1. 29 U.S.C. 20 *et seq.* (1976). As in *Jones & Laughlin*, with regard to the NLRA the Court upheld the constitutionality of the FLSA in *United States* v. *Darby*, 312 U.S. 100 (1941). Initially, however, the Court held that the FLSA could not be applied constitutionally to state and local governments in *National League of Cities* v. *Usery*, 426 U.S. 833 (1976). But the Court has reversed that decision by 5–4 vote in *Garcia* v. *San Antonio Metropolitan Transit Authority*, ___U.S.___, 105 S. Ct. 1005 (1985).

2. 40 U.S.C. §276a (1976).

3. 41 U.S.C. §§35–45 (1976).

4. 44 Stat. 577 (1926), as amended 45 U.S.C. §§151 *et seq.* (1976).

5. 48 Stat. 195 (1933).

6. *Schechter Poultry Corp.* v. *United States*, 295 U.S. 495 (1935).

7. 301 U.S. 1 (1937). For an excellent treatment of the early development of the NLRB see J. Gross, *The Making of the National Labor Relations Board: A Study in Economics, Politics and the Law*, vol. I (1974).

8. W. Galenson, *The CIO Challenge to the AFL* (1960).

9. L. Keyserling, "The Wagner Act: Its Origin and Current Significance," 29 Geo. Wash. L. Rev. 199 (1960).

10. *Textile Workers' Union* v. *Lincoln Mills*, 353 U.S. 448 (1957).

11. *United Steelworkers* v. *American Manufacturing Co.*, 363 U.S. 564 (1960); *United Steelworkers* v. *Warner & Gulf Navigation Co.*, 363 U.S. 574 (1960); *United Steelworkers* v. *Enterprise Wheel & Car Co.*, 363 U.S. 593 (1960); W. Gould, "On Labor Injunctions, Unions, and the Judges: The Boys Market Case," 1970 Supreme Court Rev. 215; B. Aaron, "Arbitration in the Federal Courts," 9 UCLA L. Rev. 360 (1962).

12. Section 8: "The Congress shall have Power . . . To regulate Commerce with foreign Nations, and among the several States, and with the Indian Tribes. . . . "

13. The occupation-of-the-field test is vividly exemplified in *Oregon-Washington Ry. & Nav. Co.* v. *Washington*, 270 U.S. 87 (1926). In this case, the Court struck down the Washington plant-quarantine regulation. Congress had precluded state action because a previous congressional statute on the same subject was of such immensity as to indicate the Congress intended to occupy the field. Cf. *Mintz* v. *Baldwin*, 289 U.S. 346 (1933), which upheld a New York statute on the grounds that congressional legislation was specific as to ground that it would not cover.

14. *San Diego Building Trades Council* v. *Garmon*, 359 U.S. 236, 245 (1959).

15. But there are exceptions: "It is true that we have allowed the States to grant compensation for the consequences, as defined by the traditional law of torts, of conduct marked by violence and imminent threats to the public order . . . ; *International Union, United Automobile, Aircraft and Agricultural Implement Workers, etc.* v. *Russell*, 356 U.S. 634, 78 S. Ct. 932, 2 L. Ed. 2d 1020: (b) *United Construction Workers* v. *Laburnum Const. Corp.*, 347 U.S. 656, 74 S. Ct. 833, 98 L. Ed. 1026 (c).; We have also allowed the States to enjoin such conduct . . . . State jurisdiction has prevailed in these situations because the compelling state interest, in the scheme of our federalism, in the maintenance of domestic peace is not overriden in the absence of clearly expressed congressional direction. We recognize the opinion in *United Construction Workers, etc.* v. *Laburnum Const. Corp.*, 347 U.S. 656, 74 S. Ct. 833, 835, 98 L. Ed. 1025, found support in the fact that the state remedy had no federal counterpart. But the decision was determined, as is demonstrated by the question to which review was restricted, by the 'type of conduct' involved, i.e., 'intimidation and threats of violence.' " (*Id.* at 247–48.).

16. E.g., *Metropolitan Life Insurance Co.* v. *Commonwealth of Massachusetts*, ___U.S.___, 53 U.S.L.W. 4616 (1985); *New York Telephone Co.* v. *New York State Dept. of Labor*, 440 U.S. 519 (1979); *Amalgamated Association of Street, Electric Railway & Motor Coach Employees* v. *Lockridge*, 404 U.S. 274 (1971); *International Association of Machinists* v. *Gonzales*, 356 U.S. 617 (1958); *Machinists, Lodge 76* v. *Wisconsin Employment Relations Commission*, 427 U.S. 132 (1976).

17. *Linn* v. *Plant Guard Workers*, 383 U.S. 53 (1966).

18. *Farmer* v. *United Brotherhood of Carpenters*, 430 U.S. 290 (1977).

19. *Sears, Roebuck & Co.* v. *San Diego County District Council of Carpenters*, 436 U.S. 180 (1978).

20. *Brown* v. *Hotel Employees, Local 54*, ___ U.S. ___, 104 S.Ct. 3179 (1984) Although the state courts are not deprived of jurisdiction where arbitration clauses in labor contracts are at issue, the federal labor law of contract

preempts tort law based upon a violation of the collective agreement, *Allis-Chalmers Corp.* v. *Lueck*, ___U.S.___, 105 S. Ct. 1904 (1985).

21. See notes 16, 18, and 19 *supra* and note 25 *infra.*

22. *Guss* v. *Utah Labor Relations Board*, 353 U.S. 1 (1957); *Polish National Alliance* v. *NLRB*, 322 U.S. 643 (1944). In 1983 the Court adopted a strong preemption stand when concluding that a supervisor could not sue a union for alleged interference with employment because the state court would have to decide whether the union conduct was coercive or noncoercive. *Local 926, Operating Engineers* v. *Jones*, 440 U.S. 669, (1983).

23. "The Board, in its discretion, may, by rule of decision or by published rules adopted pursuant to the Administrative Procedure Act, decline to assert jurisdiction over any labor dispute involving any class or category of employers, where, in the opinion of the Board, the effect of such labor dispute on commerce is not sufficiently substantial to warrant the exercise of its jurisdiction: provided, That the Board shall not decline to assert jurisdiction over any labor dispute over which it would assert jurisdiction under the standards prevailing upon August 1, 1959." NLRA §14(c)(1). 29 U.S.C. §164(c)(1) (1976).

24. *NLRB* v. *Fainblatt*, 306 U.S. 601, 605–607 (1939); *NLRB* v. *Reliance Fuel Oil Corp.*, 371 U.S. 224 (1963).

25. *McCulloch* v. *Sociedad Nacional de Marineros de Honduras*, 372 U.S. 10 (1963). Accord, *Benz* v. *Compania Naviero Hidalgo*, S.A. 353 U.S. 138 (1957); *Incres Steam Ship Co.* v. *International Maritime Workers Union*, 372 U.S. 24 (1963); *Windward Shipping (London) Limited, et al.* v. *American Radio Association, AFL-CIO, et al.*, 415 U.S. 104 (1974); *American Radio Association, AFL-CIO, et al.* v. *Mobile Steamship Association, Inc.*, 419 U.S. 215 (1974).

26. *International Longshoremen's Local 1416, AFL- CIO* v. *Ariadne Shipping Ltd., et al.*, 397 U.S. 195 (1970).

27. The Board so held in *Allied International, Inc.*, 257 NLRB No. 151 (1981). This view was confirmed by the Supreme Court in *International Longshoremen's Association* v. *Allied International, Inc.*, 456 U.S. 212 (1982).

28. This preference contrasts with those of individual employees and minority-group organizations (such as the NAACP), who do not have the involvement in the appointment of Board members and the General Counsel that labor and management organizations such as the AFL-CIO, the Chambers of Commerce, and the National Association of Manufacturers possess.

29. A minor extension of coverage occurred in 1974 to include the employees of nonprofit health-care institutions. Act of July 26, 1974, Pub. L. No. 93-360, 88 Stat. 395 amended the definition of "employer" in 29 U.S.C. §152(2) (1976) to give this effect.

30. Agricultural Labor Relations Act of 1975, Cal. Labor Code §§1140 et seq. (West Supp. 1980). See H. Levy, "The Agricultural Labor Relations Act of 1975," 15 Santa Clara Law. 783 (1975).

31. D. Bok, "Reflections on the Distinctive Character of American Labor Laws," 84 Harv. L. Rev. 1394 (1971).

32. NLRA §2 (3), 29 U.S.C. 152 (11) (1976). Independent contractors were excluded under the Taft-Hartley amendments. *NLRB* v. *Hearst Publications, Inc.*, 322 U.S. 111 (1944). Illegal aliens are employees within the Act's meaning; *Sure-Tan, Inc.* v. *NLRB*, ___ U.S. ___ 104 S. Ct. 2803 (1984); so are nonresident aliens who are here lawfully; *NLRB* v. *Actors' Equity Assn.*, 644 F.2d 939 (2d Cir. 1981). However, in *Sure-Tan* the Court held, by a 5–4 vote, that the Court of Appeals had exceeded its authority by awarding a minimum amount of back pay to illegally discharged illegal aliens without regard to their availability for work.

33. *NLRB* v. *The Catholic Bishops of Chicago*, 440 U.S. 490 (1980). This doctrine has been extended to commercial operations in *Faith Center — WHCT Channel 18*, 261 NLRB No. 111 (1982) But the appellate courts have rejected attacks on the Board's jurisdiction over nursing homes with religious connections. *NLRB* v. *St. Louis Christian Home* 663 F.2d 60 (8th Cir. 1981); *Tressler Lutheran Home* v. *NLRB*, 677 F.2d 302 (3rd Cir. 1982). The Court of Appeals for the Second Circuit has held that the New York State Labor Relations Board may constitutionally assert jurisdiction over lay teachers in church-operated schools. *Catholic High School Association* v. *Culvert* 753 F.2d 1161 (2d Cir. 1985). See also *St. Elizabeth Hospital* v. *NLRB*, 715 F.2d 1193 (11th Cir. 1983) (religious atmosphere of hospital was secondary to promises of health care services, involvement of NLRB in collective bargaining mediation was constitutional); *Denver Post of the National Society of Volunteers of America* v. *NLRB*, 732 F.2d 769 (10th Cir. 1984) (the VOA programs were not pervasively religious in character and they functioned in a secular fashion, especially since counselors were not required to have any particular religious background or training); *Volunteers of America–Minnesota Bar None Boys Ranch* v. *NLRB*, 752 F.2d 345 (8th Cir. 1985) (NLRB's assertion of jurisdiction does not violate the constitution where center has as its primary purpose the care of children, not propagation of the faith); *Volunteers of America, Los Angeles* v. *NLRB*, 120 LRRM 3547 (9th Cir. 1985) (NLRB properly asserted jurisdiction over alcohol center inasmuch as program is carried out in secular fashion.)
  The Court of Appeals for the First Circuit has held that the principles of *Catholic Bishops* are inapplicable to a religious university that describes itself as a "Catholic-oriented civil institution" governed by a board of trustees, a majority of whom must be the members of the Dominican Order. *Universidad Central DeBaya* v. *NLRB*, 120 LRRM 3457 (1st Cir. 1985).

34. *NLRB* v. *Bell Aerospace Co.*, 416 U.S. 267 (1974). Nonmanagerial "confidential" employees are also excluded when they are engaged in labor relations functions; *NLRB* v. *Hendricks County Rural Electric Membership Corp.*, 454 U.S. 170 (1982). The Board may exclude from bargaining units close relatives of

owner-managers of a closely held corporation without a finding that such employees possess special job-related privileges. *NLRB* v. *Action Automotive, Inc.*, ___U.S.___, 105 S. Ct. 984 (1985). Children and spouse of the employer are not an "employee" under the Act. "In the context of corporations, the Board has limited the . . . exclusion to the children or spouses of an individual with at least a 50% ownership interest." *Id.* at 989, n. 7.

35. *NLRB* v. *Yeshiva University*, 444 U.S. 627 (1980).

36. The Board so held in *R.C.A. Mfg. Co.*, 2 NLRB 168 (1936). The circuit courts agreed. See, e.g., *New York Handkerchief Mtg. Co.* v. *NLRB*, 114 F.2d 144 (7th Cir.) *cert. denied*, 311 U.S. 704 (1940); *NLRB* v. *Deutsch Co.*, 265 F.2d 473 (9th Cir. 1959), *cert. denied*, 361 U.S. 963, *rehearing denied*, 362 U.S. 945 (1960) (citing cases from fifth and seventh circuits and from the Board).

37. NLRA §2(5), 29 U.S.C. 152 (5) (1970). A union may be disqualified as a labor organization if supervisors play an active and leadership role in the union. See *Sierra Vista Hospital, Inc.*, 241 NLRB 631 (1979); *Bausch & Lomb Optical Co.*, 108 NLRB 1555 (1954). By virtue of §9(b)(3) of the Act, unions which have—or are affiliated with labor organizations which have—guard and non-guard members may not be certified by the Board. Over the strong dissent of member Zimmerman, the Board placed more stringent limitations upon the representative functions of such "mixed" unions. See *The University of Chicago*, 272 NLRB No. 126 (1984); *Wells Fargo Armored Service Corporation*, 270 NLRB No. 106 (1984), enforcement granted *sub. nom. Teamsters Local 807* v. *NLRB*, 118 LRRM 2613 (2nd Cir. 1985).

38. NLRA §9(b)(2) states in part: "The Board shall not . . . decide that any craft unit is inappropriate for such purposes on the ground that a different unit has been established by a prior Board determination. . . . " See also *American Potash & Chemical Corp.*, 107 NLRB 1418, 1422 (1954). ("It is not the province of this Board to dictate the course and pattern of labor organization in our vast industrial complex.") But see *Mallinckrodt Chemical Works*, 162 NLRB 367 (1966) (in which the Board overruled *American Potash* and reinstated history and existing patterns of collective bargaining as factors relevant to the determination of the appropriate bargaining unit) and *General Motors Corp. (Cadillac Motor Car Div.)*, 120 NLRB 1215 (1958) (in which the Board, relying on the long bargaining history of exclusive UAW representation on a multi-plant, national basis, denied severance of single-plant units as too narrow in scope, and thus inappropriate).

39. See generally R. Berry and W. Gould, "A Long Deep Drive to Collective Bargaining: Of Players, Owners, Brawls, and Strikes," 32 Case Western L. Rev. 685 (1981); R. Berry et al., *Labor Relations in Professional Sports* (1986).

40. Labor-Management Relations Act, Pub. L. No. 101, 80th Cong., 1st Sess. (1947). 61 Stat. 136, 29 U.S.C. §149(b)(5) *et seq.* (1976).

41. *NLRB* v. *Action Automotive, Inc.*, ___U.S.___, 105 S. Ct. 984 (1985).

42. *NLRB* v. *Metropolitan Life Ins. Co.*, 380 U.S. 438 (1965). The Board has held that an appropriate unit (there may be more than one) in multilocation industries is presumptively a single location. See *Sav-On Drugs, Inc.*, 138 NLRB 1032 (1962); *Frisch's Big Boy Ill-Mar, Inc.*, 147 NLRB 551 (1964) *enf. denied*, 356 F. 2d 895 (7th Cir. 1966); *F. W. Woolworth Co.*, 144 NLRB 307 (1963); *Dixie Belle Mills, Inc.*, 139 NLRB 629 (1962); *Metropolitan Life Ins. Co.*, 156 NLRB 1408 (1966); *Wyandotte Savings Bank*, 245 NLRB No. 129 (1979).

43. See cases cited in footnote 42 *supra*. Where new employees or jobs are added, it is possible for them to be declared part of an existing unit, as an accretion to it, without a new election. See Judge Winter's discussion of this principle in *NLRB* v. *Stevens Ford, Inc.*, 120 LRRM 2589, 2592–2595 (2d Cir. 1985).

44. *President and Fellows of Harvard College*, 269 NLRB No. 151 (1984).

45. *St. Francis Hospital*, 271 NLRB No. 160 (1984) A large unit has been fashioned for hotels. *ACL Corporation*, 273 NLRB No. 9 (1984).

46. *Hampton Roads Broadcasting Corp. (WCH)*, 100 NLRB 238, 239 (1952).

47. 272 NLRB No. 21 (1984). Member Zimmerman dissented.

48. *Id.* at 5.

49. *The Globe Machine and Stamping Co.*, 3 NLRB 294 (1937).

50. The Board first required this in *Excelsior Underwear, Inc.*, 156 NLRB 1236 (1966). This decision was approved by the Supreme Court in *NLRB* v. *Wyman-Gordon Co.*, 394 U.S. 759 (1969).

51. *Todd Shipyards Corp.* , 5 NLRB 20, 25 (1938); *Edwin J. Schlacter Meat Co.*, 100 NLRB 1171 (1952).

52. *Leedom* v. *Kyne*, 358 U.A. 184 (1958) Xd. *Boire* v. *Greyhound Corp.*, 376 U.S. 473 (1964).

53. See generally *American Federation of Labor* v. *NLRB*, 308 U.S. 401 (1940). See also *Raley's, Inc.* v. *NLRB*, 725 F.2d 1204 (9th Cir. 1984) and member Zimmerman's dissent in *ACL Corporation*, 273 NLRB No. 9 (1984).

Chapter 4

1. With respect to spies, see *NLRB* v. *Fansteel Manufacturing Corp.*, 306 U.S. 240, 251 (1939). The Court of Appeals for the Third Circuit has taken the position that photographing peaceful employee union demonstrations is not *per se* unlawful surveillance but must be considered in light of all the circumstances. *U.S. Steel Corp.* v. *NLRB*, 682 F.2d 98 (3rd Cir. 1982). But see *Kallman* v. *NLRB*, 640 F.2d 1094 (9th Cir. 1981); *NLRB* v. *Colonial Haven Nursing Home*,

542 F.2d 691 (7th Cir. 1976); *Flambeau Plastics Corp.*, 167 NLRB 735 (1967) *enf'd* 501 F.2d 128 (7th Cir. 1968); *Captain Nemo's*, 258 NLRB 537 (1981); *Cutting, Inc.*, 255 NLRB 534 (1981). The policy of the Board concerning interrogation is that, absent unusual circumstances, polling of employees is a violation unless certain specified criteria are met; *Struksnes Construction Co.*, 165 NLRB 1062, 1063 (1967). The Second Circuit has refused to enforce this policy, preferring the Board's own earlier view that the question was whether the interrogation was coercive in the totality of circumstances; *NLRB* v. *Lorben Corp.*, 345 F.2d 346 (2d Cir. 1965). The Court of Appeals for the Ninth Circuit has applied these rules to post-recognition disputes about majority status. Promises and threats are distinguished from objective predictions in *NLRB* v. *Gissel Packing Co.*, 395 U.S. 575 (1969); *Weather Tamer* v. *NLRB*, 676 F.2d 483 (11th Cir. 1982). Where an employer interrogates employees to verify a union's claim of majority status or to prepare a defense for an unfair-labor-practice trial, the employer must communicate the purpose of the interrogation, assure the worker that no reprisals will take place, and obtain his participation voluntarily. Moreover, the questioning must take place in a context "free from employer hostility to union activity" and the employer must not "pry into" other union activities. See *Johnnie's Poultry Co.*, 146 NLRB 770 (1964).

2. *PPG Industries, Inc.*, 251 NLRB No. 156 (1980).

3. *Blue Flash Express*, 109 NLRB 591 (1954).

4. *Rossmore House*, 269 NLRB No. 198 (1984) *enforced sub. nom.. Hotel Employees Local 2* v. *NLRB*, 760 F.2d 1006 (9th Cir. 1985). The Board has held *Rossmore* applicable to "open" union sympathizers because the employee wears a union button. *Premier Rubber Co.*, 272 NLRB No. 76 (1984). The circuit courts are split between the positions taken in *PPG Industries, Inc.* and *Rossmore House.* See *Midwest Stock Exchange* v. *NLRB*, 635 F. 2d 1255 (7th Cir. 1980); *Graham Architectural Products* v. *NLRB*, 697 F. 2d 534 (3rd Cir. 1983); *TRW-United Greenfield Division* v. *NLRB*, 637 F. 2d 410 (5th Cir. 1981); *Hotel Employees Local 2* v. *NLRB, supra.*

5. 375 U.S. 405 (1964). See Jackson and Heller, "Promises and Grants of Benefits Under the National Labor Relations Act," 131 U. of Penna. L. Rev. 1 (1982).

6. 375 U.S. at 409.

7. *NLRB* v. *Savair Mfg.*, 414 U.S. 270 (1973). However, where a waiver of initiation fees and a lower-than-usual dues structure are open to all employees, regardless of whether they support or vote for the union, the union's conduct is lawful. See, e.g., *NLRB* v. *Whitney Museum of American Art*, 636 F.2d 19 (2d Cir. 1980). Similarly lawful is a union's insistence that employees pay initiation fees and dues before the organizational campaign commences; *Hickory Springs Mfg. Co.* v. *NLRB*, 645 F.2d 506 (5th Cir. Unit A, 1980).

8. 29 U.S.C. §158(a)(2) (1976) is the relevant provision. There is considerable debate about how expansively this provision should be interpreted. See *Chi-*

cago Rawhide Mfg. Co. v. NLRB, 221 F.2d 165 (7th Cir. 1955); NLRB v. Scott & Fetzer, 691 F.2d 288 (6th Cir. 1982); W. Gould, Japan's Reshaping of American Labor Law (1984), pp. 95-99. For another view see Note, "Collective Bargaining As An Industrial System: An Argument Against Judicial Revision of Section 8(a)(2) of the National Labor Relations Act," 96 Harv. L. Rev. 1664 (1983). On the use of company time and property by an incumbent union and the question of unlawful assistance see, e.g., Base Wyandotte Corp., 274 NLRB No. 147 (1985); Coamo Knitting Mills, 150 NLRB 579, 582 (1964); Elias Mallouk Realty Corp., 265 NLRB 1225, 1236 (1982); Duquesne University of the Holy Ghost, 198 NLRB 891 (1971); Summer Products, 189 NLRB 826, 828 (1971); Longchamps, Inc., 205 NLRB 1025, 1026 (1973). See Sockell, "The Legality of Employee-Participation Programs in Unionized Firms," 37 Industrial and Labor Relations Rev. 541 (1984).

9. 29 U.S.C. §160(c) (1976) provides in part that when it finds a person to be engaged in an unfair labor practice "the Board . . . shall issue an order requiring such person to cease and desist from such unfair labor practices, and take such affirmative action . . . as will effectuate the policies of this subchapter. . . . " See, e.g., NLRB v. Getlan Iron Works, Inc., 377 F.2d 894, 896 (2d Cir. 1967).

10. Second Annual Report of the National Labor Relations Board, p. 156. "The statute clearly calls for the posting of notices as part of the enforcement procedures of the NLRB. NLRB is charged with serving the public interest to enforce labor relations rights which are public, not private rights." NLRB v. Hiney Printing Co., 733 F.2d 1170, 2405 (6th Cir. 1984). See generally W. Gould, Japan's Reshaping of American Labor Law (1984), pp. 68-69.

11. H. J. Heinz Co. v. NLRB, 311 U.S. 514, 522-23 (1941) (Board may order disestablishment if continued existence of a union is an obstacle to the employees' right of self-organization); NLRB v. Pennsylvania Greyhound Lines, 303 U.S. 261 (1938) (Board has power to require an employer to withdraw recognition from a union that it sponsors and dominates, and may sometimes order disestablishment); NLRB v. Metropolitan Alloys Corp., 624 F.2d 743 (6th Cir. 1980) (disestablishment "clearly the appropriate remedy" when union is a "company-created sham"). However, when an employer had assisted in the formation of a union but no longer dominated it "the Board did not err in failing to order disestablishment": International Union of United Brewery Workers v. NLRB, 298 F. 2d 297, 300 (D.C. Cir. 1961), cert. denied, sub nom. Gulf Bottlers, Inc. v. NLRB, 369 U.S. 843 (1962). Until the 1947 Taft-Hartley amendments the Board disestablished a company union if it was unaffiliated with a national union, but it cannot fashion a remedy on this basis now. See Carpenter Steel Co., 76 NLRB 670 (1948).

12. However, the lawfulness of the exclusive hiring hall frequently establishes a de facto closed shop. Local 357, Teamsters v. NLRB, 365 U.S. 667 (1961).

13. Alabama, Arizona, Arkansas, Florida, Georgia, Idaho, Iowa, Kansas, Louisiana, Mississippi, Nebraska, Nevada, North Carolina, North Dakota, South

Carolina, South Dakota, Tennessee, Texas, Utah, Virginia, Wyoming. The Court of Appeals for the District of Columbia has held that a union violates federal labor law when it insists upon a contract clause assessing nonunion employees for the costs of union representation in a right-to-work state. Judge Mikva dissented. *Plumbers Local Union 141* v. *NLRB*, 675 F.2d 1257 (D.C. Cir. 1982). See also *Oil, Chemical & Atomic Workers Int'l Union* v. *Mobil Oil Corp.*, 426 U.S. 407 (1976); *Retail Clerks* v. *Schemmerhorn*, 373 U.S. 746 (1963).

14. P.L. 96-593 (December 24, 1980). *Service Employees International Union, Local 6*, Case No. 19-CB- 5151, Advice Memoranda of the NLRB General Counsel, 117 LRRM 1503 (September 27, 1984).

15. *United States* v. *Emmons*, 410 U.S. 396 (1973).

16. *United States* v. *Thorodarson*, 646 F.2d 1323 (9th Cir. 1981).

17. Pub. L. No. 257, 86th Cong., 1st Sess. (1959). This provision has its origins in the so-called *Sand Door* loophole to the secondary boycott provisions which, while they prohibited strikes and other concerted activity to enforce "hot cargo" agreements, permitted employers and unions to voluntarily enter into such agreements. See *Local 1976, United Brotherhood of Carpenters* v. *NLRB (Sand Door)*, 357 U.S. 93 (1958).

18. *National Woodwork Manufacturing Assoc.* v. *NLRB*, 386 U.S. 612 (1967); *Truck Driver's Union, Local 413* v. *NLRB*, 334 F.2d, 539 (D.C. Cir. 1964), *cert. denied*, 379 U.S. 916 (1964).

19. 29 U.S.C. §158(e) (garment industry) and §158(f) (1976) (construction industry).

20. Restrictions on payments by employers to labor organizations "shall not be applicable . . . with respect to money deducted from the wages of employees in payment of membership dues in a labor organization: *Provided*, That the employer has received from each employee, on whose account such deductions are made, a written assignment which shall not be irrevocable for a period of more than one year, or beyond the termination date of the applicable collective agreement, whichever occurs sooner. . . . " 29 U.S.C. §186(c) (1976).

21. *NLRB* v. *Plasterers' International Ass'n Local 79*, 404 U.S. 116 (1971). See generally "The Employer as a Necessary Party to Voluntary Settlement of Work Assignment Disputes Under Section 10(k) of the NLRA" (comment), 38 U. Chi. L. Rev. 389 (1971).

22. *NLRB* v. *Radio and Television Broadcast Engineers Union, Local 1212*, 364 U.S. 573 (1961).

23. 29 U.S.C. 160(b) (1976).

24. This is an unfair labor practice, just as a recognition agreement according a minority union exclusive representation status is an unfair labor practice in that it coerces the majority of employees. *ILGWU* v. *NLRB*, 366 U.S. 731 (1961).

25. *Local Lodge No. 1424, International Association of Machinists* v. *NLRB*, 362 U.S. 411 (1960) (*Bryan Manufacturing*).

26. *United States Postal Service Marina Mail*, 271 NLRB No. 61, (1984) slip op. at 9. The Board, Member Zimmerman dissenting, purported to apply principles established in the area of employment discrimination and tenure denial. *Delaware State College* v. *Ricks*, 449 U.S. 250 (1980); *Chardon* v. *Fernandez*, 454 U.S. 6 (1981).

27. Rules and Regulation of the NLRB (Procedure) §101.8, 29 CFR §101.8 (1979).

28. Rosenbloom, "A New Look at the General Counsel's Unreviewable Discretion Not to Issue a Complaint Under the NLRA," 86 Yale L. J. 1349 (1977). See also *NLRB* v. *Sears, Roebuck & Co.*, 421 U.S. 132 (1975); *United Electrical Contractors* v. *Ordman*, 366 F.2d 776 (2d Cir. 1966); *International Association of Machinists and Aerospace Workers, AFL-CIO* v. *Lubbers*, 681 F.2d 598 (9th Cir. 1982).

29. "He has the right to appear at the hearing in person or by counsel and to call, examine and cross-examine witnesses. 29 C.F.R. 102.38 and 101.10 (b)(2). He is entitled to a review of an adverse Board decision by the Court of Appeals, 29 U.S.C.A. §160(f)." *Kellwood Co.* v. *NLRB*, 411 F.2d 493, 499–500 (8th Cir. 1968). Charging parties who are wholly successful before the Board may intervene in review proceeding by the Court of Appeals; *International Union, Local 283* v. *Scofield*, 382 U.S. 205 (1965). However, in injunctive proceedings under 29 U.S.C. §160(e) (1976) the charging party may appear by counsel and present any relevant testimony but may not initiate an appeal nor intervene as a party; *Solien* v. *Miscellaneous Drivers & Helpers U., Local No. 610*, 440 F.2d 124, 130–31 (8th Cir.), *cert. denied*, 403 U.S. 905, *rehearing denied*, 404 U.S. 960, *rehearing denied*, 405 U.S. 999 (1971).

30. "The Board shall have the power to petition a court of appeals of the United States . . . within any circuit . . . wherein the unfair labor practice in question occurred or wherein such person resides or transacts business, for the enforcement of such order and for the appropriate temporary relief or restraining order, and shall file in the court the record in the proceedings . . . ."; NLRA §10(e); 29 U.S.C. §160(e) (1976). While the statute vests the Board with this authority, the Board has delegated these powers to the General Counsel since at least 1955. Recently, however, the Board has begun to cut back on the General Counsel's enforcement powers, requiring that all appeals court briefs and pleadings be reviewed by the Board's Solicitor one week before they are to be filed in court. See *Labor Relations Yearbook* (BNA) (1983), p. 230. There is also frequent controversy about whether an appeal

should go to the Court of Appeals for the District of Columbia (the location of the Board) or one of the other circuits where the unfair labor practice occurred. See remarks by Abner J. Mikva, "Court Shoppers: And They're Off and Running," Annual Luncheon of Section of Labor and Employment Law, American Bar Association, August 12, 1981 (unpublished). In *Universal Camera Corp.* v. *NLRB*, 340 U.S. 474 (1951), the Court held that judicial review of Board orders should be based on the "record considered as a whole" and that the courts of appeals should defer to Board decisions unless they "cannot conscientiously find that the evidence supporting the decision is substantial.".

31. See Congressional Quarterly Inc., *The Supreme Court and Its Work* (1981), pp. 61–62.

Chapter 5

1. Even when an exclusive bargaining agent has been chosen, the law says that "any individual employee or a group of employees shall have the right at any time to present grievances to their employer and to have such grievances adjusted, without the intervention of the bargaining representative, as long as the adjustment is not inconsistent with the terms of a collective bargaining contract or agreement then in effect: *Provided further*, That the bargaining representative has been given opportunity to be present." 29 U.S. §159(a).

2. The Board so ruled in *Excelsior Underwear, Inc.*, 156 NLRB 1236 (1966). Seven justices approved of the rule in *NLRB* v. *Wyman-Gordon Co.*, 394 U.S. 759 (1969) (Fortas, J. for the court, and Black, J. concurring).

3. See *NLRB* v. *S & H Grossinger's, Inc.*, 372 F.2d 26, 29 (2d Cir. 1967). For some of the general problems see W. Gould, "Taft-Hartley Revisited: The Contrariety of the Collective Bargaining Agreement and the Plight of the Unorganized," 13 Labor L. J. 348 (1962).

4. *Wiese Plow Welding Co., Inc.*, 123 NLRB 616 (1959) Cf. *Allied Lettercraft Co., Inc.*, 272 NLRB No. 97 (1984).

5. 321 U.S. 322 (1944).

6. *Id.* at 336.

7. *Id.* at 337–39.

8. *Edward G. Budd Mfg. Co.* v. *NLRB*, 138 F.2d 86, 90 (3d Cir. 1943).

9. For example, *NLRB* v. *Jacob E. Decker & Sons*, 636 F.2d 129 (5th Cir., Unit A, 1981); *NLRB* v. *Big Three Welding Equipment Company*, 359 F.2d 77 (5th Cir. 1966).

10. *Mt. Healthy City Board of Education* v. *Doyle*, 429 U.S. 274 (1977).

11. *Givhan v. Western Line Consolidated School District*, 439 U.S. 410 (1979).

12. W. Gould, "The Supreme Court and Labor Law: The October 1978 Term," 21 Arizona L. Rev. 621, 622–625 (1979).

13. 251 NLRB No. 150, (1980). *NLRB v. Great Dane Trailers, Inc.*, 388 U.S. 26 (1967).

14. 251 NLRB No. 150 (1980), slip op. at 20–21.

15. 462 U.S. 393, 103 S.Ct. 2469 (1983).

16. *Id.* at 403.

17. *Id.* at 401 n.6.

18. *NLRB v. Great Dane Trailers, Inc.*, 388 U.S. 26 (1967); *American Ship Building Co. v. NLRB*, 380 U.S. 300 (1965); *Radio Officers' Union v. NLRB*, 347 U.S. 17 (1954); *Local 357, Teamsters v. NLRB*, 365 U.S. 667 (1961). One of a wide variety of issues relating to discrimination is whether the award of superseniority to union stewards is lawful. See, e.g., *NLRB v. Milk Drivers & Dairy Employees, Local 338*, 531 F.2d 1162 (2d Cir. 1976); *United Electrical Radio & Machine Workers of America, Local 623 (Linpco)*, 230 NLRB 406 (1977) *enforced sub. nom. D'Amico v. NLRB*, 582 F.2d 820 (3rd Cir. 1978); *Gulton Electro-Voice, Inc.*, 266 NLRB 406, *enforced sub. nom. Local 900, International Union of Electrical, Radio & Machine Workers v. NLRB*, 727 F.2d 1184 (D.C. Cir. 1984); *NLRB v. Niagara Machine & Tool Workers*, 746 F.2d 143 (2d Cir. 1984); *Local 1384, UAW v. NLRB*, 756 F.2d 482 (7th Cir. 1985); *NLRB v. Harvey Hubble, Inc.*, 119 LRRM 3460 (4th Cir. 1985); *NLRB v. Wayne Corp.*, 120 LRRM 3321 (7th Cir. 1985).

19. *NLRB v. Burnup and Sims, Inc.*, 379 U.S. 21 (1964).

20. 324 U.S. 793 (1945); W. Gould, "The Question of Union Activity on Company Property," 18 Vanderbilt L. Rev. 73 (1964); W. Gould, "Union Organizational Rights and the Concept of Quasi-Public Property," 49 Minn. L. Rev. 505 (1965).

21. *Id.* at 802–803 and 802n.8.

22. *Id.* at 803n.10.

23. *T.R.W. Bearings*, 257 NLRB 442 (1981).

24. *Our Way, Inc.*, 268 NLRB No. 61 (1984).

25. *Id.* at p. 4. The Board, Member Zimmerman's dissent notwithstanding, was of the view that, until *T.R.W. Bearings*, "working time" rules were presumptively lawful. The Board relied upon *Essex International*, 211 NLRB 749 (1974).

26. *Hammary Manufacturing Corp.*, 265 NLRB No. 7 (1982); *Saint Vincent's Hospital*, 265 NLRB No. 6 (1982).

27. *Id.* at 2-3, n.4; *Serv-Air, Inc.* v. *NLRB*, 395 F.2d 557 (10th Cir. 1968).

28. *Emerson Electric Co., U.S. Electrical Motor Division*, 187 NLRB 294 (1970).

29. *NLRB* v. *Babcock and Wilcox Co.*, 351 U.S. 105, 112 (1956). The rule relating to nonemployee access under the California Agricultural Relations Act appears to be more liberal. See *Agricultural Labor Relations Board* v. *Superior Court*, 16 Cal. 3d 392 (1976), *appeal dismissed*, 429 U.S. 802 (1976).

30. *NLRB* v. *Babcock and Wilcox Co.*, 351 U.S. at 107 n.1, 113.

31. *Id.* at 112-113.

32. *NLRB* v. *Magnavox Co.*, 415 U.S. 322, 325 (1974).

33. *Eastex, Inc.* v. *NLRB*, 437 U.S. 556 (1978).

34. See *Local 174, International Union, UAW* v. *NLRB*, 645 F.2d 1151 (D.C. Cir., 1981), in which distributing literature on company property was held unprotected when "the principal thrust of the leaflet was to induce employees to vote for specific candidates, not to educate them on political issues relevant to their employment conditions." *Id.* at 2563 Compare *Fun Striders, Inc.* v. *NLRB*, 686 F.2d 659 (9th Cir. 1981).

35. 406 U.S. 539 (1972).

36. *Id.* at 545.

37. *Id.* at 544-45.

38. *Id.* at 547.

39. 424 U.S. 507 (1976).

40. *Id.* at 521-22. A footnote is omitted.

41. *Scott Hudgens*, 230 NLRB 414 (1977).

42. *Amalgamated Food Employees Union* v. *Logan Valley Plaza*, 391 U.S. 308 (1968) (overruled in *Hudgens*, 424 U.S. at 518).

43. *Pruneyard Shopping Center* v. *Robins*, 447 U.S. 74 (1980).

44. *Seattle First National Bank*, 243 NLRB No. 145 (1979), *modified*, 651 F.2d 1272 (9th Cir. 1980). See also *Grant Food Store Markets* v. *NLRB*, 241 NLRB 727 (1979) *rev'd.*, 633 F.2d 18 (6th Cir. 1980).

45. *Hutzler Bros.* v. *NLRB*, 630 F.2d 1012 (4th Cir. 1980).

46. *San Diego Building Trades Council* v. *Garmon*, 359 U.S. 236 (1959).

47. *Sears, Roebuck & Co.* v. *San Diego County District Council of Carpenters*, 436 U.S. 180, 198–207 (1978).

48. *Marshall Field & Co.*, 98 NLRB 88 (1952), *enforced as modified, Marshall Field & Co.* v. *NLRB*, 200 F.2d 375 (7th Cir. 1953); *May Department Stores Co.*, 59 NLRB 976 (1944), *enforced as modified*, 154 F.2d 533 (8th Cir. 1946); *Goldblatt Bros., Inc.*, 77 NLRB 1262 (1948); *Montgomery Ward & Co., Inc.* v. *NLRB*, 692 F.2d 1115 (7th Cir. 1982) *cert. denied* 103 S. Ct. 1892 (1983); *Montgomery Ward & Co.* v. *NLRB*, 728 F.2d 389 (6th Cir. 1984); *Ameron Automotive Center, a Division of the Kelly-Springfield Tire Co.*, 265 NLRB No. 76 (1982); *F.W. Woolworth Company d/b/a Woolco Division*, 265 NLRB No. 58 (1982); *Hughes Properties, Inc. d/b/a Harolds Club*, 267 NLRB No. 141 (1983) enforced 758 F.2d 1320 (9th Cir. 1985).

49. *Marriot Corp.*, 223 NLRB 978 (1976); *Bankers Club, Inc.*, 218 NLRB 22 (1975); *McDonald's Corp.*, 205 NLRB 404 (1973). See generally *Beth Israel Hospital* v. *NLRB*, 437 U.S. 483 (1978); *Times Publishing Co.* v. *NLRB*, 605 F.2d 847 (5th Cir. 1979).

50. See *supra* note 1, chapter 3.

51. *St. John's Hospital and School of Nursing, Inc.*, 222 NLRB 1150 (1976).

52. *Beth Israel Hospital* v. *NLRB*, 437 U.S. 483, 495 (1978).

53. *NLRB* v. *Baptist Hospital, Inc.*, 442 U.S. 773 (1979). The wearing of union insignia or button as a statutory Section 7 right has frequently conflicted with dress codes. *Holladay Park Hospital and Oregon Nurses Association, Inc.*, 262 NLRB 26 (1982); *Pay'n Save Corp.* v. *NLRB*, 641 F.2d 697 (9th Cir. 1981); *NLRB* v. *Harrah's Club*, 337 F.2d 177 (9th Cir. 1964); *Davison-Paxor Co.* v. *NLRB*, 462 F.2d 364 (5th Cir. 1972); *Midstate Telephone Corp.* v. *NLRB*, 706 F.2d 401 (2d. Cir. 1983); *Southern California Edison Company*, 274 NLRB No. 167 (1985).

54. *Cashway Lumber, Inc.*, 202 NLRB 380 (1973).

55. *Vincent's Steak House*, 216 NLRB 647 (1975); *Helton* v. *NLRB*, 658 F.2d 583 (D.C. Cir. 1981); *Container Corporation of America*, 244 NLRB No. 53 (1979), *enforced in part sub. nom.. NLRB* v. *Container Corporation of America*, 649 F.2d 1213 (6th Cir. 1981); *NLRB* v. *Honeywell, Inc.*, 722 F.2d 405 (8th Cir. 1983); *ITT McDonnel and Miller*, 267 NLRB No. 181 (1983). Apparently, literature that might not be tolerated as a union insignia can be protected when it is displayed on a bulletin board; *Southwestern Bell Telephone Company*, 276 NLRB No. 110 (1985).

56. *May Department Store*, 136 NLRB 797 (1962), *enforcement denied*, 316 F.2d 797 (6th Cir. 1963). But the Sixth Circuit did find an imbalance where there

were also unfair labor practices in *Montgomery Ward and Co.* v. *NLRB*, 339 F.2d 889 (6th Cir. 1965).

57. *NLRB* v. *Drivers, Chauffeurs, Helpers, Local Union No. 639*, 362 U.S. 274 (1960).

58. *Id.* at 284.

59. *Id.*

60. 29 U.S.C. §158(b)(7) (1976) provides that it shall be an unfair labor practice for a labor organization or its agents

to picket or cause to be picketed, or threaten to picket or cause to be picketed, any employer where an object thereof is forcing or requiring an employer to recognize or bargain with a labor organization as the representative of his employees, or forcing or requiring the employees of an employer to accept or select such labor organization as their collective bargaining representative, unless such labor organization is currently certified as the representative of such employees:

(A) where the employer has lawfully recognized in accordance with this subchapter any other labor organization and a question concerning representation may not appropriately be raised under section 159(c) of this title.

(B) where within the preceding twelve months a valid election under section 159(c) has been conducted, or

(C) where such picketing has been conducted without a petition under section 159(c) of this title being filed within a reasonable period of time not to exceed thirty days from the commencement of such picketing: Provided, That when such a petition has been filed the Board shall forthwith, without regard to the provisions of section 159(c) (1) of this title or the absence of a showing of substantial interest on the part of the labor organization, direct an election in such a unit as the Board finds to be appropriate and shall certify the results thereof: Provided further, That nothing in this subparagraph (C) shall be construed to prohibit picketing or other publicity for the purpose of truthfully advising the public (including consumers) that an employer does not employ members of, or have a contract with, a labor organization, unless an effect of such picketing is to induce any individual employed by any other person in the course of his employment, not to pick up, deliver or transport any goods or not to perform any services.
Nothing in this paragraph (7) shall be construed to permit any act which would otherwise be an unfair labor practice under this subsection.

61. For example, *Giant Food Markets, Inc.*, 241 NLRB No. 105, *enforcement denied*, 633 F.2d 18 (6th Cir.) (1980). See also *International Hod Carriers, Local No. 41 (Calumet Contractors Association)*, 133 NLRB 512 (1961) and *Houston Building and Construction Trades Council ("Claude Everett Construction")*, 136 NLRB 321 (1962). The Supreme Court has had to address difficult problems involving an uncertified union's picket line in the construction industry prior to its estab-

lishment of majority status. See *NLRB* v. *Local 103, International Association of Bridge Workers*, 434 U.S. 335 (1978).

62. *Thornhill* v. *Alabama*, 310 U.S. 88 (1940).

63. *International Brotherhood of Teamsters, Local 695* v. *Vogt, Inc.*, 354 U.S. 284 (1957). The Court there discussed earlier cases, including *Building Service Employees* v. *Gazzam*, 339 U.S. 532 (1950), *International Brotherhood of Teamsters* v. *Hanke*, 339 U.S. 470 (1950) and *Giboney* v. *Empire Storage and Ice Co.*, 336 U.S. 490 (1949). The distinction is discussed in A. Cox, "Strikes, Picketing, and the Constitution," 4 Vanderbilt L. Rev. 574, 591–602 (1950–51). Picketing in furtherance of an unlawful objective is not protected by the First Amendment. See, most recently, *NLRB* v. *Retail Store Employees' Union*, 447 U.S. 607, 616 (1980); *Carvel Corporation*, 273 NLRB No. 81 (1984) But see *Miller* v. *United Food and Commercial Workers Union, Local 498*, 708 F.2d 467 (9th Cir. 1983); *Johansen* v. *San Diego County Council of Carpenters*, 745 F.2d 1289 (9th Cir. 1984).

64. *Connell Construction Co.* v. *Plumbers Local 100*, 421 U.S. 616 (1965). Cf. *United Mine Workers* v. *Pennington*, 381 U.S. 657 (1965).

65. *NLRB* v. *International Rice Milling Co.*, 341 U.S. 665 (1951). Cf. *NLRB* v. *Local 825, Operating Engineers*, 400 U.S. 297 (1971).

66. *NLRB* v. *Business Machines and Office Appliance Mechanics Conference Board, Local 459 IUE ("Royal Typewriter")*, 228 F.2d 553 (2d Cir. 1955), *cert. denied*, 351 U.S. 962 (1956); *Douds* v. *Metropolitan Federation of Architects*, 75 F. Supp. 672 (S.D.N.Y. 1948).

67. See *supra* note 14, chapter 4.

68. The Court has held that a valid work-preservation objective may exist even where technological innovation makes it impossible for the union to pursue the identical work performed in the past by bargaining-unit members. See *NLRB* v. *International Longshoremen's Union, AFL-CIO*, 447 U.S. 125 (1980) (ILAI); *NLRB* v. *International Longshoremen's Association, AFL-CIO*, ___U.S.___, 53 U.S.L.W. 4919 (June 27, 1985) (ILAII).

69. 341 U.S. 675 (1951).

70. *Id.* at 690.

71. *Local 761, International Union of Electrical, Radio and Machine Workers, AFL-CIO* v. *NLRB*, 366 U.S. 667 (1961).

72. The bill (H.R. 4250) was approved by the House Education and Labor Committee; 94 Labor Relations Reporter No. 23, p. 1 (March 21, 1977). The full House defeated the bill on March 23 by a vote of 217–205; *Id.* no. 25, p. 1 (March 28, 1977). See also *J. F. Hoff Electric Co.* v. *NLRB*, 642 F.2d 1266 (D.C. Cir. 1980). See especially the standards for common situs picketing set forth in *Moore Dry Dock*, 92 NLRB 547 (1950).

73. The veto occurred on January 5, 1976 (Bureau of National Affairs, Labor Relations Yearbook, 1976, p. 3).

74. *Connell Constr. Co.* v. *Plumbers Local 100*, 421 U.S. 616 (1975). The obverse of the *Connell* question, i.e., whether unions can complain under the antitrust law against employer conspiracies to boycott unionized contractors, was answered negatively in an 8-1 decision of the Court. *Associated General Contractors of California, Inc.* v. *California State Council of Carpenters*, ___ U.S. ___, 103 S.Ct. 897 (1983).

75. 456 U.S. 645 (1982).

76. *Id.* at 660. The Court stated that the top-down effect was "limited" in a number of ways by other provisions of the NLRA: (1) prohibitions against recognitional picketing; (2) the right of employees to challenge a construction union's representative status despite a valid pre-hire agreement; (3) prohibitions against discrimination against non-union members in the hiring hall; the *Denver Building Trades* protection of employees employed by non-union contractors.

77. *Id.* at 663-64.

78. *NLRB* v. *Fruit and Vegetable Packers, Local 760 ("Tree Fruits")*, 377 U.S. 58 (1964).

79. *Id.* at 61n.3. Moreover, secondary leafletting in and of itself may create secondary problems. See *NLRB* v. *Servette, Inc.*, 377 U.S. 46 (1964); *Pet, Inc.* v. *NLRB*, 641 F.2d 545 (8th Cir. 1981). An interesting discussion of the *Pet* decision and the right of unions to urge boycotts of separate corporations or subsidiaries that are part of a conglomerate is contained in "Unions, Conglomerates and Secondary Activity" (comment), 129 U. of Penna. L. Rev. 221 (1981). The constitutional issues have been avoided thus far. *Edward J. De Bartolo* v. *NLRB*, 463 U.S. 147, 103 S.Ct. 2926 (1983). On remand the Board has applied the "struck product" analysis utilized by the Supreme Court in secondary consumer picketing cases. *The Edward J. De Bartolo Corporation*, 273 NLRB No. 172, p.5., n. 8 (1985); see generally *Service Employees, Local 399* v. *NLRB*, 723 F.2d 746 (9th Cir. 1984); Goldman, "The First Amendment and Nonpicketing Labor Publicity Under Section 8(b)(4)(ii)(B) of the National Labor Relations Act," 36 Vand. L. Rev. 1469 (1983).

80. *Id.* at 72. See also *Carey* v. *Brown*, 447 U.S. 455 (1980).

81. *NLRB* v. *Retail Store Emp. Union Local 1001*, 447 U.S. 607 (1980).

82. *Id.* at 616. The Court acted upon the earliest NLRA secondary boycott case in which First Amendment arguments had been rejected. *Electrical Workers* v. *NLRB*, 341 U.S. 694, 705 (1951).

83. 447 U.S. at 619 (Stevens, J., concurring).

84. *International Longshoremen's Ass'n* v. *Allied International*, 456 U.S. 212, 226-27 n. 26 (1982).

85. *NAACP* v. *Claiborne Hardware*, 458 U.S. 886 (1982). See generally Harper, "The Consumer's Emerging to Boycott: *NAACP* v. *Claiborne Hardware* and its Implications for American Labor Law," 93 Yale L. J. 409 (1984).

86. *NLRB* v. *Gissel Packing Co.*, 395 U.S. 575 (1969).

87. *Id.* at 602. The Fourth Circuit had found the cards to be inherently unreliable. See *Id.* at 585. Employees are presumed to have designated the union as their bargaining agent where the authorization card so states unless oral misrepresentations clearly cancel the language on the card. The Board, over Member Dennis's dissent, will not use or rely upon English-language cards for Spanish speakers. *Superior Container, Inc.*, 276 NLRB No. 55 (1985). But see *NLRB* v. *American Art Industries*, 415 F. 2nd 1223 (5th Cir. 1969).

88. *Id.* at 602.

89. 29 U.S.C. §159 (c)(1)(B) (1976). See Gissel, 395 U.S. at 594-95.

90. *Linden Lumber Division, Summer & Co.* v. *NLRB*, 419 U.S. 301 (1974).

91. *J. P. Stevens & Co., Gulistan Div.* v. *NLRB*, 441 F.2d 514 (5th Cir. 1971). Where two unions are competing, the Board has regarded the cards as unreliable; *Midwest Piping & Supply Co.*, 63 NLRB 1060 (1945). However, the Board has modified *Midwest Piping* so that an employer is obliged to bargain with an incumbent union despite the filing of a rival union representation petition, *RCA Del Caribe, Inc.*, 262 NLRB No. 116 (1982). Moreover, unlawful company assistance will not be equated with company recognition of a rival union in an initial organizational context before a valid election petition has been filed and where the recognized union's majority is uncoerced and unassisted.

92. 242 NLRB No. 179 (1979). See also "United Dairy Farmers Cooperative Association: NLRB Bargaining Orders in the Absence of a Clear Showing of a Pro-Union Majority" (comment), 80 Columbia Law Rev. 840 (1980). The discussion of this case is taken from W. Gould, "Recent Developments Under the National Labor Act: The Board and the Circuit Courts," 14 U.C.D. L. Rev. 497 (1981).

93. *Id.*

94. *Id.*

95. *United Dairy Farmers Cooperative Assn.* v. *NLRB*, 633 F.2d 1054, 1066 (3d Cir. 1980).

96. The Third Circuit has also had occasion to deal with the *Gissel* bargaining-order problem in a case where the union did not hold a minority of authori-

zation cards: *NLRB* v. *K & K Gourmet Meats, Inc.*, 640 F.2d 460 (3d Cir. 1981). See also *NLRB* v. *Unit Train Sales*, 636 F.2d 1121 (6th Cir. 1980).

97. 633 F.2d at 1066.

98. *Id.* at 1067.

99. *Id.* at 1068.

100. *Id.* at 1069.

101. *Id.* at 1069, n.16. On remand, Chairman Fanning and Member Jenkins adhered to their original view that the Board possesses the requisite authority to fashion a bargaining order. Member Zimmerman, without expressing a view, acceded to the Third Circuit view; *United Dairy Farmers*, 257 NLRB No. 129 (1981).

102. *Conair Corp.*, 261 NLRB No.178 (1982)

103. *Conair Corp.* v. *NLRB*, 721 F.2d 1355 (D.C. Cir. 1983).

104. 270 NLRB No.113 (1984).

105. *Id.* at 10.

106. The presumption of majority status during the one year certification period is irrebuttable. *Brooks* v. *NLRB*, 348 U.S. 96(1954).

107. Indeed, the Board has recently held that four weeks of bargaining and less than three months of recognition was a reasonable period of time in which majority status could be questioned. *Tajon, Inc.*, 269 NLRB No. 62 (1984). See also *Brennan's Cadillac, Inc.*, 231 NLRB 225 (1977) (3 months adequate; two members dissenting). Cf. *Vantran Elec. Corp.*, 231 NLRB 1014 (1977) (4 1/2 months inadequate; one member dissenting), *enforcement denied*, 580 F.2d 921 (7th Cir. 1978). After a reasonable period of time has elapsed, a good faith doubt about the incumbent union's majority status may be manifested through either a good-faith doubt that the union possesses majority status or actual evidence of lack of majority status. *Sofro, Inc.*, 268 NLRB No. 15 (1983); *Celanese Corporation of America*, 95 NLRB 664 (1951); *Terrell Machine Company*, 173 NLRB 1480 (1969) *enforced*, 427 F.2d 1008 (4th Cir. 1970); *Dalewood Rehabilitation Hospital Inc.* d/b/a *Golden State Habilitation Convalescent Center* v. *NLRB*, 566 F.2d 77 (9th Cir. 1977); *National Cash Register Co.* v. *NLRB, 494 F.2d 189 (8th Cir. 1974); Laystrom Manufacturing Co.*, 151 NLRB 1482 (1965), *enforcement denied*, 359 F.2d 799 (7th Cir. 1966).

108. AFL-CIO No-Raiding Pact. There are problems in bringing together all parties in one proceeding. See *Transportation-Communication Employees Union* v. *Union Pacific Railroad*, 385 U.S. 157 (1966); *Columbia Broadcasting System* v. *American Recording & Broadcasting Association*, 414 F.2d 1326 (2d Cir. 1969).

109. *Appalachian Shale Products Co.*, 121 NLRB 1160 (1958).

110. *Id.*

111. *Id.*

112. *Hershey Chocolate Corp.*, 121 NLRB 90 (1958); *General Extrusion Co.*, 121 NLRB 1165 (1958).

113. *General Cable Corp.*, 139 NLRB 1123 (1962), set the maximum time at 3 years. *American Seating Corp.*, 106 NLRB 250 (1953), had set the bar at the lesser period of the agreement and a permitted maximum period (then 2 years).

Chapter 6

1. *NLRB* v. *Insurance Agents' International Union*, 361 U.S. 477 (1960).

2. *Id.* at 488–89.

3. Two of the leading cases taking opposite sides are *Anchortank, Inc.* v. *NLRB*, 618 F.2d 1153 (5th Cir. 1980) and *Ontario Knife* v. *NLRB*, 637 F.2d 840 (2d Cir. 1980). These and other decisions are discussed in W. Gould, "Recent Developments Under the National Labor Relations Act: The Board and the Circuit Courts," 14 Univ. Calif. Davis L. Rev. 497 (1981). See generally A. Cox, "The Right to Engage in Concerted Activities," 26 Ind. L. J. 319 (1951).

4. The Board's rule is set forth in *Alleluia Cushion Company*, 211 NLRB No. 162 (1975). The Sixth Circuit approved the rule in *NLRB* v. *Lloyd A. Fry Co.*, 651 F.2d 442 (6th Cir. 1981). But see *Krispy Kreme Doughnut Corp.* v. *NLRB*, 635 F.2d 304 (4th Cir. 1980).

5. *Meyers Industries, Inc.*, 268 NLRB No. 73 (1984), slip. op. at 12 remanded sub. nom. *Price* v. *NLRB*, 755 F.2d 941 (D.C. Cir. 1985). The Second Circuit has been less patient with the Board. *Ewing* v. *NLRB*, 119 LLRM 3273 (2nd Cir. 1985). See also *JMC Transport, Inc.* v. *NLRB*, 120 LRRM 3217 (6th Cir. 1985). Application of the *Meyers Industries* rule is set forth in *Access Control Systems*, 270 NLRB No. 118 (1984); *Mannington Mills, Inc.*, 272 NLRB No. 15 (1984); *Bearden and Company* d/b/a, *D.A. Collins Refractories*, 272 NLRB No. 135 (1984).

6. ___ U.S. ___ 104 S.Ct. 1505 (1984).

7. 104 S.Ct. at 1516.

8. *ABF Freight Systems, Inc.*, 271 NLRB No. 6 (1984).

9. *NLRB* v. *Weingarten, Inc.*, 420 U.S. 251 (1975).

10. *Taracorp Industries, A Division of Taracorp, Inc.*, 273 NLRB No. 54 (1984).

11. *Materials Research Corp.*, 262 NLRB 1010 (1982).

12. *E.I. du Pont de Nemours* v. *NLRB*, 707 F.2d 1076 (9th Cir. 1983); *ITT Corporation* v. *NLRB*, 719 F.2d 851 (6th Cir. 1983); *E.I. du Pont de Nemours* v. *NLRB*, 724 F.2d 1061 (3rd Cir. 1983).

13. *Sears, Roebuck and Co.*, 274 NLRB No. 55 (1985). Cf. *Taracorp Industries*, supra note 10, at 9.

14. *New York Times* v. *Sullivan*, 376 U.S. 254 (1964); *Letter Carriers* v. *Austin*, 448 U.S. 264 (1974); *NLRB* v. *Greyhound Lines, Inc.*, 660 F.2d 354 (8th Cir. 1981). But see *Connick* v. *Myers*, 461 U.S. 138 (1983).

15. *Jeannette Corporation* v. *NLRB*, 532 F.2d 916 (3d Cir. 1976).

16. For example, *NLRB* v. *Red Top, Inc.*, 455 F.2d 721 (8th Cir. 1972); *Bettcher Mfg. Corp.*, 76 NLRB 526 (1948).

17. *Linn* v. *Plant Guard Workers*, 383 U.S. 53, 58 (1966). However, an employer may institute a well founded libel and business interference action which has a reasonable basis in state court regardless of retaliatory motive under the First Amendment and the Board may not enjoin the action. *Bill Johnson's Restaurant* v. *NLRB*, ___ U.S. ___, 103 S.Ct. 2161 (1983). Contrarily, a divided Court has concluded that unions are not liable under Reconstruction statutes to deprive non-union workers of First Amendment rights through violent behavior. *Carpenters Local 610* v. *Scott*, 463 U.S. 825, (1983).

18. *Great Lakes Steel*, 236 NLRB No. 115 (1978). Accord, *Samsonite Corporation*, 206 NLRB 343 (1973).

19. "Animal exuberance," referred to in *NLRB* v. *Illinois Tool Works*, 153 F.2d 811, 815–16 (7th Cir. 1946), it is taken from the Supreme Court's language in *Milk Wagon Drivers* v. *Meadowmoor Dairies, Inc.*, 312 U.S. 287, 293 (1941). In *NLRB* v. *Thor Power Tool Company*, 351 F.2d 584, 587 (7th Cir. 1965), the court stated that employees are permitted "some leeway for impulsive behavior which must be balanced against the employer's right to maintain order and respect."

20. *Tyler Business Services, Inc.*, 256 NLRB No. 88, (1981), enforcement denied, 680 F.2d 338 (4th Cir. 1982).

21. 346 U.S. 464 (1953).

22. *The Patterson-Sargent Company*, 115 NLRB 1627 (1956).

23. *Coors Container Co.* v. *NLRB*, 628 F.2d 1283, 1288 (10th Cir. 1980). The Board has also held that a union sticker on an employee's crane is protected. *Malta Construction Company*, 276 NLRB No. 171 (1985). Chairman Dotson dissented.

24. *Sullair P.T.O., Inc.* v. *NLRB*, 641 F.2d 500, 503 (7th Cir. 1981). See also *Timpte, Inc.* v. *NLRB*, 590 F.2d 871 (10th Cir. 1979); *Maryland Drydock Co.* v. *NLRB*, 183 F.2d 538 (4th Cir. 1950); *NLRB* v. *Garner Tool & Die Manufacturing, Inc.*, 493 F.2d 263 (8th Cir. 1974); *Coors Container Co.* v. *NLRB*, *supra* note 15.

25. *NLRB* v. *Prescott Industrial Products Company*, 500 F.2d 6, 11 (8th Cir. 1974).

26. *Southwestern Bell Telephone Company*, 200 NLRB 667 (1972). The language was more obviously obscene and similarly unprotected in *Caterpillar Tractor Company*, 276 NLRB No. 151 (1985).

27. *Inland Steel Company*, 257 NLRB No. 13 (1981) See also, *Borman's Inc.* v. *NLRB*, 676 F.2d 1138 (6th Cir. 1982); *Southern California Edison Company*, 274 NLRB No. 167 (1985).

28. *NLRB* v. *Nevis Industries*, 647 F.2d 905 (9th Cir. 1981).

29. *NLRB* v. *Sheraton Puerto Rico Corp.*, 651 F.2d 49 (1st Cir. 1981).

30. 262 NLRB 402 (1982) aff'd sub. nom. *Automobile Salesmen's Union Local 1095* v. *NLRB*, 711 F.2d 383 (D.C. Cir. 1983).

31. *Id.* at 404.

32. *NLRB* v. *Washington Aluminum Co.*, 370 U.S. 9 (1962).

33. *NLRB* v. *Sands Mfg. Co.*, 306 U.S. 332 (1938). There are exceptions to this rule in the case of "serious" unfair labor practices: see *Arlan's Department Store*, 133 NLRB 802, 807 (1961); *Mastro Plastics* v. *NLRB*, 350 U.S. 270 (1956); *NLRB* v. *Northeast Oklahoma City Mfg. Co.*, 631 F.2d 6691 (10th Cir. 1980); *Dow Chemical Co.* v. *NLRB*, 636 F.2d 1352 (3rd Cir. 1980); *Caterpillar Tractor Co.* v. *NLRB*, 658 F.2d 1242 (7th Cir. 1981). The Board has held that sympathy strikes are unprotected activity when there is a broad no-strike clause in the collective bargaining agreement. *Indianapolis Power & Light Company*, 273 NLRB No. 211 (1985) Meanwhile, a cooling-off period imposed prior to the contract's expiration by section 8(d) of the Act obliges the parties not to engage in strikes or lockouts, *NLRB* v. *Lion Oil Co.*, 352 U.S. 282 (1957), and where unions violate the obligation workers lose their status as "employees" under the Act, *Fort Smith Chair Co.*, 143 NLRB 514, *enforced* 336 F. 2d 738 (D.C. Cir. 1963), *cert. den.*, 379 U.S. 838 (1964). The Board has held that the burden of filing statutory notification with mediation agencies rests exclusively with the initiating party (proposing contract modification) and that the initiating party's failure to file such a notice cannot serve to preclude the nominating party from undertaking otherwise lawful economic action. *United Artists Communications, Inc.*, 274 NLRB No. 17 (1985), p. 7, overruling *Hooker Chemical Corp.*, 224 NLRB 1535 (1976 *enf. denied* 573 F.2d 965 (7th Cir. 1978).

34. *Elk Lumber Co.*, 91 NLRB 333 (1950); *NLRB* v. *Montgomery Ward & Co., Inc.*, 157 F.2d 486, 496 (8th Cir. 1946). See generally W. Gould, "The Status of

Unauthorized and (Wildcat) Strikes under the National Labor Relations Act," 52 Cornell L. Q. 672 (1967).

35. *NLRB* v. *Fansteel Metallurgical Corp.*, 306 U.S. 240 (1939); *Johns-Manville Products Corp.* v. *NLRB*, 557 F.2d 1126 (5th Cir. 1977); *NLRB* v. *Pepsi-Cola Bottling Company*, 449 F.2d 824 (5th Cir. 1971). See member Dennis's dissent in *Waco, Inc.*, 273 NLRB No. 101 (1985). See Gould, *op. cit.* The Board has taken the position that words as well as physical conduct can constitute strike misconduct which justifies the employer's refusal to reinstate the striker. *Clear Pine Mouldings, Inc.*, 268 NLRB No. 173 (1984). In this decision the Board repudiated the *Thayer* doctrine which balanced the severity of the employer's unfair labor practice against the gravity of the striker's misconduct.

36. *The Emporium Capwell Co.* v. *Western Addison Community Organization*, 420 U.S. 50 (1975); *NLRB* v. *Draper Corp.*, 145 F.2d 199 (4th Cir. 1944); Gould, *op. cit.* The refusal to cross a picket line as well as the strike is protected. *NLRB* v. *Rockaway News Supply Co., Inc.*, 345 U.S. 871 (1953); *NLRB* v. *Southern Greyhound Lines*, 426 F.2d 1299 (5th Cir. 1970); *NLRB* v. *L.G. Everist, Inc.*, 334 F.2d 312 (8th Cir. 1964); *ABS Co.*, 269 NLRB No. 138 (1984); *Business Services by Manpower, Inc.*, 272 NLRB No. 119 (1984); *Dave Castellino & Sons*, 277 NLRB No. 50 (1985).

37. *NLRB* v. *R. C. Can Co.*, 328 F.2d 974 (5th Cir. 1964); Gould, *op. cit.*, pp. 678–80, pp. 682–90. However, the Court of Appeals subsequently warned that *R.C. Can* must be applied with "great care," *NLRB* v. *Shop Rite Foods*, 430 F.2d 786, 790 (5th Cir. 1970), and the Board appears to concur in this view, *Energy Coal Income Partnership 1981-1*, 269 NLRB No. 137 (1984); *AAL, Inc.*, 275 NLRB No. 12 (1985).

38. 29 U.S.C. §§176 *et seq.* (1976). See, e.g., *United Steelworkers* v. *United States*, 361 U.S. 39 (1959); *Youngstown Sheet and Tube Co.* v. *Sawyer*, 343 U.S. 579 (1952) (the steel seizure case).

39. NLRA §§206–210.

40. Sen. Rep. No. 105 on S.B. 11 1126. Cong. Rec. 3951 Sen. (April 23, 1947) (remarks of Sen. Taft).

41. *Dorchy* v. *Kansas*, 272 U.S. 306 (1926); *UAW* v. *Wisconsin Employment Relations Board*, 336 U.S. 245 (1949); *United Federation of Postal Clerks* v. *Blount*, 325 F. Supp. 879 (D.D.C.), *aff'd*, 404 U.S. 802 (1971). 304 U.S. 333 (1938). By virtue of the doctrine of preemption, however, states have been unable to restrict emergency strikes in the private sector. *International Union UAW* v. *O'Brien*, 339 U.S. 454 (1950); *Street Employees Division 1287* v. *Missouri*, 374 U.S., 74 (1963).

42. 304 U.S. 333 (1938).

43. 29 U.S.C. §159 (c)(3) (1976).

44. *NLRB* v. *International Van Lines*, 409 U.S. 48 (1972); *Climate Control Corporation*, 251 NLRB No. 102 (1980). Moreover, strikers who are discharged are entitled to back pay from the date of discharge without a request for reinstatement. *Abilities & Goodwill, Inc.*, 241 NLRB No. 5 (1979); *NLRB* v. *Lyon & Ryan Ford, Inc.*, 647 F.2d 745 (7th Cir. 1981).

45. *NLRB* v. *Erie Resistor Corp.*, 373 U.S. 221 (1963).

46. *Brotherhood of Railroad Trainmen* v. *Jacksonville Terminal Co.*, 394 U.S. 369 (1969).

47. Indeed, prior to *Erie Resistor*, a lower court held that *Mackay* permits employers to award superseniority. United also refused to hire trainees who did not cross the picket line. "United Strike: It's A Matter of Principle Now," *Business Week*, June 10, 1985, p.48, col. 1. While this conduct would be unlawful under the NLRA, *Phelps Dodge* v. *NLRB*, 313 U.S. 177 (1941), the answer has yet to be provided by the Supreme Court under the RLA. But United's practices were held unlawful by a federal district court. *Airline Pilots* v. *United Airlines*, 119 LRRM 3483 (N.D. Ill. 1985). Cf. *Nelson* v. *Piedmont Airlines*, 750 F.2d 1234 (4th Cir. 1984). Cf. *Brotherhood of Locomotive Firemen and Engineermen* v. *National Mediation Board*, 410 F.2d 1025 (D.C. Cir. 1969); *Airline Pilots Association* v. *Alaska Airlines*, 735 F.2d 328 (9th Cir. 1984).

48. *NLRB* v. *Fleetwood Trailer Co.*, 389 U.S. 375 (1967).

49. *Id.* at 378.

50. *Laidlaw* v. *NLRB*, 414 F.2d 99 (7th Cir. 1969), *cert. denied*, 397 U.S. 920 (1970); *American Machinery Corp.* v. *NLRB*, 424 F.2d 1321 (5th Cir. 1970). For some of the problems in determining whether replacements are laid off or discharged by virtue of strikers Section 7 rights, see *Harrison Ready Mix Concrete, Inc.*, 272 NLRB No. 47 (1984).

51. *Brooks Research and Manufacturing*, 202 NLRB 634 (1973). But the Court of Appeals for the Seventh Circuit has recognized business justification defenses. See *Giddings & Lewis, Inc.* v. *NLRB*, 113 LRRM 3361 (7th Cir. 1983).

52. *Giddings & Lewis* v. *NLRB*, 675 F.2d 926 (7th Cir. 1982).

53. ___ U.S. ___, 103 S.Ct. 3172 (1983).

54. Justice Blackmun wrote a separate concurring opinion.

55. *Machinists* v. *Wisconsin Employment Relations Commission*, 427 U.S. 132, 140 (1976); *NLRB* v. *Nash-Finch*, 404 U.S. 138, 144 (1971). Compare the New Jersey Supreme Court's treatment of state law prohibiting some strikebreaking. *U.S. Chamber of Commerce* v. *New Jersey*, 110 LRRM 2328 (N.J. 1982). Cf. *Gould, Inc.* v. *Wisconsin Department of Industry, Labor and Human Relations*, 117 LRRM 3337 (7th Cir. 1984).

56. See *Belknap, Inc.* v. *Hale, supra* note 51, at 3198-99. ("The Court's change in the law of permanency weakens the rights of strikers and undermines the protection afforded those rights by the Act. Such adjustments in the balance of power between labor and management are for Congress, not this Court.")

57. 380 U.S. 300 (1965).

58. In *American Shipbuilding*, 380 U.S. at 307, the Court lists some lockouts previously found exempt by the Board. These include the response to a "whipsaw" strike in *NLRB* v. *Truck Drivers Local 449 ("Buffalo Linen")*, 353 U.S. 87 (1957).

59. *American Shipbuilding*, 380 U.S. at 305.

60. *NLRB* v. *Truck Drivers Local 449 ("Buffalo Linen")*, 353 U.S. 87 (1957). But employer withdrawal from multiemployer bargaining is carefully circumscribed; *Charles D. Bonanno Linen Service, Inc.* v. *NLRB*, 454 U.S. 404 (1982).

61. *NLRB* v. *Brown*, 380 U.S. 278 (1965).

62. See, for example, *Inland Trucking Co.* v. *NLRB*, 440 F.2d 562 (7th Cir. 1971) (use of temporary replacements and a lockout when no strike *per se* a violation). But cf. *Inter-collegiate Press, Graphic Arts Div.*, 486 F.2d 837 (8th Cir. 1973), *cert. denied*, 416 U.S. 938 (1974) (interests must be balanced case by case).

63. See also Case Comment, 85 Harv. L. Rev. 680 (1972).

64. *Insurance Agents*, 361 U.S. at 484.

65. *NLRB* v. *Reed & Prince Mfg. Co.*, 205 F.2d 131 (1st Cir.), *cert. denied*, 346 U.S. 887 (1953); *Pittsburgh-Des Moines Corp.* v. *NLRB*, 663 F.2d 956 (9th Cir. 1981); *Pease Company* v. *NLRB*, 666 F.2d 1044 (6th Cir. 1981) *NLRB* v. *A-1 King Size Sandwiches*, 116 LRRM 2658 (11th Cir. 1984).

66. 343 U.S. 395 (1952).

67. *Id.* at 404.

68. 29 U.S.C. §158(d).

69. *NLRB* v. *Bildisco and Bildisco*, ___ U.S. ___, 104 S. Ct., 1188 (1984).

70. 11 U.S.C. §1113, congressional statute modifying *NLRB* v. *Bildisco and Bildisco*, ___ U.S. ___, 104 U.S. S. Ct., 1188 (1984). This statute requires an employer filing for bankruptcy to "bargain" with the union over necessary modifications of the collective bargaining agreement before filing an application seeking rejection of the collective bargaining agreement. The court can only approve rejecting the collective bargaining agreement if the union re-

fuses to accept the employer's proposal without good cause and "the balance of the equities" favors rejection. If the court does not rule on the employer's application within 30 days, the employer can terminate or alter the collective bargaining agreement.

71. *NLRB* v. *Wooster Division of Borg-Warner Corp.*, 356 U.S. 342 (1958).

72. *NLRB* v. *Katz*, 369 U.S. 736 (1962). Subsequent to impasse, an employer may institute its conditions. But the implementation of something more substantial than what was offered is bad-faith bargaining. *NLRB* v. *Crompton-Highland Mills*, 337 U.S. 217 (1949). Cf. *NLRB* v. *Exchange Parts Co.*, 375 U.S. 405 (1964). However, the Second Circuit Court has held that an employer did not violate the Act when it hired replacements at a rate of pay higher than that offered to strikers. *Auto Workers Local 259* v. *NLRB*, 120 LRRM 3102 (2d Cir. 1985).

73. See, e.g., *NLRB* v. *Tomco Communication Inc.*, 567 F.2d 871, 881 (9th Cir. 1978). The leading case defining impasse is *Taft Broadcasting Co.*, 163 NLRB 475, 478 (1967) *enforced*, 395 F.2d 622 (D.C. Cir. 1968). The Board has found an impasse where there were only 3 meetings between labor and management. *Lou Stecher's Super Markets*, 275 NLRB No. 71 (1985). See also Bell Transit Company, 271 NLRB No. 184 (1984). In establishing that an unfair refusal to bargain exists because of insistence upon a nonmandatory subject to the point of impasse, it needs to be proven that the nonmandatory subject is the sole cause of impasse. *Phillip Carey* v. *NLRB*, 331 F.2d 720 (6th Cir. 1964) *cert. denied*, 379 U.S. 888.

74. The contrast is stated in *NLRB* v. *International Van Lines*, 409 U.S. 48, 50–51 (1972). The decision rested on other grounds.

75. *NLRB* v. *Columbus Printing Pressmen Local 252*, 543 F.2d 1161 (5th Cir. 1976); *La Crosse Electrical Contractors Association*, 271 NLRB No. 36(1984); *Sheet Metal Workers Local 59*, 227 NLRB 520 (1976).

76. *Borg-Warner*, 356 U.S. at 350.

77. *Id.*

78. See W. Gould, *Japan's Reshaping of American Labor Law* (1984), pp. 124–128.

79. See *Fitzsimmons Manufacturing Company*, 251 NLRB No. 53 (1980), *enforced*, 670 F.2d 663 (6th Cir. 1982); *KDEN Broadcasting Co.*, 225 NLRB 25 (1976); *Cascade Corporation*, 192 NLRB 533 (1971).

80. The Board's current position is set forth in *Amoco Production Company*, 262 NLRB No. 160 (1982). Compare *Financial Institution Employees of America Local No. 1182* v. *NLRB*, 752 F.2d 356 (9th Cir. 1984) *cert. granted*, 105 S. Ct. 2318 (1985).

81. *General Electric Co.* v. *NLRB*, 415 F.2d 512 (2d Cir. 1969) ("coalition bargaining"). For an excellent discussion of this subject see S. Goldberg, "Coordinated Bargaining Tactics of Unions," 54 Cornell L. Rev. 897 (1969). Cf. *NLRB* v. *St. Joseph's Hospital*, 118 2765 LRRM (2nd Cir. 1985).

82. *NLRB* v. *Bartlett-Collins Co.*, 639 F.2d 652 (10th Cir. 1981); *Latrobe Steel Co.* v. *NLRB*, 630 F.2d 171 (3d Cir. 1980); *Hutchinson Fruit Company, Inc.*, 277 NLRB No. 54 (1985). See "AMC Objects to the Taping of Contract Talks," *Wall Street Journal*, June 19, 1985, p. 39.

83. *Fibreboard Paper Products Corp.* v. *NLRB*, 379 U.S. 203 (1964).

84. *Id.* at 225.

85. *First National Maintenance Corp.* v. *NLRB*, 452 U.S. 666, 677-78, 4772 (1981).

86. *Textile Workers Union* v. *Darlington Manufacturing Co.*, 380 U.S. 263 (1965).

87. *NLRB* v. *Adams Dairy, Inc.*, 350 F.2d 108, 113 (8th Cir. 1965), *cert. denied*, 382 U.S. 1011 (1966); *Royal Typewriter Co.* v. *NLRB*, 533 F.2d 1030, 1039 (8th Cir. 1976) (dicta); *NLRB* v. *Thompson Transport Co.*, 406 F.2d 698, 703 (10th Cir. 1969); *NLRB* v. *Transmarine Navigation Corp.*, 380 F.2d 933, 939 (9th Cir. 1967); *NLRB* v. *Royal Plating and Polishing Co.*, 350 F.2d 191, 196 (3rd Cir. 1965).

88. *NLRB* v. *First National Maintenance Corp.*, 627 F.2d 596 (2d Cir. 1980); *Brockway Motor Trucks* v. *NLRB*, 582 F.2d 720 (3d Cir. 1978).

89. *NLRB* v. *First National Maintenance Corp.*, 627 F.2d at 601-02 (footnote omitted).

90. *First National Maintenance Corp.* v. *NLRB*, *supra* note 78, at 686-87. Justice Brennan dissented in an opinion joined in by Justice Marshall. See W. Gould, "The Supreme Court's Labor and Employment Docket in the October 1980 Term: Justice Brennan's Term," 53 Univ. Colo. L. Rev. 1 6-18 (1981).

91. *Bob's Big Boy Family Restaurant*, 264 NLRB No. 178 (1982).

92. *The Liberal Market, Inc.*, 264 NLRB No. 109 (1982); *Otis Elevator Company*, 269 NLRB No. 162 (1984); *Bostrom Discussion, VOP, Inc.*, 272 NLRB No. 153 (1984); *Fraser Shipyards, Inc.*, 272 NLRB No. 80 (1984); *The Kroger Company*, 273 NLRB No. 70 (1984); *Garwood-Detroit Truck Equipment, Inc.*, 274 NLRB No. 23 (1985). See *Newspaper Guild Greater Philadelphia, Local 100* v. *NLRB*, 636 F.2d 550 (D.C. Cir. 1980) (holding that rules designed to prevent employees from engaging in activities which might compromise editorials and journalism is central to ultimate products and therefore not subject to mandatory bargaining).

93. *Milwaukee Spring Division of Illinois Coil Spring Company*, 265 NLRB No. 28 (1982).

94. *Milwaukee Spring Division*, 268 NLRB No. 87 (1984) *enforcement granted sub. nom. International Union, UAW* v. *NLRB*, 119 LRRM 2801 (D.C. Cir. 1985).

95. *NLRB* v. *General Electric Co.*, 418 F.2d 736 (2d Cir. 1969), *cert. denied*, 397 U.S. 965 (1970).

96. *NLRB* v. *Truitt Manufacturing Co.*, 351 U.S. 149 (1956). Cf. *Advertisers Manufacturing Company*, 275 NLRB No. 19 (1985). See also *NLRB* v. *Acme Industrial Co.*, 385 U.S. 432 (1967). See generally Bartosic and Hartley, "The Employer's Duty to Supply Information to the Union," 58 Cornell L. Rev. 23 (1972).
Similarly, the Court has limited information about employee test scores which are characterized as confidential. *NLRB* v. *Detroit Edison Co.*, 440 U.S. 301 (1979). There are frequent disputes about employee personnel records. Compare *Washington Gas Light Company*, 273 NLRB No. 20 (1984) with *New Jersey Bell Telephone Co.* v. *NLRB*, 720 F.2d. 789 (3rd Cir. 1983). Unions have had difficulty in obtaining access to information regarding non-unit work, *Bohemia, Inc.*, 272 NLRB No. 178 (1984); *United States Postal Service*, 261 NLRB No. 68 (1982). But see *E. I. Dupont de Nemours v. NLRB*, 117 LRRM 2497 (6th Cir. 1984). Employers have, however, been obliged to disclose relevant information on some bargaining issues. *Minnesota Mining and Mfg. Co.*, 261 NLRB 27 (1982) enfd. 711 F. 2d. 348 (D.C. Cir. 1983).

Chapter 7

1. *Proposed Amendments to the National Labor Relations Act: Hearings on H.R. 8410 Before the Subcommittee on Labor-Management Relations of the House Committee on Education and Labor*, 95th Cong., 1st Sess. 389 (statement of John H. Fanning). In fact, this proved to be a slight exaggeration. See, moreover, chapter 1, note 14.

2. H.R. Rep. No. 95–637, 95th Cong., 1st Sess. 21 (1977). See *Weiler, Promises To Keep: Securing Workers' Rights & Self-Organization Under the NLRA*, 96 Harv. L. Rev. 1769 (1983).

3. *Local 60, United Brotherhood of Carpenters* v. *NLRB*, 365 U.S. 651, 655 (1961); *NLRB* v. *Seven-Up Bottling*, 344 U.S. 344, 346 (1953). See also, e.g., *NLRB* v. *J. S. Alberici Construction Co.*, 591 F.2d 463, 470 n.8 (8th Cir. 1979); *Packing House and Industrial Services* v. *NLRB*, 590 F.2d 688, 697 (8th Cir. 1978).

4. The circuit courts have gone farther, holding that the proper test is what the employees would have earned but for the wrongful dismissal and that this may be less than the result of multiplying the actual wage before dismissal by the time since dismissal if the employer would have discharged the employee anyway for legitimate reasons; *NLRB* v. *Fort Vancouver Plywood Co.*, 604 F.2d 596 (9th Cir. 1979); *J. S. Alberici Construction Co.; Florsheim Shoe Store Co.* v. *NLRB*, 565 F. 2d 1240 (2d Cir. 1977); *Sunderstrand Heat Transfer, Inc.* v. *NLRB*, 538 F.2d 1257 (7th Cir. 1976); *NLRB* v. *Local No. 2 of United Association of Plumbing and Pipefitting Industry*, 360 F.2d 428, 434 (2d Cir. 1966). Support for the "but for" test was found in *Golden State Bottling Co.* v. *NLRB*, 414 U.S.

168, 189–90 (1974). But see *Packing House and Industrial Services* v. *NLRB*, 590 F.2d at 697–98 (antiunion animus justifies order reinstating entire work force of predecessor company), following *NLRB* v. *International Van Lines*, 409 U.S. 48, 53 (1972).

5. *NLRB* v. *Gullett Gin Co.*, 340 U.S. 361 (1951).

6. S. Rep. No. 95-628, 95th Cong. 2d Sess. 11 (1978).

7. W. Gould, "Prospects for Labor Law Reform: The Unions and Carter," *The Nation*, April 16, 1977, at pp. 466 and 467.

8. In response to J. P. Stevens's many unfair labor practices, the Board has devised extraordinary remedies. For example, 380 F.2d 292 (2d Cir. 1967) requires that the employer post the Board notice of its violation in the plant where the unfair labor practice occurred, and also in all of the company's 43 plants, and that the notice be mailed to all employees in all plants; 441 F.2d 514 (5th Cir. 1971) and 461 F.2d 490 (4th Cir. 1972) require that the employer give the union, upon request, reasonable access to plant bulletin boards for a period of one year and that the Board order to be read to employees during working time; 406 F.2d 1017 (4th Cir. 1968) and 417 F.2d 533 (5th Cir. 1969) require the employer to give a list of names and addresses of all employees in all plants to the union; and 464 F.2d 1326 (2d Cir. 1972), *cert denied*, 410 U.S. 926 (1973) provides for the payment to the NLRB of costs and expenses, counsel fees, and salaries in a civil contempt proceeding. Traditional remedies were regarded as insufficient for J. P. Stevens in 475 F.2d 973 (D.C. Cir. 1973) and compliance fines were imposed in 563 F.2d (2d Cir. 1977) but denied in 434 U.S. 1064 (1978). The history has been recounted in the context of more violations in *J. P. Stevens* v. *NLRB*, 638 F.2d 676 (4th Cir. 1980).

9. Oversight Hearings on the National Labor Relations Board: Hearings Before the Sub-committee on Labor-Management Relations of the House Committee on Education and Labor, 94th Cong., 1st Sess. 295–489.

10. See *supra* note 31, chapter 4.

11. There is no duty to bargain after an election and before certification where there are unresolved objections not claimed to be frivolous [*Sunderstrand Heat Transfers, Inc.* v. *NLRB*, 538 F.2d 1257, 1259 (7th Cir. 1976), overruling the Board citing *General Electric Co.*, 163 NLRB 198 (1967); *Trinity Steel Co.*, 103 NLRB 1470 (1953); *Harbor Chevrolet Co.*, 93 NLRB 1326 (1951)]. If the Board certifies a union, the employer may refuse to bargain and not be guilty of an unfair labor practice if the employer carries the heavy burden of showing that the certification was incorrect [*NLRB* v. *Allis- Chalmers Corp.*, 601 F.2d 870, 871–72 (5th Cir. 1979); *NLRB* v. *Newton-New Haven Co.*, 506 F.2d 1035 (2d Cir. 1974); *NLRB* v. *Clarytona Manor, Inc.*, 479 F.2d 976 (7th Cir. 1973)].

12. *Ex-Cell-O Corp.*, 185 NLRB 107 (1970), *rev'd and remanded to the Board, sub nom., International Union, U.A.W.* v. *NLRB*, 449 F. 2d 1046, 1050 (D.C. Cir. 1971). The Board later reaffirmed its position in a case where the violation was "clear and flagrant" [*Tiidee Products, Inc.*, 194 NLRB 1234 (1972), *enforced*, 502 F.2d 349 (D. C. Cir. 1974), *cert. denied*, 421 U.S. 991 (1975)].

13. *Tiidee Products, Inc.* But the Court of Appeals eliminated the award of litigation expenses. In a later case the Board refused litigation expenses, the Court of Appeals awarded them, but the Supreme Court reversed, saying this determination was for the Board [*NLRB* v. *Food Store Employees Local 347 (Hecks Inc.)*, 417 U.S. 1 (1974)]. On remand, the Board stood by the rule of *Tiidee Products*, but distinguished *Hecks, Inc.* on the ground that here the employer's position was debatable [*Hecks, Inc.*, 215 NLRB 765, 767 (1974)].

14. 29 U.S.C. §160 (j) (1976).

15. 29 U.S.C. §160 (1) (1976).

16. These are those practices that violate 8(b)(4)(A)–(C) or 8(b)(7) or 8(e), i.e., 29 U.S.C. §§158 (b)(4)(A)–(C), 158 (b)(7), 158(e)(1976). Included are the rules against secondary boycotts and recognitional picketing. See chapter 3.

17. W. Gould, *Black Workers in White Unions* (1977), pp. 281–315.

18. Oversight Hearings on the National Labor Relations Board: Hearings Before the Subcommittee on Labor-Management Relations of the House Committee on Education and Labor, 94th Cong., 1st Sess. 348 (statement of Jack Crowley).

19. "AFL-CIO Chief Calls Labor Laws A (Dead Letter)," *Wall Street Journal*, August 16, 1984, p. 8; "Kirkland's Call to Void Labor Laws Ignites a Growing National Debate," *Wall Street Journal*, November 6, 1984, p. 29, col. 3; Gould, "Mistaken Opposition to the N.L.R.B.," *New York Times*, June 20, 1985, p. 31, col. 2.

Chapter 8

1. See generally Proceedings of the Twenty-Sixth Annual Meeting, National Academy of Arbitrators: Arbitration of Interest Disputes (1974).

2. Noble, "Postal Contract Includes a Raise and Concession," *New York Times*, December 25, 1984. 39 U.S.C. §101 *et seq. (1984 Supp.)*.

3. Bureau of National Affairs, Government Employee Relations Reporter 51:1011 to 51:6024 (1985). Connecticut Gen. Stat. Title 7, Sec. 7-467 *et seq.* (1965) as last amended eff. 10-1-84 (mandatory issue by issue, for all municipal employees); Hawaii Rev. Stat. Ch. 89, Sec. 89-1 *et seq.* as last amended eff. 7-1-84 (mandatory, package, firefighters only); Illinois, Illinois Rev. Stat. Ch. 48, Sec. 1614 (1983) eff. 7-1-84 (at request of either party, for security em-

ployees, state peace officers and state firefighter disputes, issue by issue on economic issues); Code of Iowa, Ch. 20, Sec. 20-1 *et seq.* (1974) as last amended eff. 1-1-79 (at request of either party, issue by issue with extra options as recommended by fact finder, all public employees); Massachusetts, M.G.L.A. Ch. 1078, Sec. 4 (1973) as last amended 1982, expires June 30, 1985 (for police and firefighters but with different subject matter scope for each); Michigan, M.C.L.A., Sec. 423-231 *et seq.* (1969) as last amended eff. 1-4-78 (on petition by either party, police, firefighters and certain other emergency personnel employed by police and fire departments, issue by issue on economic issues); Montana, Title 39, Ch. 31, Parts 1-4, MCA (1973) as last amended eff. 7/1/83 (at request of either party, package, for firefighters in municipalities); Nevada, N.R.S. Sec. 288.101 *et seq.* (1969) as last amended eff. 7-1-83 (package, mandatory for firefighters and used under some conditions for other local government employees); New Jersey, Ch. 85, Sec. 1 *et seq.* (1977) as last amended eff. 7/30/82 (a variety of procedures for police and firefighters); Ohio, Ohio Rev. Code Title 41, Ch. 4117 Sec. 4117.14 (1983) eff. 4-1-84 (mandatory issue by issue for safety personnel); Wisconsin, W.S.A. Ch. 111, Sec. 111.70 *et seq.* as last amended eff. 3-20-84 (agreement of parties on order of Wisconsin Employment Relations Commission leads to either final offer or conventional arbitration for police and firefighters).

4. The 29 jurisdictions that currently have interest-arbitration statutes are Alaska, Connecticut, Delaware, District of Columbia, Hawaii, Illinois, Indiana, Iowa, Maine, Massachusetts, Michigan, Minnesota, Montana, Nebraska, Nevada, New Jersey, New York, Ohio, Oklahoma, Oregon, Pennsylvania, Rhode Island, Texas, Vermont, Washington, Wisconsin, Wyoming, New York City, and Eugene, Oregon. See generally R. Lester, *Labor Arbitration in State and Local Government: An Examination of Experience in Eight States and New York City* (1984).

5. For example, S.560, 92d Cong., 1st Sess. (1971).

6. Proceedings of the Twenty-Sixth Annual Meeting, National Academy of Arbitrators, Arbitration of Interest Disputes (1976), pp. 79–80.

7. *NLRB* v. *Weingarten, Inc.*, 420 U.S. 251 (1975).

8. *Baton Rouge Waterworks Co.*, 246 N.L.R.B. No. 161 (1979).

9. The Supreme Court has rejected the proposition that failure to adhere to two arbitration awards and not to give them any "effect would impair the effectiveness of the dispute resolution process for which the parties bargained." *Metropolitan Edison Co.* v. *NLRB*, ___ U.S. ___, *103 S.Ct. 1467 (1983)*. *See also Oil, Chemical and Atomic Workers, Local 4-16000* v. *Ethyl Corp.*, 644 F.2d 1044 (5th Cir. 1981); *Boston Shipping Association, Inc.* v. *International Longshoremen's Association (AFL-CIO)*, 108 LRRM 2449 (1st Cir., 1981).

10. 29 U.S.C. §158(a)(5) (1976).

11. W. Usery, "Why Strikes Occur During the Term of Contract Agreements," 1976 *Labor Relations Yearbook* 131, 132 (Bureau of National Affairs); Southeastern Conference on Bargaining Trends (remarks of John Canestraight), 1976 *Labor Relations Yearbook* 175 (Bureau of National Affairs).

12. W. Gould, *Black Workers in White Unions* (1977), pp. 211–42; W. Gould, "Labor Arbitration of Grievances Involving Racial Discrimination," 118 U. Penn. L. Rev. 40 (1969).

13. 42 U.S.C. §2000 (1976).

14. W. Gould, "Labor Arbitration of Grievances Involving Racial Discrimination," 118 Penna. L. Rev. 40, 46 (1969).

15. For example, *Acuff* v. *United Paperworks*, 404 F.2d 169 (5th Cir. 1968), *cert. denied*, 394 U.S. 987 (1969).

16. 353 U.S. 448 (1957).

17. *United Steelworkers* v. *American Manufacturing Co.*, 363 U.S. 564 (1960); *United Steelworkers* v. *Warrior and Gulf Navigation Co.*, 363 U.S. 574 (1960); *United Steelworkers* v. *Enterprise Wheel and Car Corp.*, 363 U.S. 593 (1960).

18. In *Pennoyer* v. *Neff*, 95 U.S. 714 (1878), the Supreme Court found that due process demanded the traditional rule of the common law: that jurisdiction over an individual could be achieved only by his voluntary appearance or by personal service of process within the state. This position was gradually liberalized in two ways. First, the need for presence within the state was given up (at first for particular sorts of cases, and then generally) when the court decided that it was enough for the person to have certain minimum contacts with the state sufficient to satisfy traditional notions of fair play and substantial justice [*International Shoe Co.* v. *Washington*, 326 U.S. 310 (1945)]. The various states are free to take as much of this constitutionally permitted jurisdiction as they desire. Second, the permissible means of service have been liberalized. The means must be reasonably calculated to apprise the out-of-state person of the suit (*International Shoe Co.*). Once again, within those limits, the states are free to specify the permissible means of service.

19. The Court decided that the statute authorized federal courts to fashion a body of federal common law, and that the statute, as thus interpreted, was constitutional.

20. 353 U.S. at 458. The Court extended the reach of section 301, and the authority of the courts to establish a federal common law to union constitutions and suits by local unions against internationals to enforce them, in *Plumbers and Pipefitters* v. *Local 334*, 452 U.S. 615 (1981).

21. "Final adjustment by a method agreed upon by the parties is declared to be the desirable method for the settlement of grievance disputes arising over

the application or interpretation of an existing collective bargaining agreement." 1129 U.S.C. §173(d) (1976).

22. *International Association of Machinists* v. *Cutler-Hammer, Inc.*, 271 App. Div. 917, 67 N.Y.S.2d 317 (1947), *affirmed* 297 N.Y. 519, 74 N.E.2d 464 (1948).

23. *Warrior and Gulf Navigation Co.*, 363 U.S. 574 (1960).

24. *Id.* at 581–82.

25. *Id.* at 578.

26. *Id.* at 580.

27. *W.R. Grace & Company* v. *Local Union 759, International Union of the United Rubber, Cork, Linoleum and Plastic Workers of America*, 461 U.S. 757 (1983). Subsequent to *W.R. Grace*, courts have identified "well-defined and dominant" public policies, see, e.g., *Amalgamated Meat Cutters and Butcher Workmen of North America* v. *Great Western Food Company*, 712 F.2d 122 (5th Cir. 1983) (arbitration award reinstating driver caught drinking on duty violated public policy against professional drivers drinking and driving); *U.S. Postal Service* v. *American Postal Workers Union, AFL-CIO*, 736 F.2d 822 (1st Cir. 1984) (arbitration award reinstating postal employee convicted of embezzling postal funds violated public policy of trust and efficiency for the postal service); *Northrop Corporation* v. *Triad Financial Establishment*, 593 F.Supp. 928 (C.D. CA. 1984) (portion of arbitration award vacated because public policy involving Department of Defense regulations and a Saudi Arabian decree prevented performance of certain phases of a marketing agreement). The principle that arbitrators must be faithful to the contract and not "manifest an infidelity to this obligation" can be found in *United Steelworkers of America* v. *Enterprise Wheel and Car Corp.*, 363 U.S. 593, 597 (1960).

28. 398 U.S. 235 (1970).

29. *Id.* at 244.

30. *Id.* at 245. See *Dowd Box Co.* v. *Courtney*, 368 U.S. 502 (1962).

31. *Id.* at 248 (footnote omitted).

32. *Id.* at 251.

33. *Id.* at 250.

34. *Buffalo Forge Co.* v. *United Steelworkers*, 428 U.S. 397 (1976); W. Gould, "On Labor Injunctions Pending Arbitration: Recasting Buffalo Forge," 30 Stanford L. Rev. 533 (1978); see also W. Gould, "On Labor Injunctions, Unions and the Judges: The Boys Market Case," 1970 Supreme Court Review 215. The Supreme Court later relied on both *Boys Markets* and *Buffalo Forge* in ruling

that an injunction could not be issued against the International Longshoremen's Association for refusing to handle cargo bound to or coming from the Soviet Union in protest of the invasion of Afghanistan. *Jacksonville Bulk Terminals, Inc.* v. *International Longshoremen's Assoc.*, 457 U.S. 702 (1982). The Court found that the underlying dispute, "whether viewed as an expression of the Union's 'moral outrage' at Soviet military policy or as an expression of sympathy for the people of Afghanistan, is plainly not arbitrable under the collective bargaining agreement." *Id.* at 711.

35. *Teamsters, Local 174* v. *Lucas Flour Co.*, 369 U.S. 95 (1962).

36. *Drake Bakeries* v. *Bakery Workers*, 370 U.S. 257 (1962).

37. *Carbon Fuel* v. *Mine Workers*, 444 U.S. 212 (1979). This decision does not deal with local union liability. The question is often an academic one, since locals often do not have much money in their treasuries.

38. *Atkinson* v. *Sinclair Roofing Co.*, 370 U.S. 238 (1962).

39. *Complete Auto Transit, Inc.* v. *Reis*, 451 U.S. 401 (1981).

40. See note 34. Local union liability was established on one or another of these theories in *Easzor Express, Inc.* v. *International Brotherhood of Teamsters*, 520 F.2d 951 (3d Cir. 1975), *cert. denied*, 424 U.S. 935 (1976); *United Steelworkers of America* v. *Lorain*, 616 F.2d 919 (6th Cir. 1980); *Keebler* v. *Bakery Workers, Local 492-A*, 104 LRRM 2625 (E.D. Pa., 1980). See generally M. Whitman, "Wildcat Strikes: The Union's Narrowing Path to Rectitude," 50 Ind. L.J. 472 (1975); W. Gould, "Taft-Hartley Comes to Great Britain," 81 Yale L.J. 1421 (1972).

41. *Metropolitan Edison Co.* v. *NLRB*, ___ U.S. ___, 103 S.Ct. 1467 (1983). The Court also concluded that statutory immunization may be waived in the collective bargaining agreement.

42. *Id.* at 1472.

43. The leading case in which the deferral doctrine was developed is *Spielberg Manufacturing Co.*, 112 NLRB 1080 (1955). See also *International Harvester Co.*, 138 NLRB 923 (1962), *enforced sub nom.* Ramsey v. *NLRB* 327 F.2d 784 (7th Cir.), *cert. denied*, 377 U.S. 1003 (1964). The problems involved in applying *Spielberg* are still considerable. See, e.g., *NLRB* v. *Pincus Bros. Inc.-Maxwell*, 620 F.2d 367 (3d Cir. 1980); *NLRB* v. *Max Factor & Co.*, 640 F.2s 197 (9th Cir. 1980), *cert. denied*, 451 U.S. 983 (1981); "Judicial Review and the Trend Toward More Stringent NLRB Standards on Arbitral Deferrals" (comment), 129 U. Penna. L.R. 738 (1981).

44. *Olin Corporation*, 268 NLRB No. 86 (1984), slip. op. at 5.

45. *Id.*

46. *Collyer Insulated Wire*, 192 NLRB 837 (1971). See *William E. Arnold Co.* v. *Carpenters District Council*, 417 U.S. 12, 16–17 (1974); *Carey* v. *Westinghouse Electric Corp.*, 375 U.S. 261, 270–272 (1964).

47. For example, *General American Transport Corp.*, 228 NLRB No. 102 (1977) (the Board refused to extend Collyer to 8(a)(3) cases); *Machinists Lodges 700, 743, 1746* v. *NLRB*, 525 F.2d 237 (2d Cir. 1975); *IBEW Local 2188* v. *NLRB*, 494 F.2d 1087 (D.C. Cir. 1974), *cert. denied*, 419 U.S. 834 (1974); *Kansas Meat Packers*, 198 NLRB 543 (1972); *Anaconda Wire and Cable Co.*, 201 NLRB 839 (1973).

48. *United Technologies Corporation*, 268 NLRB, No. 83 (1984).

49. 376 U.S. 543 (1964).

50. *NLRB* v. *Burns International Security Services*, 406 U.S. 272 (1972).

51. *H. K. Porter* v. *NLRB*, 397 U.S. 99 (1970).

52. *Howard Johnson Co.* v. *Detroit Local Joint Executive Board, Hotel Employees International Union*, 417 U.S. 249 (1974).

53. *Republic Steel Corp.* v. *Maddox*, 379 U.S. 650 (1965). The decision authorizing individual actions is *Smith* v. *Evening News Association*, 371 U.S. 195 (1962).

54. 386 U.S. 171 (1967).

55. ___ U.S. ___, 103 S.Ct. 588 (1983).

56. *Id.* at 602–03 (White, J., dissenting).

57. 415 U.S. 36, 60 (1974).

58. *Id.* footnote 21.

59. Basic Vegetable Products, Inc., 64 Labor Arbitration Reports 620 (1975); Settlement Agreement between Weyerhauser Co. and International Woodworkers of America, May 1979 (in the author's files).

60. *Barrentine* v. *Arkansas-Best Freight System*, 24 WH Cases 1284 (1981). Chief Justice Burger dissented, in an opinion joined in by Justice Rehnquist.

61. *McDonald* v. *City of Westbranch*, ___U.S.___, 104 S. Ct. 1799, 1801 (1984).

62. *Service Employees International Union* v. *County of Napa*, 99 Cal. App. 3d 946, 160 Cal. Rptr. 810 (1979); J. Toole, "Judicial Activism in Public Sector Grievance Arbitration: A Study of Recent Developments," 33 Arbitration, J. 6 (1978); *In the matter of the Arbitration between the City of Plattsburgh* v. *Local 788 and New York Council 66, AFSCME, AFL-CIO*, 485 N.Y.S.2d 618, 619 (A.D. 3d

1985) (the policy of favoring arbitration in private sector labor relations does not apply equally in the field of public employment. . . . Absent a clear, unequivocal agreement to the contrary, it must be taken for granted that the public body did not intend to refer a particular matter to arbitration). But see *The City and County of Denver* v. *Denver Firefighters, Local 858 AFL-CIO*, 663 P.2d 1032, 1041 (Colo. 1983) (firefighters filed complaint against the city claiming city breached collective bargaining agreement in refusing to submit a grievance to binding arbitration. Court found that "on its face . . . claim is arbitrable because it requires interpretation and application of standards of employer conduct agreed to by the City"); *In the matter of Arbitration: Nicolet High School District* v. *Nicolet Education Assocation*, 348 N.W.2d 175, 178 118 W.2d 707 (Wis. 1984) ("This court has developed several well-settled rules governing review of arbitrator's decisions. An arbitrator's award is presumptively valid, and it will be disturbed only when its invalidity is demonstrated by clear and convincing evidence"); *Board of Control of Ferris State College* v. *Michigan AFSCME, Council 25, Local 1609*, 361 N.W.2d 342, 343 Mich. App. 1984) (Court follows the standard of limited review from the *Steelworkers Trilogy*, "drawing its essence from the collective bargaining agreement," a position that has also been adopted by the Michigan Supreme Court).

63. T. Kochan, "Dynamics of Dispute Resolution in the Public Sector," in *Public Sector Bargaining* (Industrial Relations Research Association Series, 1979), pp. 150, 154.

64. *Id.* at 175.

Chapter 9

1. *Steele* v. *Louisville and Nashville Railroad*, 323 U.S. 192 (1944) (a duty of fair representation under the Railway Labor Act, 45 U.S.C. §§ 151 *et seq.*). The Supreme Court found a duty of fair representation under the NLRA in *Syres* v. *Oil Workers Local 23*, 350 U.S. 829 (1955) (*per curiam*), reversing 223 F.2d 739 (5th Cir. 1955). The Board first found a breach of the duty of fair representation to violate §8(b) in *Miranda Fuel Co.*, 140 N.L.R.B. 181 (1962), *enforcement denied* 326 F.2d 172 (2d Cir. 1963).

2. *Vaca* v. *Sipes*, 386 U.S. at 190.

3. The decision that seems to have gone furthest in establishing duty of fair representation obligation for negligent union behavior is *Dutrisac* v. *Caterpillar Tractor Co.* 749 F.2d 1270 (9th Cir. 1983); See also *De Anyo* v. *Sindicato de Trabajadores Packing, AFL-CIO*, 425 F.2d 281, LRRM (1st Cir. 1970) (union's total failure to investigate and process grievances is deemed arbitrary and thus a breach of its duty of fair representation); *Ruzicka* v. *General Motors Corp.*, 523 F.2d 306, 90 LRRM 2497, *affirmed on rehearing*, 528 F.2d 912, 91 LRRM 3054 (6th Cir. 1975) (union's negligent failure to file for arbitration of employee's grievance within prescribed time limits held to constitute a breach of its duty of fair representation); *Malone* v. *U.S. Postal Service*, 526 F.2d 1099, 90 LRRM 3287 (6th Cir. 1975) (union's negligent failure to take any action in processing

employee's grievance held to be a breach of its duty of fair representation); *Robesky* v. *Quantas Empire Airways*, 573 F.2d 1082, 98 LRRM 2090 (9th Cir. 1978) (duty of fair representation violated by union's nondisclosure of information critical to employee's determination of whether to accept employer's settlement offer); cf. *Price* v. *Southern Pacific Transp. Co.*, 586 F.2d 750, 100 LRRM 2671 (9th Cir. 1978) (union's failure to file a grievance held to be neither egregious nor arbitrary). See generally A. Cox, "Rights Under a Labor Agreement," 69 Harv. L. Rev. 601 (1956); K. Hanslowe, "Individual Rights in Collective Labor Relations," 45 Cornell L.Q. 25 (1959); C. Summers, "The Individual Employee's Rights Under the Collective Bargaining Agreement: What Constitutes Fair Representation?" 126 U. of Penna. L. Rev. 251 (1977). Punitive damages are not available when the duty is violated [*IBEW* v. *Faust*, 442 U.S. 42 (1979)].

4. *Clayton* v. *International Union, UAW*, 49 U.S.L.W. 4550 (1981). The employee has the obligation to exhaust the procedures set forth in the collective bargaining agreement [*Republic Steel Corp.* v. *Maddox*, 379 U.S. 650 (1965)].

5. *Acuff* v. *United Papermakers*, 404 F.2d 169 (5th Cir. 1968), *cert. denied*, 394 U.S. 987 (1969).

6. *Smith* v. *Hussmann Refrigerator Co.*, 619 F.2d 1229 (8th Cir. 1980). See also *Clark* v. *Hein-Werner Corp.*, 8 Wis.2d 264, 99 N.W.2d 132 (1962).

7. *Hines* v. *Anchor Motor Freight*, 424 U.S. 554 (1976).

8. *Id.* at 571.

9. *United Parcel Service, Inc.* v. *Mitchell*, 101 S. Ct. 1559 (1981). The result in *United Parcel* was to reduce the period from 6 years (contract actions) to 90 days (arbitration awards). Only Justice Stevens dissented. The statute of limitations for breach of collective-bargaining agreements is state law [*Auto Workers* v. *Hoosier Cardinal Corp.*, 383 U.S. 696 (1965)].

10. *Del Costello* v. *International Brotherhood of Teamsters*, ___U.S.___ 103 S. Ct. 2281, 2291 (1983). The majority of the circuit courts of appeal have chosen to apply *Del Costello* retroactively; see *Graves* v. *Smith's Transfer Corporation*, 736 F.2d 819 (1st Cir. 1984); *Assad* v. *Mt. Sinai Hospital*, 725 F.2d 837 (2d Cir. 1984); *Perez* v. *Dana Corporation, Parish Frame Division*, 718 F.2d 581 (3rd Cir. 1983); *Murray* v. *Branch Motor Express Company*, 723 F.2d 1146 (4th Cir. 1983); *Edwards* v. *Sea-Land Service, Inc.*, 720 F.2d 857 (5th Cir. 1983); *Lincoln* v. *Machinists and Aerospace Workers*, 723 F.2d 627 (8th Cir. 1983); *Rogers* v. *Lockheed Georgia Company*, 720 F.2d 1247 (11th Cir. 1983). The Ninth Circuit has not applied *Del Costello* retroactively, see *Edwards* v. *Teamsters Local Union No. 36, Building Material and Dump Truck Drivers*, 719 F.2d 1036 (9th Cir. 1983).

11. 373 U.S. 734 (1963).

12. 388 U.S. 175 (1967).

13. W. Gould, "Solidarity Forever—Or Hardly Ever," 66 Cornell L. Rev. 77 (1980).

14. *Pattern Makers' League of North America* v. *NLRB*, ___U.S. ___ (June 27, 1985).

15. *Id.* at ___.

16. *NLRB* v. *Boeing Co.*, 412 U.S. 67 (1973).

17. *Abood* v. *Detroit Board of Education*, 431 U.S. 209 (1977).

18. Pub. L. 86-257, Sept. 14, 1959, 73 Stat. 519, 29 U.S.C. §§401 *et seq.* (1976). This statute has spawned litigation about the union's fiduciary duty to members; see, for instance, *Morrisey* v. *Curran*, 107 LRRM 2233 (2d Cir. 1981).

19. *United Steelworkers of America, AFL-CIO-CLC* v. *Sadlowski*, 457 U.S. 102, 109 (1982).

20. *Id.* at 124.

21. *Id.* at 124.

22. *Id.*

23. *Finnegan* v. *Leu*, 456 U.S. 431 (1982).

24. *Id.* at 437.

25. *Id.* at 441 fn. 11. See *Cotter* v. *Owens* 118 LRRM 2451 (2d Cir. 1985).

26. *Alvey* v. *General Electric Co.*, 622 F.2d 1279 (7th Cir. 1980). See generally A. Cox, "Internal Affairs of Labor Unions Under the Labor Reform Act of 1959," 58 Mich. L. Rev. 819 (1960).

27. *Williams* v. *International Typographical Union*, 423 F.2d 1295 (10th Cir.), *cert. denied*, 400 U.S. 824 (1970).

28. 108 LRRM 2105 (D.C. Cir. 1981).

29. *Bauman* v. *Presser*, 117 LRRM 2393, 2399 (D.C. D.C. 1984)

30. *Id.* at 2396.

31. 29 U.S.C. §461.

32. 29 U.S.C. §§481 *et seq.*.

33. 29 U.S.C. §481 (e) (1976). See generally *Hodgson* v. *Local 6799, United Steel-workers*, 403 U.S. 333 (1971); *Wirtz* v. *Hotel, Motel and Club Employees Union, Local 6*, 391 U.S. 492 (1968); *Calhoon* v. *Harvey*, 379 U.S. 134 (1964).

34. 404 U.S. 528 (1972).

35. *Local No. 82, Furniture and Piano Moving* v. *Crowley*, ___ U.S. ___, 104 S. Ct. 2557 (1984).

36. *International Association of Machinists* v. *Street*, 367 U.S. 740 (1961). See also *Pipefitters Local 562* v. *United States*, 407 U.S. 385 (1972).

37. *Ellis* v. *Brotherhood of Railway, Airline and Steamship Clerks*, ___U.S.___, 104 S. Ct. 1883 (1984)

38. *Id.* at 1890.

Chapter 10

1. The following states have public-employee legislation: Alabama, Alaska, California, Connecticut, Delaware, Florida, Georgia, Hawaii, Idaho, Illinois, Indiana, Iowa, Kansas, Louisiana, Maine, Maryland, Massachusetts, Michigan, Minnesota, Missouri, Montana, Nebraska, Nevada, New Hampshire, New Jersey, New Mexico, New York, North Dakota, Ohio, Oklahoma, Oregon, Pennsylvania, Rhode Island, South Dakota, Tennessee, Texas, Vermont, Washington, Wisconsin, Wyoming, and Washington, D.C. The Indiana Public Employees Collective Bargaining Act was repealed effective Sept. 1, 1982. However, teachers in Indiana still have a statutory right to bargain collectively. Three states, Virginia, Louisiana and South Carolina, although they do not have any public employee bargaining laws, have recently enacted grievance procedures for some public employees. See J. Grodin, D. Wollett, R. Alleyne, *Collective Bargaining in Public Employment*, third edition (1979), GERR §51.

2. H. Edwards, "The Emerging Duty to Bargain in the Public Sector," 71 Michigan L. Rev. 885, 896 (1973).

3. 5 U.S.C. §1101 *et seq.* Pub. L. No. 95-454, 92 Stat. 1111.

4. 39 U.S.C. Sec. 1206.

5. *American Federation of State, County and Municipal Employees, AFL-CIO* v. *Woodward*, 406 F.2d 137 (8th Cir. 1969).

6. *United States Civil Service Commission* v. *National Association of Letter Carriers*, 413 U.S. 548, 564 (1973); *Pickering* v. *Board of Education*, 391 U.S. 563, 568 (1968).

7. *Shelton* v. *Tucker*, 364 U.S. 479 (1960).

8. There is authority on policemen: *Loutine* v. *Van Cleave*, 483 F.2d 966, 967 (10th Cir. 1973); *Vorbeek* v. *McNeal*, 407 F. Supp. 733 (E.D. Mo. 1976) (three-judge court), *affirmed*, 426 U.S. 943, *rehearing denied*, 429 U.S. 874.

9. It is permissible to prevent fire-department *officers* from joining the same union as rank-and-file employees. *Firefighters' Local 2498* v. *York County*, 589 F.2d 775 (4th Cir. 1978); *Elk Grove Firefighters' Local No. 2340* v. *Williss*, 400 F. Supp. 1097 (N.D. Ill. 1975), *affirmed*, 539 F.2d 714 (7th Cir. 1976); *Firefighters* v. *City of Tupelo*, 439 F.Supp. 1224 (N.D. Miss. 1977). A regulation prohibiting police officers from joining "any labor organization whose membership is not exclusively limited to full time law enforcement officers" impermissibly limits police officers' rights of association under the First Amendment; *Mescall* v. *Rochford*, 101 L.R.R.M. 3136 (N.D. Ill. 1979), aff'd 655 F.2d 111 (7th Cir. 1981).

10. *United Federation of Postal Clerks* v. *Blount*, 325 F. Supp. 879 (D.D.C. 1971) (three-judge court), *affirmed*, 404 U.S. 802; *Vorbeek* v. *McNeil, supra* note 8; *Loutine* v. *Van Cleave, supra* note 8.

11. *County Sanitation District No. 2 of Los Angeles* v. *County Employees Association SEIU*, 38 Cal.3d 564 (1985).

12. *Smith* v. *Arkansas State Highway Employees*, 441 U.S. 463 (1979).

13. *City of Madison, Joint School District No. 8* v. *Wisconsin Employment Relations Commission*, 429 U.S. 167 (1976).

14. *Perry Education Association* v. *Perry Local Educators' Association*, 460 U.S. 37 (1983).

15. *NLRB* v. *Magnavox Co.*, 415 U.S. 322 (1974); *Helton* v. *NLRB*, 656 F.2d 883 (D.C. Cir. 1981).

16. *Ysleta Federation of Teachers* v. *Ysleta Independent School District*, 720 F.2d 1429 (5th Cir. 1983).

17. *Minnesota State Board for Community Colleges* v. *Knight*, ___U.S.___, 104 S. Ct. 1058 (1984).

18. *Board of Regents* v. *Roth*, 408 U.S. 564 (1972); *Perry* v. *Sinderman*, 408 U.S. 593 (1972); *Arnett* v. *Kennedy*, 416 U.S. 134 (1974); *Goss* v. *Lopez*, 419 U.S. 565 (1975); *Bishop* v. *Wood*, 426 U.S. 341 (1976); *Davis* v. *Scherer*, ___U.S.___, 104 S. Ct. 3012 (1984); *Cleveland Board of Education* v. *Loudermill*, ___U.S.___, 105 S. Ct. 1487 (1985).

19. *Cleveland Board of Education*, 105 S. Ct. 1487, 1491 (1985).

20. Governor's Commission on Public Employment Relations, Final Report (State of New York, 1966).

21. Wellington, *Unions and the Cities* (1972); H. Wellington and R. Winter, "The Limits of Collective Bargaining in Public Employment," 78 Yale L.J. 1107 (1969).

22. J. Burton and C. Krider, "The Role and Consequences of Strikes by Public Employees," 79 Yale L.J. 419 (1969).

23. R. Smith, H. Edwards, and R. T. Clark, *Labor Relations Law in the Public Sector* (1974), pp. 259–273.

24. *Detroit Police Officers Association* v. *Detroit*, 391 Mich. 44, 214 N.W.2d 803 (1974).

25. *San Jose Peace Officers Association* v. *San Jose*, 78 Cal. App.3d 935, 144 Cal. Rpt. 638 (1978).

26. *Bureau of Alcohol, Tobacco and Firearms* v. *Federal Labor Relations Authority*, ___U.S.___(1985).

27. In early 1978 there were eight such states: the five in the text plus Montana, Oregon, and Wisconsin [T. Kochan, "Dynamics of Dispute Resolution in the Public Sector," in *Public-Sector Bargaining* (Industrial Relations Research Association Series, 1979), pp. 150, 154–55]. In 1980 only Idaho could be added to the list. California has required public employers to exhaust administrative remedies before the state labor-relations agency before seeking injunctions against strikes [*San Diego Teachers Association* v. *Superior Court*, 24 Cal.3d 1, 154 Cal. Rptr. 893 (1979)]. Cf. *Holland School District* v. *Holland Education Association*, 380 Mich. 314, 157 N.W.2d 206 (1968). But the Seventh Circuit Court of Appeals has held that the California approach does not apply under the federal statutory scheme [*United States* v. *PATCO*, 653 F.2d 1134 (7th Cir. 1981), *cert. denied*, 454 U.S. 1083 (1981)].

28. *County Sanitation of Los Angeles* v. *SEIU*, 38 Cal.3d 564, 586 (1985).

29. W. Gould, "Managing Emergency Strikes," *New Leader*, March 14, 1966; K. Hanslowe, *The Emerging Law of Labor Relations in Public Employment* (1967).

30. The Civil Service Reform Act of 1978, Pub. L. 95-454, Oct. 13, 1978, 92 Stat. 111. 5 U.S.C. §7119(c)(5)(A)(ii) (1979 Supp.).

31. Kochan, *op. cit.* at 156; W. Gould, "Public Employment: Mediation, Fact Finding and Arbitration," 55 Am. B.A.J. 835, 838 (1969).

Chapter 11

1. Labor and management must be represented equally on the board of trustees [29 U.S.C. §186(c)(5)]. Cf. *NLRB* v. *Amax Coal Co.*, 453 U.S. 322 (1981), in which the Court held, 8-1, that under both the NLRA and ERISA trustees administer the trusts in the interest of employees and their families rather than that of the appointing party.

2. 29 U.S.C. §1001(b) (1976).

3. Pub. L. 96-364, 94 Stat. 1209–1210.

4. 446 U.S. 359 (1980).

5. *Alessi* v. *Raybestos-Manhattan, Inc.*, 451 U.S. 504 (1981).

6. *Industrial Union Department, AFL-CIO* v. *American Petroleum Institute*, 448 U.S. 607, 614 (1980). See "The Significant Risk Requirement in OSHA Regulation of Carcinogens" (comment), 33 Stanford L. Rev. 551 (1981).

7. *Id.* at 615 quoting 29 U.S.C. §652 (d).

8. *Id.* at 642.

9. The Court did not reach this issue in *American Petroleum.*

10. *Id.* at 641.

11. *AFL-CIO* v. *Marshall*, 617 F.2d 636, 661 (D.C. Cir. 1979). *Industrial Union Department, AFL-CIO* v. *Hodgson*, 499 F.2d 467, 478 (D.C. Cir. 1974), contains a sentence quoted in several later cases in that circuit, e.g., *AFL-CIO* v. *Marshall*, 617 F.2d at 655 w. 4.

12. *American Textile Manufacturers Institute, Inc.* v. *Donovan*, 452 U.S. 490 (1981). Chief Justice Burger, Justice Rehnquist, and Justice Stewart were the dissenters.

13. *Id.* at 495.

14. *American Petroleum*, 448 U.S. at 652; *Whirlpool Corp.* v. *Marshall*, 445 U.S., 20–21 (1980).

15. *Marshall* v. *Barlow's, Inc.*, 436 U.S. 307 (1978). However, the Court has held that the same constitutional requirements do not apply in the case of the Federal Mine Safety and Health Act of 1977, 30 U.S.C. §301. See *Donovan* v. *Dewey*, 452 U.S. 594 (1981).

16. *Taylor* v. *Brighton Corp.*, 616 F.2d 256 (6th Cir. 1980).

17. *Bethlehem Steel Corp.* v. *Occupational Safety and Health Review Commission*, 540 F.2d 157 (3d Cir. 1976). ("Repeated" implies at least two previous instances, and application of the statute requires willfulness.) However, see *Todd Shipyards Corp.* v. *Secretary of Labor*, 589 F.2d 683 (9th Cir. 1978) (one previous instance suffices and the statute requires repeated infractions or willfulness); *George Hyman Construction Co.* v. *Occupational Safety and Health Review Commission*, 582 F.2d 834 (4th Cir. 1978); *Todd Shipyards Corp.* v. *Secretary of Labor*, 566 F.2d 1327 (9th Cir. 1977).

18. *NLRB* v. *Washington Aluminum Co.*, 370 U.S. 9 (1962).

19. *Gateway Coal Co.* v. *UMW*, 414 U.S. 368, 385 (1974); *NLRB* v. *Knight Morley Co.*, 251 F.2d 753 (6th Cir. 1957), *cert. denied*, 357 U.S. 927 (1958). See J. Atleson, "Threats to Health and Safety: Employees Self Help under the NLRA," 59 Minn. L. Rev. 647 (1975).

20. *Whirlpool Corp.* v. *Marshall*, 445 U.S. 1 (1980).

21. See *id.* at 20–21.

22. 42 U.S.C. §706(f), as amended, 86 Stat. 103 (1972).

23. 42 U.S.C. §§703–04 (1976).

24. *International Brotherhood of Teamsters c. United States*, 431 U.S. 324 (1977). See also *Hazelwood School District* v. *United States*, 433 U.S. 299 (1977) (further defining the appropriate use of statistics).

25. Statistics were first used in class-action cases such as *International Brotherhood of Teamsters*. See *Davis* v. *Califano*, 613 F.2d 957 (D.C. Cir. 1978). Earlier decisions [e.g., *EEOC* v. *New York Times Broadcasting Service*, 542 F.2d 356 (6th Cir. 1976); *King* v. *Yellow Freight System, Inc.*, 523 F.2d 879 (8th Cir. 1975)] had held only that the statistical evidence in such cases was relevant.

26. 401 U.S. 424 (1971).

27. Even when the practice which excludes disproportionately is eliminated, an individual denied employment because of a non-job-related procedure can be a victim of discrimination. *Connecticut* v. *Teal*, 457 U.S. 440 (1982); cf. *Costa* v. *Markey*, 706 F.2d 1 (1st Cir. 1982), *cert. denied*, 104 S. Ct. 547 (1984).

28. The theory was applied under §1981 to New York City school teachers in *Chance* v. *Board of Examiners*, 458 F.2d 1167 (2d Cir. 1972), *later appeal*, 561 F.2d 1079 (1977). In 1976 the Supreme Court ruled that the theory could not be applied to cases brought on constitutional grounds [*Washington* v. *Davis*, 426 U.S. 299 (1976)]. Title VII now applies to governmental bodies [Public Law 92-261, §2(1), 86 Stat. 103 amending 42 U.S.C. §2000e(a)]. See *New York City Transit Authority* v. *Beazer*, 440 U.S. 568 (1979).

29. *General Building Contractors Association* v. *Pennsylvania*, 458 U.S. 375 (1982). Indeed, where employers have required college degrees for positions with responsibility and risk, *Griggs* has not been followed. *Davis* v. *City of Dallas*, 39 F.E.P. Cases 744 (5th Cir. 1985). See especially *Spurlock* v. *United Airlines, Inc.*, 475 F. 2d 216 (10th Cir. 1972).

30. *Dothard* v. *Rawlinson*, 433 U.S. 321 (1977).

31. *Western Airlines, Inc.* v. *Criswell*, 53 U.S.L.W. 4776, 4770 (1985). See also *Johnson* v. *Mayor*, 53 U.S.L.W. 4754 (1985); *Trans World Airlines* v. *Thurston*, ___ U.S. ___, 105 S. Ct. 613 (1985).

32. *McDonnell Douglas Corp.* v. *Green*, 411 U.S. 792 (1973); *Furnco Construction Co.* v. *Waters*, 438 U.S. 567 (1978).

33. *Texas Dept. of Community Affairs* v. *Burdine*, 450 U.S. 248 (1981). See also *United States Postal Service Board of Governors* v. *Aikens*, 460 U.S. 711 (1983); *Anderson* v. *City of Bessemer*, ___ U.S. ___ , 105 S. Ct. 1504 (1985).

34. *Bell* v. *Birmingham Linen Service*, 715 F.2d 1552 (11th Cir. 1983), *cert.denied*, 104 S. Ct. 2385 (1984).

35. *Conner* v. *Fort Gordon Bus Company*, 37 FEP Cases 1574 (11th Cir. 1985); *Miles* v. *M.N.C. Corporation*, 750 F.2d. 867 (11th Cir. 1985).

36. *Bibbs* v. *Block*, 749 F.2d 508 (8th Cir. 1984) (discernible factor test); *Cazalas* v. *United States Department of Justice*, 731 F.2d 280 (5th Cir. 1984), *cert. denied*, 105 S. Ct. 1169 (1985) (significant motivating factor test); *Lewis* v. *University of Pittsburgh*, 725 F.2d 910 (3d Cir. 1983) (any consideration of impermissible factor); *Coleman* v. *Missouri Pacific Railroad Company*, 622 F.2d 408 (8th Cir. 1980) (contributing factor test).

36a. *Bibbs* v. *Block*, 39 FEP Cases 970, 975 (8th Cir. 1985) (rehearing *en banc*).

37. *International Brotherhood of Teamsters* v. *U.S.*, 431 U.S. 324 (1977). See also, *American Tobacco Co.* v. *Patterson*, 456 U.S. 63 (1982) (not an unlawful employment practice to apply different standards pursuant to a bona fide seniority plan as long as differences are not a result of intentional discrimination and are not limited to seniority systems adopted before effective date of Civil Rights Act); *Pullman-Standard* v. *Swint*, 456 U.S. 273 (1982) (a showing of disparate impact is insufficient to invalidate a seniority system, even though the result may be to perpetuate pre-Act discrimination).

38. For example, *id.* at 337 (of 6,742 employees, 314 were black and 257 Spanish surnamed).

39. It was included in an amendment by Representative Howard Smith of Virginia, an opponent of the bill, in an attempt to prevent passage of the bill. See 88 Cong. Rec. 2576–584 and 2804.

40. 77 Stat. 56, 29 U.S.C §206(d) (1976).

41. 3 C.F.R. 169 (1974).

42. April 9, 1866, Ch. 31, 14 Stat. 27. Now 42 U.S.C. §§ 1981, 1983.

43. 42 U.S.C. §2000e-5(e) (1976).

44. *General Electric Co.* v. *Gilbert*, 429 U.S. 125 (1976).

45. 42 U.S.C. §2000e(k) (1979 Supp.) Some states have passed legislation explicitly providing for pregnancy leave and the validity of such legislation has

withstood challenge. See *Miller-Wohl Co.* v. *Commissioner of Labor*, 692 P.2d 1243 (Mont. 1984); *California Federal Savings & Loan Ass'n* v. *Guerra*, 758 F.2d 390 (9th Cir. 1985). The issue is now pending before the Supreme Court. Cert. granted, ___ U.S. ___ (Jan. 13, 1986).

46. *Newport News Shipbuilding and Dry Dock Co.* v. *EEOC*, ___ U.S. ___ , 103 S. Ct. 2622 (1983), ___ U.S. ___ .

47. *City of Los Angeles Dept. of Water & Power* v. *Manhart*, 435 U.S. 702 (1978).

48. *Arizona Governing Committee for Tax Deferred Annuity* v. *Norris*, ___ U.S. ___ , 103 S. Ct. 3492 (1983).

49. *Phillips* v. *Martin Marietta Corp.*, 400 U.S. 542 (1971).

50. For example, *Willingham* v. *Macon Telegraph Publishing Co.*, 507 F.2d 1084 (5th Cir. 1975) (*en banc*); *Gerdom* v. *Continental Airlines, Inc.*, 692 F.2d 602 (9th Cir. 1982), *cert. denied*, 460 U.S. 1074 (1983) (policy requiring an exclusively female category of flight attendants to adhere to weight restrictions constitutes discriminatory treatment on basis of sex); *Ulane* v. *Eastern Airlines*, 742 F.2d 1081 (7th Cir. 1984) (Title VII is not so expansive in scope as to prohibit discrimination against transsexuals).

51. *Garcia* v. *Gloor*, 609 F.2d 156 (5th Cir. 1980).

52. For example, *Tomkins* v. *Public Service Electric & Gas Co.*, 568 F.2d 1044 (3rd Cir. 1977); *Barnes* v. *Castle*, 561 F.2d 983 (D.C. Cir. 1977); *Garber* v. *Saxon Business Products, Inc.*, 552 F.2d 1032 (4th Cir. 1977); *Vinson* v. *Taylor*, 36 FEP Cases 1425 (D.C. Cir. 1985). Where a sexual relationship is a substantial factor in the denial of a job to the plaintiff employee, title VII is violated. *King* v. *Palmer*, 39 FEP Cases 877 (D.C. Cir. 1985).

53. *County of Washington* v. *Gunther*, 452 U.S. 161 (1981). See also *IUE* v. *Westinghouse Electric Corp.*, 631 F.2d 1094 (3d Cir. 1980).; *Spaulding* v. *Univ. of Washington*, 740 F. 2d 686 (9th Cir. 1984).

54. *Id.* at 166–67. See also *American Federation of State, County and Municipal Employees* v. *State of Washington*, 32 FEP Cases 1577 (W.D.W.A. 1983); *American Federation of State, County and Municipal Employees* v. *State of Washington*, 578 F.Supp. 846 (W.D.W.A. 1983); reversed, 38 FEP Cases 1353 (9th Cir. 1985). Federal District Judge Tanner ordered $800 million in back pay to 15,000 women who earned less then men on the state payroll for jobs deemed to be of comparable worth. "U.S. Drops a Fight on Comparable Worth," *New York Times,* September 15, 1984, p. 6. *Spaulding* v. *University of Washington*, 740 F.2d 686 (9th Cir. 1984), *cert. denied* 105 S. Ct. 511 (1985).

55. *Trans World Airlines, Inc.* v. *Hardison*, 432 U.S. 63 (1977).

56. 29 U.S.C. §§31–41c, 42-1 to 426, 701–709, 720–724, 730–32, 740, 741, 750, 760–64, 770–76, 780–87, 790–94 (1976) and 41 C.F.R. §60–741.1 *et seq.*.

57. 29 U.S.C. §621 *et seq.* (1976).

58. Pub. L. 95-256, §1, 92 Stat. 189 (1978), so amended, 29 U.S.C. §§621 *et seq.* 29 U.S.C. §623 (f)(2) (1979 Supp.). See also state legislation banning mandatory retirement: Alaska Stat. Title 18, Ch. 80, Sec. 18.80.220 (1965) as last amended eff. 5-26-82 (public and private sector); California Gov't Code Sec. 7295.0 (1980) as last amended eff. 6-11-83 (public & private sector); Connecticut Gen. Stat. Title 462, Sec. 462-60 (1984) as last amended eff. 10-1-84 (private sector); Florida Stat. Title XLIV, Ch. 760, Sec. 760-10(8)(b)(1978) as last amended eff. 10-1-81 (private sector), Sec. 112.044 (1982) as last amended eff. 10-1-79 (public sector); Georgia Code Annot. Title 34, Sec. 34-1-2 as last amended 1981 (private sector); Hawaii Rev. Stat. Title 21, Ch.378, Sec. 378-3 (1981) as last amended 1984 (private sector), Title 7, Ch. 76 Sec. 76-44 (1955) as last amended 1975 (public sector); Maine Rev. Stat. Title 5, Sec. 4574 (1974) as last amended eff. 6-22-79 (public and private sector); Maryland Annot. Code Article 49B, Sec. 16 (1979) as last amended 1978 (public & private sector); Massachusetts Annot. Laws. Ch. 151B Sec. 4 (17)(1976) as last amended eff. 6-16-84 (private sector); Michigan Stat. Annot. Title 3, Art. 453 Sec. 3.548 (202)(1976) as last amended eff. 5-22-78 (private sector); Montana Code Annot. Title 49, Sec. 49-2-303 (1974) as last amended 1983, Sec. 49-3-103 (1975) as last amended 1983 (public and private sector); New Hampshire Rev. Stat. Ch. 354 Sec. 354- A:4 (VIII)(1965) as last amended 1979 (public and private sector); New York Exec. Law Sec. 296 (3)(a)(1984) eff. 9-17-84 for public sector, eff. 1-1-86 for private sector; North Carolina Gen. Stat. Ch. 143(8)-181 as last amended 1983 (public and private sector); Tennessee Code Annot. Title 4, Ch. 21 Secs. 4-21-126, 4-21-125 (1980)(public sector); Utah Code Annot. Title 34, Ch. 35 Sec. 34-35-6(3)(b) as last amended eff. 4-29-85 (public and private sector); Vermont Stat. Annot. Title 21, Ch. 5 Sec. 495 (c)(f) as last amended eff. 7-1-81 (public and private) Bureau of National Affairs, Labor Relations Reporter, State Fair Employment Practice Laws (1985).

59. Aaron Bernstein, "Putting Mandatory Retirement Out to Pasture," *Business Week*, June 10, 1985, at pp. 104 and 105.

60. 422 U.S. 405 (1975).

61. *Id.* at 419–422. The Court, by a 6-3 vote, has held that an employer's unconditional offer of a previously denied job to a job applicant who charged the employer with hiring discrimination generally tolls back pay liability even if the employer does not offer retroactive seniority. *Ford Motor Co.* v. *EEOC*, 458 U.S. 219 (1982).

62. *Great American Savings and Loan Association* v. *Novotny*, 442 U.S. 366, 374–75 (1979) ("the majority of federal courts have held that the Act does not allow a court to award general or punitive damages"). See *De Grace* v. *Rumsfeld*, 614 F.2d 796, 808 (1st Cir. 1980) (agreeing with "all the 808 circuits which have addressed the matter"); *Harrington* v. *Vandalia-Butler Board of Education*, 585 F.2d 192 (6th Cir. 1978), *cert. denied*, 441 U.S. 932 (1979); *Richerson* v. *Jones*, 551 F.2d 918, 926–28 (3d Cir. 1977); *EEOC* v. *Detroit Edison Co.*, 515 F.2d 301,

308–310 (6th Cir. 1975), *vacated on other grounds and remanded sub nom., Detroit Edison Co. v. EEOC*, 431 U.S. 951 (1977). But see *Clairborne* v. *Illinois Central Railroad*, 583 F.2d 143, 154 (5th Cir. 1978), *cert. denied*, 442 U.S. 934 (1979) (*dicta*).

63. *Johnson* v. *Railway Express*, 421 U.S. 454, 459–60 (1975).

64. For example, *Scott* v. *University of Delaware*, 601 F.2d 76, 81 n.8 (3d Cir. 1979), *cert. denied*, 444 U.S. 931; *Clairborne* v. *Illinois Central Railroad*, 583 F.2d at 153–54 (punitive damages under 42 U.S.C. §1981 even if action brought under both that and Title VII); *Allen* v. *Amalgamated Transit Union*, 554 F.2d 876, 883 (8th Cir. 1977), *cert. denied*, 434 U.S. 891; *Gill* v. *Manuel*, 488 F.2d 799, 801 (9th Cir. 1973); *Caperci* v. *Huntoon*, 397 F.2d 799 (1st Cir. 1968), *cert. denied*, 393 U.S. 940; *Mansell* v. *Saunders*, 372 F.2d 573 (5th Cir. 1967).

65. For example, *United States* v. *Trucking Employers, Inc.*, 561 F.2d 313, 318 (D.C. Cir. 1977).

66. *United States* v. *City of Chicago*, 549 F.2d 415 (7th Cir. 1977), *cert. denied*, 434 U.S. 875; *Patterson* v. *American Tobacco Co.*, 535 F.2d 257 (4th Cir. 1976); *Rios* v. *Steamfitters Local 638*, 501 F.2d 622 (2d Cir. 1974); *Erie Human Relations Commission* v. *Tullio*, 493 F.2d 371 (3d Cir. 1974); *United States* v. *N.L. Industries, Inc.*, 479 F.2d 354 (8th Cir. 1973); *United States* v. *Ironworkers Local 86*, 443 F.2d 544 (9th Cir. 1971); *United States* v. *Local 38, IBEW*, 428 F.2d 144 (6th Cir. 1970); *Local 53, Heat Workers* v. *Vogler*, 407 F.2d 1047 (5th Cir. 1969). On occasion, an appellate court may remand because the district court failed to order sufficient affirmative relief; see, e.g., *Morrow* v. *Grisler*, 491 F.2d 1053 (5th Cir. 1974) (*en banc*), *cert. denied*, 419 U.S. 895. An affirmative-action consent decree may be approved without admission of past discriminatory intent [*United States* v. *City of Miami, Florida*, 614 F.2d 1322 (5th Cir. 1980), *rehearing en banc ordered* August 26, 1980, 625 F.2d 1310)].

67. See, e.g., *Associated Contractors of Massachusetts, Inc.* v. *Altshuler*, 490 F.2d 9 (1st Cir. 1973), *cert. denied*, 416 U.S. 957 (1974); *Contractors Association of Eastern Pennsylvania* v. *Secretary of Labor*, 442 F.2d 159 (3d Cir. 1971), *cert. denied*, 404 U.S. 854; *Weiner* v. *Cuyahoga Community College District*, 19 Ohio St. 2d 35, 249 N.E.2d 907 (1969), *cert. denied*, 396 U.S. 1004 (1970). See also *Regents of the University of California* v. *Bakke*, 438 U.S. 265, 301–02 (1978).

68. *Regents of the University of California* v. *Bakke*, 438 U.S. 265 (1978).

69. *United Steelworkers of America* v. *Weber*, 443 U.S. 193 (1979). See also *Detroit Police Officers' Association* v. *Young*, 808 F.2d 671 (6th Cir. 1979).

70. *Wygant* v. *Jackson Board of Education*, 746 F.2d 1152 (6th Cir. 1984), *cert. granted* (U.S. Apr. 15, 1985) (No. 84-1340).

71. *Firefighters Local 1784* v. *Stotts*, ___U.S.___, 104 S. Ct. 2576, (1984)

72. *Id.* at 2587.

73. See 53 *Am. Jur.* 2d *Master & Servant* 27 (1970).

74. *Woolley* v. *Hoffmann-La Roche, Inc.,* 491 A.2d 1257, 1266 (N.J. 1985).

75. *Novosel* v. *Nationwide Insurance Co.,* 721 F.2d 894 (3d Cir. 1983).

76. *Woolley,* 491 A.2d 1257; *Weiner* v. *McGraw-Hill, Inc.,* 57 N.Y. 2d 458, 457 N.Y.S.2d 193 (1982); *Touissant* v. *Blue Cross & Blue Shield of Michigan,* 408 Mich. 579, 292 N.W.2d 880 (1980).

77. *Cleary* v. *American Airlines, Inc.,* 111 Cal.App.3d 443, 168 Cal. Rptr. 722 (1980); *Crenshaw* v. *Bozeman Deaconess Hospital,* 693 P.2d 487 (Mont.1984)

78. Arizona, California, Connecticut, Florida, Hawaii, Idaho, Illinois, Indiana, Kansas, Kentucky, Maryland, Massachusetts, Michigan, Missouri, Montana, Nevada, New Hampshire, New Jersey, New Mexico, Oregon, Pennsylvania, Tennessee, Texas, Washington, West Virginia, and Wisconsin.

79. Alabama, Alaska, Arizona, Arkansas, California, Colorado, Idaho, Illinois, Kansas, Kentucky, Maine, Massachusetts, Michigan, Minnesota, Nebraska, Nevada, New Mexico, New York, North Carolina, Ohio, Oklahoma, Oregon, South Dakota, Virginia, Washington, and Wisconsin.

80. Alaska, California, Connecticut, Iowa, Massachusetts, Montana, and New Hampshire.

81. *Tameny* v. *Atlantic Richfield Co.,* 27 Cal.3d 167 (1980).

82. *Pugh* v. *See's Candy, Inc.,* 116 Cal.App.3d 311, 171 Cal.Rptr. 917 (1981).

83. 111 Cal. App. 3d 443 (1980).

84. *Garibaldi* v. *Lucky Food Stores, Inc.,* 726 F.2d 1367 (9th Cir. 1984); *Midgett* v. *Sackett–Chicago, Inc.,* 105 Ill.2d 143, 473 N.E.2d 1280 (1984).

85. Connecticut, Delaware, Illinois, Iowa, Kansas, Louisiana, Maine, Maryland, Michigan, New York, Oklahoma, Oregon, Texas, Washington, and Wisconsin. Address by William B. Gould, American Arbitration Association, 7th Annual Arbitration Day Conference in Los Angeles, California (Nov. 15, 1984).

86. "To Strike A New Balance: A Report of the Ad Hoc Committee on Termination at Will and Wrongful Discharge," *Labor and Employment Law News,* State Bar of California (February 8, 1984).

Chapter 12

1. "Protecting at Will Employees Against Wrongful Discharge: The Duty to Terminate Only in Good Faith," 93 Harv. L. Rev. 1816 (1980); C. Summers,

"Individual Protection Against Unjust Dismissal: Time for a Statute," 62 Va. L. Rev. 481 (1976); C. Peck, "Unjust Discharges from Employment: A Necessary Change in the Law," 40 Ohio St. L. J. 1 (1979).

2. *NLRB* v. *Insurance Agents' International Union*, 361 U.S. 477, 488 (1960).

3. For example, L. Thurow, *The Zero-Sum Society* (1980). For a perceptive discussion of recent and unsuccessful efforts see R. Flanagan, "The National Accord As a Social Contract," 34 Indus. & Lab. Rel. Rev. 35 (1981).

Index

Taft-Hartley amendments to. *See* Taft-
Hartley amendments
and trusteeships, 166, 182
and union access to company property,
69–70
and union security agreements, 163
National Labor Relations Board (NLRB)
appellate procedure for decisions of, 31,
61–62
arbitration and, 152–153
back-pay hearings before, 61, 123–124,
129
caseload of, 122–123
delays in decisions of, 61–62, 125–129
elections held by, 46–47
enforcement of orders of, 31
filing and prosecution before, 56–61, 125
General Counsel of. *See* General Counsel
(NLRB)
organizational structure of, 32–33
preemption and primary jurisdiction of,
33–37, 76
short-form opinions of, 60
statute of limitations for complaints
before, 55–56
unfair-labor-practice decisions of, 7,
53–54, 68–70, 76, 80
National Trucking Agreement, 136
New Jersey, 196
Newspaper industry, 179
New York City, 157, 178
New York State, 174
NLRA. *See* National Labor Relations Act
NLRB. *See* National Labor Relations
Board *and names of specific cases*
NLRB v. *Allis-Chalmers Mfg. Co.*, 32–33,
162–163
NLRB v. *American National Insurance Co.*,
109
NLRB v. *Bell Aerospace Co.*, 38
NLRB v. *City Disposal System*, 96
NLRB v. *Exchange Parts Co.*, 49
NLRB v. *General Motors Corp.*, 162
NLRB v. *Gissel*, 86–89
NLRB v. *Jones & Laughlin Steel Corp.*, 97
NLRB v. *Local Union No. 1229, IBEW*, 97
NLRB v. *Mackay Radio & Telegraph Co.*,
101–103
NLRB v. *Transportation Management Corp.*,
68

No-raiding agreements, 6, 91
Norris-LaGuardia Act, 3, 24–28, 31, 80,
145, 148–149, 151
No-strike clauses, 99, 144–145, 148–152

Objections to elections, 47
Occupational Health and Safety Act of
1970, 156, 183–186
Occupational Health and Safety
Administration, 184–186
Office of Federal Contracts Compliance
Program, 193
Open shops, 17
Organizational campaigns, 7
blackmail picketing in, 55, 79
and compulsory recognition of union,
86–92
conflicts between craft and industrial
unions in, 44–45
discriminatory discipline and dismissal
during, 66–69
and exclusivity doctrine, 64–66
picketing during, 54–55, 73–75, 77–86
posting of notices during, 50
recruitment in, 63–64
remedies and, 124
right of free speech during, 49–50
secondary picketing during, 80–86
union access to company property
during, 46–47, 69–77

Pennsylvania, 177
Pension Benefit Guaranty Corp. case, 183
Picketing, 12–13, 21–25, 52–55, 73–75,
79–86
Plant closings, 7, 85, 116–118, 183, 185
Plant occupations, 99
Police
arbitration for, 135, 157
strikes by, 178–179
unions for, 172, 177
Political power of unions, 2, 168–170,
176–177
Postal Reorganization Act of 1970, 135,
171
Powell, Justice Lewis, 38, 104, 155
Preemption and primary jurisdiction
doctrine, 34–37, 76, 145
Prima facie tort doctrine, 12–13